Marilynne Robinson, Theologian of the Ordinary

Marilynne Robinson, Theologian of the Ordinary

Andrew Cunning

BLOOMSBURY ACADEMIC
NEW YORK • LONDON • OXFORD • NEW DELHI • SYDNEY

BLOOMSBURY ACADEMIC
Bloomsbury Publishing Inc
1385 Broadway, New York, NY 10018, USA
50 Bedford Square, London, WC1B 3DP, UK

BLOOMSBURY, BLOOMSBURY ACADEMIC and the Diana logo are trademarks of
Bloomsbury Publishing Plc

First published in the United States of America 2021

This paperback edition published 2022

Copyright © Andrew Cunning, 2021

Cover design by Eleanor Rose
Cover photograph: Portrait of Marilynne Robinson, 2007 © Ulf Andersen / Getty Images

For legal purposes the Acknowledgements on p. viii constitute
an extension of this copyright page

All rights reserved. No part of this publication may be reproduced or transmitted
in any form or by any means, electronic or mechanical, including photocopying,
recording, or any information storage or retrieval system, without
prior permission in writing from the publishers.

Bloomsbury Publishing Inc does not have any control over, or responsibility for, any third-party websites referred to or in this book. All internet addresses given in this book were correct at the time of going to press. The author and publisher regret any inconvenience caused if addresses have changed or sites have ceased to exist, but can accept no responsibility for any such changes.

Library of Congress Cataloging-in-Publication Data
Names: Cunning, Andrew, author.
Title: Marilynne Robinson, theologian of the ordinary / Andrew Cunning.
Description: New York: Bloomsbury Academic, 2021. | Includes bibliographical references and index. | Summary: "This book outlines the foundational theology of Marilynne Robinson's work through sustained analysis of her novels, essays, unpublished notebooks, drafts, and an original interview with the author"–Provided by publisher.
Identifiers: LCCN 2020023600 | ISBN 9781501371349 (paperback) | ISBN 9781501358999 (hardback) | ISBN 9781501359019 (pdf) | ISBN 9781501359002 (epub)
Subjects: LCSH: Robinson, Marilynne–Criticism and interpretation. | Robinson, Marilynne–Religion. | Theology in literature. | Christianity and literature.
Classification: LCC PS3568.O3125 Z63 2021 | DDC 813/.54–dc23
LC record available at https://lccn.loc.gov/2020023600

ISBN: HB: 978-1-5013-5899-9
PB: 978-1-5013-7134-9
ePDF: 978-1-5013-5901-9
eBook: 978-1-5013-5900-2

Typeset by Deanta Global Publishing Services, Chennai, India

To find out more about our authors and books visit www.bloomsbury.com
and sign up for our newsletters.

Turning upward
to the real thing
my eyes
are lit.

Mícheál McCann, 'Prayer'

Contents

Acknowledgements   viii

Introduction   1
1   Marilynne Robinson, the American Ordinary and *Housekeeping*   17
2   *Gilead* and the intersection of language   55
3   *Home*: Robinson's radical grace   93
4   *Lila*: The myth of the self   129
5   Reflections on the Ordinary: An interview with Marilynne Robinson   171

References   187
Index   195

Acknowledgements

This book is the product of five years of work, and exists in the real world because of many people's support and encouragement. I want to thank Philip McGowan for his astute and calming supervision of my PhD; Stephen Williams for many years of mentoring; David Coughlan for a lovely year at the University of Limerick and for reading rubbish drafts! A thank you also to Catherine Gander for being a wonderful believer that I could write this; to Lesley Emerson for teaching me the word 'problematize' (as both a word to write and as a word to live by); and to Stephen Kelly, for observations and asides that ended up in here.

Thank you to my family for all their love and support. My expectation of finding grace in the everyday has been learned from being a part of this mad family.

I want to thank Michelle, for sharing her talent with me; Jan, for being such a positive force; Hannah for songs I write with; and Paul, for letting me finish this book at the magical River Mill.

A big thanks are due to Michael and Maria, for brain-sparking chats; to Patrick for respite at Nandos and letting me win the odd set of tennis; and to Mícheál for his reading, talking and personification of grace.

To all my students, thank you for all that you have taught me.

Introduction

'Hello. Lovely to meet you. Would you mind helping me open this door? I can't seem to get the key turned.' These were Marilynne Robinson's first words to me when we met outside the Iowa Writers' Workshop in Iowa City on 10 November 2017, and seeing the multi-prize-winning author of *Housekeeping* (1980) and *Gilead* (2004) fumbling to open a door, clutching a folded and battered copy of Dante's *Inferno* was something of a surreal experience. And yet the scene was absolutely fitting as an introduction to the conversation that followed. For an hour we chatted theology, American writing, the philosophy of time and the war between science and religion; but we began by talking about ordinariness and Robinson's common use of the word 'Ordinary'. And what better way to open a discussion with the writer that gave us Ames, Ruth and Lila than with the seemingly mundane things they seem to find ultimate meaning in. That Marilynne Robinson opens doors and underlines passages she finds interesting in books shouldn't be a surprise; but the peculiarity of the realization underlines one of Robinson's most fundamental premises: that everything is Ordinary and, by extension, worthy of our proper attention. The conversation wrapped up after about an hour and Marilynne insisted on giving me a tour of her old workplace, a gesture that signifies the generosity with time that comes across in her novels. I, for my part, managed to get a selfie out of the encounter. It now hangs in my office.

The approach

Much has been written about Marilynne Robinson's work, and a not-so insignificant portion of that has proposed to tackle her theology. Yet this is the first book-length work devoted to Robinson's theology and this work attends to what seems to be foundational to her world view. A number of readers will, undoubtedly, immediately leap to Calvin and Calvinism at the mention of Robinson and theology; however, Robinson came to Calvin at some point in the twenty-four-year gap between *Housekeeping* and *Gilead*, so her attraction to his thinking may well have a substantial 'beneath' to it. Indeed, it is clear that Robinson's family, like so many Protestant families, were Calvinist by tradition without ever speaking his name, or even being too aware of what he wrote. So Robinson's *Housekeeping* does not bear the marks of the theology she would later go on to claim. But she eventually ends up claiming it is not an explanation of anything, but rather something that requires explanation.

The aim of this book is to provide a sustained analysis of something Robinson scholars increasingly agree is, at the very least, important to her world view: the Ordinary. In a sentence or two, this book takes seriously Robinson's heightened attention to the Ordinary in novels and essays and demonstrates how a radical theology emerges from this attentiveness. This book wants to argue that Robinson is best viewed as a theologian. And while Robinson does write often of food and drink, water and wind, the book takes as its 'Ordinary' themes language, grace and time. Examining Robinson on these rather more capacious themes still leaves room for the more seemingly mundane elements like conversation, subtle familial kindnesses and memories, but also allows for the connection Robinson makes between the most Ordinary phenomena and the more apparently abstracted theology she holds. In other words, Robinson sees no tension or incongruence between holding a high Christology and writing pages of a novel on the maintenance of an old car. These concerns are distinct but they are by no means separable. And this fact takes us by the hand right into the heart of Robinson's theology.

> I am as firmly persuaded as anyone that things can be explained, or usefully described but that our methods at this point are crude, and premature, and that they lead us to ignore such experience or intuition as cannot be accompanied by them. Bad assumptions are never better than no assumptions at all. ('Language is Smarter')

The parsing of reality into the explained and the unexplained, the discussed and the unspoken, as well as the acknowledged and the ignored is a tendency common to modern thinking, for Robinson. And as reality is reduced to data to be plugged into a theory, human experience as a legitimate means of knowing becomes increasingly delegitimized. That the world is itself blind to, and ignorant of, human designations is a central concern of Robinson's work; it follows from this that a huge acknowledgement must be made to the fact that our store of knowledge is vastly outweighed by mystery and mistakes. For Marilynne Robinson reality *is*, while we have made it our business to divide and dissect it. Her Christianity is, above all, a way of seeing that seeks to maintain and gesture towards the wholeness and infinite plurality of reality and human experience, a way of seeing that refuses not to see anything.

Robinson's theology, in other words, shares the distinctly Whitminian conviction that what *is* ought to be engaged with, and what is *seen* is fit for representation, for it too is a constituent of reality. Whitman's most well-known work, the American epic, 'Song of Myself' (1855) took Emerson's emphasis on sight seriously, and constructed a vision of the continent more grounded in the odours and messes of reality than in anything Emerson conjures in 'Nature' (1836). Putting the important debate about the ethics of Whitman's representation of diverse America to one side, we can front the essential facts of his fundamental assumptions and intentions. His work evidences an unparalleled belief in the unifying work of observation and reveals an implicit belief that to refuse to see an element of the world is to capitulate to serious moral, artistic and, by extension, theological blindness.

In Whitman, consciously or unconsciously, 'unseeing' is just a few steps away from a dangerous failure of moral vision. Marilynne Robinson makes the compelling case for fully inhabiting the business of perception in *Gilead*, a novel that represents the moral blindness of a truly good man. And 'goodness' is brought into question in that text not to posit evil as the only other alternative, but to trouble the ease with which the distinction is often made. In Robinson's work, original sin is not wickedness (although it may result in wickedness) but a failure to see in that prelapsarian way, prior to the knowledge of good and evil. Robinson's attraction to Christianity, then, is not the final stop on a search for a theory of everything. Theologically, the faith is not an exploration of reality as much as it is a framework within which the world is rightly to be seen. Christianity does not exclude mystery, but acknowledges and attends to it. And the existence of mystery does not, and cannot, invalidate it; nor, indeed, is there a risk of invalidation from the progress of science or philosophy. This kind of thinking would, surely, place Christianity as a theory among theories. Indeed, should the Christian faith be thought to compete with science then it could never really be a faith worth the name. The wholeness of the world is a fascination of Robinson's thinking and this necessarily means she eschews any kind of binary thinking. And, when faced with a choice between one explanation or theory and another, it is almost inevitable she will question the necessity of the choice.

Overview

The book is divided into four chapters and finishes with an interview I carried out with Marilynne Robinson in Iowa City in 2017. Each chapter is broadly dedicated to a single novel, in chronological order, beginning with Robinson's 1980 novel, *Housekeeping*. This initial chapter makes the case that this debut novel does not sit in the same theological register, nor was it produced with the same prior theology as the following *Gilead* novels. However, this chapter is crucial to the overarching argument of the book in that it positions Robinson as a self-conscious inheritor of the American Renaissance, and argues her theology is just as much gleaned from her reading of Emerson, Whitman, Melville and Dickinson as it is from Calvin. In terms of pure theology, this chapter has the least and instead focuses on the 'literariness' of Robinson's novel, and her distinctly American use of language and metaphor. Theology is not absent here though (it never is with any of Robinson's writing), as Robinson herself in the interview with me states clearly that all her characters are theologians. So, to do justice to this claim, the chapter engages with metaphorical theology, the transcendentalism of the American Renaissance and the 'death-of-God' theology of Mark C. Taylor. The other three chapters dig in to the three core theological themes of Robinson's work. Taking *Gilead*, *Home* (2008) and *Lila* (2014), respectively, Robinson's theology is 'drawn out' under the banner of important themes of the texts. Carrying on from *Housekeeping*'s use of language, the second chapter takes up 'horizontal' and 'vertical' language in *Gilead*, and argues that in Robinson's novel language necessarily fails in all directions. And granting this failing, *Gilead* implies the necessity of physical and embodied blessing as the only response to linguistic frailty. Chapter 3 is the most overtly political, taking up the theme of grace in *Home*. And planting metaphysical grace firmly in the domestic sphere of a ruptured family, Robinson asks her readers to pay attention to the ordinariness of grace and, by extension, the politics of its theology. Jack emerges in this chapter as one of Robinson's most important theological inventions, and his Christlike disruption of sedate, 'white' theological consensus is crucial to the theology of grace constructed by her third novel. The chapter unpacks the theological and political significance of the predestination debate in *Home* and draws significantly on Robinson's non-fiction to make the case for the implied universalism of Robinson's writing. Moving from the political to the philosophical, Chapter 4 tackles the writing of the self in time in Robinson's fourth novel, *Lila*. Beginning with her writing on myth, the case is made that the self in Robinson's fiction is written like a myth: a narrative containing narratives and shifting interpretative potentialities. Arguing that memories in *Lila* become the access point to Lila herself, it is suggested that the self exists in an analogous way that the 'sacred story' of scripture exists: that is, in the stories it gives shape to. That everything can change, that people can change emerges here as Robinson's most important theological statement, and the possibility of change in a world in which time is a given is hope itself. Before beginning with *Housekeeping*, it is important to devote a little time to defining some of the key terms this book takes for granted, beginning with 'the Ordinary'.

Defining terms: The Ordinary and attention

Marilynne Robinson's written work, both novels and essays, returns most often to the fundamental importance of attentiveness.[1] Whether it

---

[1] Holberg, in a similar vein, has written, 'if one generalisation might be made about Marilynne Robinson's body of work, both fiction and nonfiction [. . .] it is that her writing urges us again to pay attention to what she calls in her first novel, *Housekeeping*, the "resurrection of the ordinary"'. Although this is a minor – and verging on pedantic – criticism of Holberg's choice of words, it would

be attention to primary sources often overlooked, to memories, to the natural world, to another person, the theme of intentional, concentrated attention emerges as the central concern of Robinson's thinking. 'We are poor observers, rarely seeing more than we intend to see', writes Robinson, arguing, 'our expectations are received, therefore static, which makes it certain that they will be like nothing in reality' (Robinson 2018: 91). Behind this vocal call for a renewed attentiveness is Robinson's conviction that reality is both worthy of and demands all the attention one can give. 'No doubt we will never know or find words for any meaningful fraction even of the aspects of reality that are available to our strategies of comprehension', she writes, and this admission of the apophatic nature of reality is her impetus for perpetual attention (Robinson 2018: 208). With the richness of reality in mind, Robinson's essays aim to convict their readers of the cardinal sins of inattentiveness and shallow experience. As Aronociwz puts it, 'mystery, as [Robinson] presents it, is not a puzzle yet unsolved, but the individual's experience of a reality that constantly reveals itself in unexpected ways' (Aronociwz 2017: 42). A repeated motif of Robinson's work is the theological imperative of inhabiting one's experience as fully as possible and being open to this mystery, Aronociwz notes, a task that overrides the natural tendency of individuals to mask complexity, in prescriptive and reductive certainty, and overlooks beauty as the mark of divinity in the natural world. And this divine presence in beauty is pure Calvin, for Robinson, as she puts it: 'his [Calvin's] conception of this world is utterly visionary' and that 'God clothes himself in the image of the world' (Robinson 1998: 225). For Robinson, experience is of a kind to infinitely deepen, an inexhaustible trove simply because reality itself exceeds the mind's capacity to master. 'This is an interesting planet', Ames posits in *Gilead*, 'it deserves all the attention you can give it'; certainly Ames' voice here is Robinson's own (Robinson 2004: 32). 'What is the world that art takes for granted?', asks Rowan Williams in *Grace and Necessity* (2005),

---

be more faithful to Robinson's thought to say that her work urges a return to attentiveness to the Ordinary *in order that it may be resurrected* (Holberg 2010: 182). It is attentiveness that is both key and causal here, as the rest of this discussion will demonstrate.

and suggests, 'it is one in which perception is always incomplete' (Williams 2005: 135). This is true, certainly, of Robinson's work. Her novels question the shallowness of habitual perception, challenging their readers to encounter more fully the moment they are in. Perception will always be incomplete for Robinson, due to the irreducible strangeness of the Ordinary. In order to unpick what is meant by 'Ordinary', it is crucial to set out Robinson's thinking against the philosophical, theological and literary conversations in which she places herself.

In *Gilead*, Ames muses on his use of the word 'just' as a means of 'indicat[ing] a stress on the word that follows it' (Robinson 2004: 32): 'the sun just *shone* and the tree just *glistened*', he records (Robinson 2004: 32). This linguistic strategy emphasizes the verb in order that the rich experience of the thing described in some way be communicated: 'people talk that way when they want to call attention to a thing existing in excess of itself, so to speak, a sort of purity or lavishness, at any rate something ordinary in kind but exceptional in degree' (Robinson 2004: 32). Ames' use of Ordinary here is crucial as it signals a foundational site of Robinson's theological thinking. Her novels have a distinctive focus on the seemingly Ordinary – light and water, memory and family, food and conversation – that, as this book argues, is neither ornamental nor incidental to her theology, but rather the foundation of it. For Robinson, the Ordinary is excessively meaningful: meaningful to the extent that 'Ordinary' becomes an almost ironic term to describe it, a misnomer. Olson rightly notes that 'the ordinary [. . .] consists of activities and things that are most frequently characterised by our inattention to them [. . .] unheroic events and overlooked things, neither crucial moments of plot development nor temporal points that signify accomplishments' (Olson 2009: 6). 'I think that the ordinary is very mysterious', Robinson comments, 'I think the ordinary, given a reasonable span of time, might also be called the ephemeral', and certainly this ephemerality ought to undercut the inattention Olson notes earlier (Chapter 5). This ephemerality, conjured vividly by Robinson in her novels, is represented in moments of transfigured perception, when the Ordinary itself seems to contain more than human cognition can accommodate comfortably. Ploeg also picks up on the distinctly Robinsonian 'excess of the Ordinary', noting that in her work 'there is always more, always surplus, "proper language" (namely representation) does not, and, arguably, cannot take it into account' (Ploeg 2016: 9). Robinson, as a theologian, begins with the fleeting experience of the strangeness of the Ordinary, with the uncanniness of the natural world and human encounters with it. Asked about her conviction of the strangeness of experience, Robinson comments, 'we have no way to make an account of it [the natural world] except in its terms, yet at the same time it continually surprises us, continually surprises us, continually seems to present itself as alien' (Chapter 5). Ames fills pages on the seemingly emblematic experience of light, or of the way water falls off a tree, because he, like Robinson, seeks to be attentive to the flickering moments of transfigured experience, moments in which reality itself seems to exist in excess of itself, seems to communicate more than can ever be interpreted.

Robinson and the sources of theology

The excessiveness of experience and the belief that the only fit response is a commitment to excavating inwardness and consulting one's own subjectivity is a central theme of American Renaissance writing and is one Robinson takes as the beginnings of theology. She connects her intuitive sense of excess with religion's capacity to encourage an embrace of subjective experience: 'let us say that religions explore the ancient human intuition that there is an energy behind experience, something not sufficiently like the reality accessible to us to be captured in the language that has developed to accommodate ordinary experience' (Robinson 2018: 228). That an individual's encounter with the Ordinary will always exceed the language available to house that experience is a recurrent theme of Robinson's writing, and is the inevitable outcome of the strangeness of the Ordinary. The 'energy behind experience' Robinson writes of here is, for her, most adequately captured in theological language, for religions themselves are responses to the utter mystery of Being and the existential questions thrown up by existence:

> The feeling of an overplus of meaning in reality, a sense that the world cannot at all be accounted for in its own terms, is a profound bond and understanding between and among religious people. It is universal in

religions to grant the meaningfulness of metaphysical thought: They all query Being itself. (Robinson 2018: 206)

For Robinson, religion in general, and Christianity in particular, provides three crucial resources for the believer: a lens through which to view the world, a set of texts that act as a repository of ancient responses to the same strangeness, and an interpretive tradition that has been felt to be a meaningful response to the world and the questions offered up by being *in* the world. 'Being', for Robinson, is under no obligation to be articulable and, crucially, the level of one's attentiveness to an aspect of Being is proportional to an awareness of this essential and ultimate ineffability. Religion, however, begins with the mystery of Being and, in the poetry, the metaphor and myth of its texts encourages an imaginative engagement with the Ordinary strangeness of reality. 'There is an overplus of experience in the consciousness of a religious person that tends to re-express itself as a sense of the beautiful', argues Robinson and, certainly in her thinking, religion provides both a vocabulary for articulating experience and an implicit faith in art to hold the excess of experience that transcends straightforward expression (Chapter 5). A commitment to art as the vocabulary of existence, and as the means of rendering the excess of experience intelligible, is crucial to Robinson's project as a writer because 'globally, people's highest art tends to be religious. Art is the vocabulary beyond vocabulary' (Chapter 5).

In her novels, particularly in the *Gilead* trilogy, Robinson seeks to represent a religious experience of reality. She does this, in part, through Lila's easy movement from nature to scripture and back to nature; in Ames' reflections on the meaning of his experiences of beauty; and in Lila's, Ames' and Glory's writing of the transfiguring power of memory on the seemingly unremarkable. Representation is a key term here. As Rowan Williams identifies, 're-presentation assumes that there is an excess in what presents itself for knowing, and that neither the initial cluster of perceptions nor any one set of responses will finally succeed in containing what is known' (Williams 2005: 139). For Williams, as with Robinson, an excess of experience demands expression that is not burdened by the human limitation so often encountered in philosophical or theological language. Instead, experience of the ephemeral Ordinary calls for art, poetry, song and myth. It insists on re-presentation in limitless forms. This representation occurs in two ways in Robinson's work. First, within the novels themselves, her characters re-present their own experience in metaphor, and in terms that suggest the excessive nature of their experience. Ames, for example, records how walking with his father back from his grandfather's grave caused him to realize 'what an amazing instrument you are, so to speak, what a power you have to experience beyond anything you might ever actually need' (Robinson 2004: 56). Second, the novels themselves are Robinson's own representation of her own conscious sense of the beautiful given voice in her essays. 'Some part of a definition of beauty', she argues, 'ought to be that it is an aspect of experience that can, and possibly should, compel attention and also reward it' (Robinson 2018: 129). It is with her non-fiction writing on beauty, experience and the Ordinary in mind that the novels emerge as Robinson's own representation of the interaction between an excess of experience and her own religious consciousness. 'The theologian can say that beauty eludes definition because it expresses the grace of God, like other elusive things, say, time and light': it is certainly the case that Robinson's novels seek not to explain the strangeness of experience her characters encounter in their interaction with the Ordinary, but instead seek to represent it in terms that Robinson herself finds satisfying (Robinson 2018: 129).

The final few sentences of the last paragraph may seem like the completion of a somewhat circular argument. Indeed, it was suggested earlier that Robinson begins with the strangeness and excessiveness of the Ordinary and finds religion and religious language adequate to her experience, yet the last paragraph claims that experience is refined and re-expressed according to the religious consciousness of a person. Granting the circularity of the argument, it should be noted that this is not a lapse in logic but rather illustrative of Robinson's approach to theology and religion. For Robinson, an initial experience of the strangeness of the Ordinary, even one prior to a religious conversion, is itself a religious one. In my interview with her she comments, 'what I've been interested in doing in both *Home* and *Lila* is complicating the sense of what the religious is' (Chapter 5). This is the very point. Robinson has no interest in drawing a line that separates the secular from the sacred, the religious from the irreligious. For her, the world is to be understood theologically in total, and that leaves little room for designating some experiences religious and other experiences as something other. So the interface between experience and religious consciousness really is not an interface at all, but a symbiotic relationship of mutual dependence, a closed loop that has no discernible beginning or end. Robinson and Kearney are of one mind here, and his *Anatheism* (2010), an important text for this book, 'reinsert[s] the hyphen between the secular and sacred where it always belonged' (Kearney 2010: 142). For Robinson, as will be developed in the discussions of transcendence later, the world's experiential depth is a product of the divine presence within it, which rules out the possibility of binary distinctions between a religious Ordinary and a secular Ordinary. Similarly, for Kearney, 'the sacred is in the secular but it is not *of* the secular per se. It is a matter of reciprocal interdependency rather than one-dimensional conflation' (Kearney 2010: 141). For Robinson, 'beauty is grandly present in the architecture of the cosmos, minutely present in the structure of the atom'; with Kearney's secular–sacred relation in mind, reality itself refuses to be parsed in human designations blind to divine beauty both in part and as a whole (Robinson 2018: 132).

So Robinson's most significant contribution to contemporary theological thinking begins to emerge when we attend to the implications of her own attention to the Ordinary. That the mundane can, and ought to, be seen as revelatory is a truth Robinson claims as foundational; and the implications of such a belief call into question the role of reason, scripture and tradition as the primary theological sources. This book seeks to take seriously Robinson's suggestion, threaded through her essays and fictions, that experience is, whether we actually recognize it or not, our greatest theological resource. Logically speaking, scripture, reason and tradition are all accessible only through experience, which means there can be no engagement with text, argumentation or historic ritual without the mediating factor of experience which makes any contact at all possible. And while she can be regularly found quoting the Bible; providing detailed exegesis of a verse; arguing for lost traditions, Robinson is more often reinstating experience – attentive, open and fully habited experience – as the first and greatest of our theological teachers.

A horizontal transcendence

It is clear, then, that Robinson's imagining of theology as a consultation between subjective experience and adequate expression ultimately finds an ideal vehicle in narrative or poetic form: as she reflects, 'only in church did I hear experience like mine acknowledged, in all those strange narratives, read and expounded and, for all that, opaque as figures of angels painted on gold' (Robinson 2012: 229). It is no accident, then, that Robinson's theology finds expression in the novel. When asked about the reality of grace as it occurs in the *Gilead* novels, Robinson comments, 'I wouldn't know how to articulate that other than through fiction', suggesting the inevitability of the novel for her way of doing theology (Chapter 5).[2] With an insistence on the richness of inner experience, Robinson creates novels with a special attentiveness to the depth and complexity of human subjectivity and, in so doing, raises the implicit argument that the novel is not merely another theological resource, but is actually the form most able to depict a way of being in the world, attentive to the inexhaustible strangeness of the Ordinary. In this way, as Weele insightfully indicates, Robinson's language achieves 'a movement that seems, like music, to progress both horizontally and vertically at the same time' (Weele 2010: 219).

Although Weele's point is a useful spatial metaphor for the movement within Robinson's novels, it should be noted that she rejects a vertical image of transcendence, if that image may be said to imply a belief in an otherworldly transcendence at the expense of encountering the physical world as it is now, and this way of thinking, although plain to see in the *Gilead* novels and in her essays, is present, too, in *Housekeeping*. As a reader of Emerson, Robinson notes the school of thought he established in the 1830s, 'Transcendentalism', was misnamed:

> I know the Americans like Emerson and his school were called Transcendentalists, but they didn't like that word – it was picked up out

---

[2] 'It was my brother who told me I should be a poet. This was not a career, as he or I understood it, but a highly respectable use of solitude', Robinson writes in *When I Was a Child I Read Books* (Robinson 2012: 28). Although a reader and admirer of poetry (Emily Dickinson and Wallace Stevens in particular), Robinson has never published any poems, instead turning to the novel. Her privileging of the novel form for the articulation of her own world view comes across in the interview included as an appendix to this book.

of Germany and imposed on them as the nearest analogy. I think if we understood things properly we would not use the word transcendence. (Chapter 5)

That Robinson emphasizes this particular point is revelatory of her reading of Emerson and of her own conception of transcendence. In Robinson's thinking, the Ordinary contains its excess of meaning due to the limited nature of human cognitive capacity and also the pervasive nature of divinity in the world. Two ways of thinking about transcendence emerge in her work, then. First, with this human limitation in mind, ignorance can be seen as the birthplace of transcendence. Simply put, it is possible to read the concept of transcendence as a name given to that which necessarily eludes understanding and conceptualization, to that which seems to imply a 'more'. 'Thinking we know more than we do, therefore rejecting what we are given as experience, blinds us to our ignorance, which is the deep darkness where truth abides', Robinson argues and, certainly for her, being attentive to ignorance allows transcendence its place (Robinson 2015: 199). This ignorance is not just of an explicitly theological order, as Robinson is also keen to remind readers of their ignorance of the physical world's true workings, noting 'I wait for the day someone will lift a corner of quantum physics and find that it is underlain by a physics yet more bizarre' (Robinson 2015: 211). This sense of the unknowable is very much present in Robinson's essays and, of course, in her fiction. Ames, as will be discussed in Chapter 2, finds nature emblematically meaningful due to his inability to finally master his own experience of it; or, in other words, he is forced to turn to metaphor as a means of interpreting the excessiveness of his encounters with nature. A true Emersonian, Ames finds a significance in the natural world that can only be relayed and represented poetically, in language that places no limit on its final meaning.

The second notion of transcendence in Robinson's thinking is an attribution of the Ordinary's surplus of meaning to the divine presence in creation. This would seem to be simply a restatement of the first connection of transcendence but in theological terms: instead of the limited nature of the human mind, this view emphasizes the mysterious nature of divinity, and this is broadly what it is. However, it should be noted that the first conception of transcendence is very much available to the atheist, and is therefore ultimately inadequate for Robinson. If transcendence emerges out of ignorance and limitation, then there is no necessary reason to posit a God or divine presence as causal. The second conception of transcendence reads the world as saturated in the ineffable and elusive presence of God and, therefore, human limitation is understood as inevitable in light of the theological nature of the Ordinary. These two notions of transcendence are clearly not mutually exclusive and, with Robinson's theism in mind, can be seen to be complementary. Robinson most often writes of a transcendence that falls into the second, more overtly theological conception. For her, the limits of human knowledge and means of knowing are crucial to bear in mind in order to avoid theological conjecture and scientific or philosophical certainty, but it is equally crucial to bear in mind the theological underpinnings of human ignorance. Robinson conceives of an 'instructive ignorance', one in which what is not understood or is not known functions as a corrective to the overstatement of simplistic dogmatism. This instructive ignorance also opens a conceptual space that allows for the divine presence operating beyond that which a strict and reductive materialism would allow.

What Robinson is calling for in her work is not a list of creedal statements that must be intellectually assented to, but an honest reappraisal of the failures of mere materialism. She writes continually of the inadequacy of positivism and scientism to everyday experience: 'so imperious is the materialist approach to reality that it considers whatever it cannot capture by its methods as effectively non-existent, for example the human self, the human mind' (Robinson 2018: 128). Robinson scorns materialism for its tendency to 'marginalize to the point of disappearance things we generally consider abstractions, for example, justice, wisdom, and beauty', and instead argues that 'the theologian may and must grant these even an especial reality' (Robinson 2018: 128–9). Transcendence is, then, the very excess of the Ordinary Robinson writes of in her essays and represents in her novels. It is not to be understood as a vertical concept, with a focus on an omniscient God residing outside of time and space, but as a horizontal concept in which the divine presence is already infused in the plane of existence humans experience from moment to moment. 'I think the concept of transcendence is based on a misreading of creation. With all respect to heaven, the scene of miracle is here, among us', she argues, and transcendence, if the word is to have a place in Robinson's work at all, must be brought 'down to earth', and folded into Ordinary experience (Robinson 1998: 243). 'Since eternity is in love with the products of time, it is of the nature of transcendence to be immanent', writes Eagleton, referring to German idealism, although the sentiment extends equally well to Robinson (Eagleton 2014: 47). Her work suggests that, in order to be transcendent or to participate in transcendence, a thing or experience must only exceed our ability to master it, assimilate it in our usual narratives of experience. In this sense, forgiveness, language, time and grace are profoundly Ordinary in the Robinsonian sense:

> experienceable in themselves but containing such a superfluity of meaning so as to point beyond themselves to a reality both unknown and unknowable. 'The immanent should not be cut off from anything that implies a larger reality at any scale', comments Robinson, and one of the most striking achievements of her work is the horizontal transcendence her fiction implies. (Chapter 5)

1

Marilynne Robinson, the American Ordinary and *Housekeeping*

Published in 1980, over two decades before her first *Gilead* novel, *Housekeeping* is anomalous in Robinson's published output. But this is only true if we expect a writer – whose work spans over four decades – to remain unerringly consistent in approach, tone and assumption over such a long period of time. Indeed, the very word 'anomaly' implies an expectation of consistency, and one that is simply too limiting for the unfolding nature of a novelist's thinking and writing. Robinson's first novel *is* different, though, but that is only a problem if we as readers are seeking to systemize her work, and this impulse to systematize is something Robinson is keen to deconstruct in her writing. So this book doesn't consider the need to smooth out contradictions between *Housekeeping* and, say, *Gilead*, but rather allows Robinson theological development, picking up on crucial ideas first set in motion in her debut, and commenting on some of the radical shifts Robinson makes over the twenty-year gap between her first and second novel.

Housekeeping, like *Gilead*, is told by a first-person narrator. It tracks the story of Ruth, the novel's narrator, beginning decades before her birth and ends with her entering transience with her aunt Sylvie. Ruth's story involves the death of her mother – almost certainly a suicide – and her early life as a child in the care of her grandmother, then two distant great aunts and, eventually and finally, her aunt Sylvie. The novel is a document of abandonments and losses, and Ruth's sister, Lucille, too leaves Ruth and takes up residence with the much more dependable Home Economics teacher, Miss Royce. The novel is densely metaphorical, proceeding like a dream told by a narrator who sees no real distinction between truth and fiction. The sparse plot, as loosely accounted for here, tells us very little of the story, and we are invited instead to enter into a subjective version of events, with the implicit notion that this is where truth lies: in the telling of a story. Scholars have approached the novel – rightly, I feel – with feminist readings. Others have approached it with an eye for metaphysics, to emphasis transience or to construct a Calvinist reading. There is no satisfactorily conclusive reading of this novel, nor will there ever be. But for this book it is important to see *Housekeeping* as a crucial part of the Robinsonian collection, and to read it with an eye for what is to come. With that in mind, it is the intention here to focus on the interplay of language, American writing and theology in the novel – central themes of Robinson's work more widely.

In tone, *Housekeeping* is set apart from the later *Gilead* novels, but thematically it has its place in the Robinsonian corpus. Like *Gilead*, *Housekeeping* is interested in the generations of a family, and how familial history produces the familial present. Where *Gilead* focuses on fathers and sons, *Housekeeping* is almost an exclusively female populated text, honing in on mothers, sisters, aunts and grandmothers. Ruth, like Lila, is a female orphan and has experience of wandering like a stranger in a strange landscape, with few people or places to call home. And this debut novel also places great value on female observation. Not that Robinson strongly insists on necessary or essentialist distinctions between male and female perception, but she does show us the world of *Housekeeping* through Ruth's eyes, just as twenty-eight years later we peer over Glory's shoulder to see the lives of Jack, Boughton, Ames and Lila in *Home*.

Unlike *Gilead*, *Home* and *Lila*, *Housekeeping* is relatively de-contextualized in terms of history and time. Geographically, it is set in Robinson's childhood Idaho landscape; but where the *Gilead* novels are inserted into the years preceding the civil rights movement, *Housekeeping* could, theoretically, take place at any stage of American history in which the trains were running. Where the later novels self-consciously interact with profoundly important American history and American issues – presidential elections, the Civil War, race riots – *Housekeeping* is altogether more inward, concerned more with individual history than with the state of the nation. The novel privileges the interior symbols of Ruth's imagination more than it engages with outward

American history, so if we are to read *Housekeeping* theologically, we must bear in mind that it does not ask to be read alongside history, but rather with an altogether more literary eye. And we begin with the American writers Robinson cites as her literary aunts and uncles.

Housekeeping and the American Ordinary: The source of the source

It has become something of a preoccupation of Robinson studies thus far to try to excavate the significance of Robinson's relation to Calvin. This is no doubt useful, especially since she claims Calvin as an influence and has sought to restore his reputation to a hostile American culture. However, as this chapter is dedicated to *Housekeeping*, it allows us the opportunity to suggest that we readers of Robinson have been too narrow in our seeking of her theological sources. To immediately unpack the Robinson–Calvin crossover is a limiting or reductive move at the best of times, but is more obviously wrongheaded when we look to this debut text. *Housekeeping* is decidedly theologically agnostic by comparison to the later *Gilead* novels and is much less immediately amenable to Calvinist interpretation. And this is not to say that it is the religious black sheep of the theological fiction family, but instead that it reveals a wider point: that Robinson has a much wider set of influences – both theological and secular – than we have allowed her. With the 'theologian of the Ordinary' moniker in mind, it is essential attention is paid to the rich tradition of nineteenth-century-American writing Robinson claims as her lineage as much as she ever does Calvin.

So before turning to Robinson's debut novel, *Housekeeping*, it will be useful to sketch out the distinctly American tradition of writing attentive to the Ordinary; for as the rest of the chapter will explore, *Housekeeping* is, in part, Robinson's fictive engagement with the American nineteenth century. The theological potential Robinson locates in the seemingly mundane is not unique to her work, but has in fact an almost 200-year American legacy in figures like Walt Whitman, Margaret Fuller, Emily Dickinson, Nathaniel Hawthorne, Ralph Waldo Emerson, Flannery O'Connor, Wallace Stevens,

Mary Oliver, Mark Doty and Marie Howe – a tradition Robinson discusses frequently. By beginning with the Ordinary and the excessive nature of experience one can expect to find there, Robinson places herself in the legacy of the transcendentalist Emerson, a key player in this chapter and a thinker she comments '[is] just a very beautiful articulator of very essential things' (Chapter 5). Emerson expanded 'church' into the fields, forests and meadows of nineteenth-century New England, and called for a democratic theology that remained uncontrolled by religious hierarchy, by meaningless tradition and untested prior doctrinal commitments. In his essays, Emerson writes of nature as if it were an inexhaustible source of spiritual riches, a world saturated with significance and always ready to give up these riches to an attentive observer. Emerson's 'Man Thinking' is immersed in the stuff of the world: 'what is nature to him? There is never a beginning, there is never an end, to the inexplicable continuity of this web of God, but always a circular power returning into itself' (Emerson 2000: 45). For Stanley, 'Emerson's "Nature" is staked on the transformative potential of perceptual attention', picking up on a faith, common to both Robinson and Emerson (Stanley 2016: 463). Self-consciously attempting to inaugurate an authentically American canon, Emerson sought to set the terms for American writing and it is crucial to note the 'ordinariness' of his sources. Emerson's 'The American Scholar' (1837) sketches an approach to thinking, writing and acting that emerges from a posture of attentiveness to the apparently Ordinary:

> I embrace the common, I explore and sit at the feet of the familiar, the low. Give me insight into to-day, and you may have the antique and future worlds. What would we really know the meaning of? The meal in the firkin; the milk in the pan; the ballad in the street; the news of the boat; the glance of the eye; the form and the gait of the body; show me the ultimate reason of these matters; show me the sublime presence of the highest spiritual case lurking, as always it does lurk, in these suburbs and extremities of nature. (Emerson 2000: 57)

Emerson builds his theology on Ordinary foundations, and has a commitment to uncovering spiritual truths in the seemingly mundane. Writers working after Emerson's 1836 'Nature' in the American nineteenth century translated and extended Emerson's basic convictions of the centrality of subjective experience and the theological potential of nature into the poetry, novels and stories that Robinson cites as her literary and theological sources. Speaking to Thomas Gardner, Robinson reflects on the sophisticated use of language in nineteenth-century American writing, noting 'it had to do with what, I suppose, one has to describe as the individualism of the culture, in the sense that the individual sensorium was assumed to be a sort of sacred place and to be a sufficient revelation of whatever there was to be understood' (Gardner 2006: 47). Jenner, whose work on Stanley Cavell and Robinson is truly revelatory, notes that 'Robinson and Cavell find a language of acknowledgement in their turn to transcendentalism' (Jenner 2019: 4). And while this language of acknowledgement leads Cavell to Ordinary language philosophy, it leads Robinson to the Ordinary in itself, and Emerson and his contemporaries are her 'way in' to a theology built on attention to the Ordinary. Cavell suggests in *Senses of Walden* (1972) that American philosophy has been used primarily in novels and stories, that is, 'in the metaphysical riot of its greatest literature' (Cavell 33). Robinson is more interested in theology than philosophy, and she would no doubt substitute her own discipline here and find much with which to agree.

For Robinson, these American writers listed earlier are instructive for the weight they place on perception as the gateway to meaningful encounter with the natural world: 'Emerson, Thoreau, and Whitman see through all convenient or dismissive categories to the actual, the vital and essential. In every case their protagonist is the perceiver. The beauty they achieve has the character of acuity rather than refinement', Robinson here noting the sheer optimism with which the American Renaissance writers approached the senses (Robinson 2018: 295). Stout makes the crucial point that Calvin, preceding these American writers, places a special focus on sight as a means of encountering God. Calvin's *Commentary on Genesis* is a useful source text for this claim, and the work where Calvin claims, 'we see, indeed, the world with our eyes, we tread the earth with our feet [. . .] but in the very things we attain some knowledge, there dwells such an immensity of divine power, goodness, and wisdom, as absorbs all our senses' (Calvin, *Commentary on Genesis*). Stout argues, with Calvin in mind, that 'the world is created with sacramental intention. Knowledge of God is mediated by the very physical capacities of sight, touch, and smell. Of these various sensory communications, it is sight that places the most prominent role' (Stout 2014: 574). From Calvin to Emerson there is a distinct and important emphasis placed on sight as a route to divinity. Emerson famously wrote of transforming himself into a 'Transparent Eyeball', but also notes in the same essay that he could survive anything as long as he retained his eyesight. Scholars have been keen to bring Calvin's theology to bear on Robinson's debut novel, but perhaps were more resistant in allowing Emerson his place in this text, which restricts interpretative potential and also underplays the shift from this initial fiction to the *Gilead* novels. The American Renaissance, for Robinson, remains the most interesting and thought-producing period of American literary history simply because of the ordinariness of its subjects and sources, and the implicit faith writers had in the individual soul as a site of revelation, central themes that run right through the heart of her written output. This book traces Robinson's own approach to the Ordinary and, as she notes here, her fascination with Emerson and his contemporaries is linked always to their fascination with this same Ordinary:

> The absence of shrines and rituals and processions that interpreted the world and guided understanding of it in England and Europe reflected, as absence, a sense of immanence that gave theological meaning to anything in itself in the moment of perception – a buzzing fly, a blade of grass. The exalted mind could understand the ordinary as visionary, given discipline and desire. (Robinson 2018: 295)

Robinson is not an anomalous literary figure, though, a sort of twentieth/twenty-first-century writer engaged with solely nineteenth-century theological and literary debates. Such a sketching of the American intellectual landscape risks leaving out key twentieth-century writers who carried Emerson's serious attention to the Ordinary forward. Elizabeth Bishop stands in this lineage, as does Wallace Stevens, William Carlos Williams and, most crucially of all, Flannery O'Connor. Each of these writers, although with different assumptions and intentions, approach the Ordinary with a sense of the utmost expectation. The red wheelbarrow upon which so much depends for Williams; the golf flourisher of Stevens' metaphysical poetics; the battered tin basin which shines like the moon in Bishop's 'The Shampoo'; all of these poems are serious in their engagement with the everyday, and their poets approach it with the assumption that a perception honouring the object itself is always rewarded with surprising insight. Phillips' insightful study, *The Poetics of the Everyday* (2010), hones in on the writing of everyday time in Frost, Bishop, Stevens and Merrill, noting that 'each of these poets works to convey the necessity of quotidian experience into an aesthetic and experiential opportunity' (Phillips 2010: 1). 'In their work, ordinary experience both shapes creative practices and directs thematic preoccupations', she argues, and her study demonstrates how the Ordinary cycles of an Ordinary day find both a home and a directing influence on these central American poets. The Ordinary, once again, is demonstrated to have a richly American tradition. Emerson's embrace of the common is complicated and deepened by the twentieth-century poets, for sure, but the very fact of their expectant engagement is indebted to Emerson's transcendental initiative.

The attention to particulars, or the allowing for the particularity of the Ordinary, is striking in these writers, and none more so than Flannery O'Connor. Famously Robinson has noted that she sees nothing resembling grace in O'Connor's stories, but the two women are closely aligned in their views on the importance of the particular for a writer's work. O'Connor writes, 'it is the peculiar burden of the fiction writer that he has to make one country do for all and that he has to evoke one country through the concrete particulars of a life that he can make believe' (O'Connor 1972: 27). Flannery O'Connor's focus on evoking particulars in order to get to something more universal has a rich American literary history. Thoreau, for example, states, 'we are acquainted with a mere pellicle of the globe on which we live. Most have not delved six feet beneath the surface, nor leaped as many above it. We know not where we are' (Thoreau 1983: 380). And Emerson, too, notes the importance of paying attention to local particulars, arguing that, 'it is for want of self-culture that the superstition of Traveling, whose idols are Italy, England, Egypt retains its fascination for all educated Americans. They who made Egypt, Italy, or Greece venerable in the imagination, did so by sticking fast where they were' (Emerson 2000: 149). This is essential transcendentalist doctrine, or at least as close as one can get to an essential transcendentalist doctrine. Attention is paramount, and the present is not in any way subservient or secondary to the past or the future in the same way that America, in all its newness, is not less than the historically rich European continent. O'Connor, defending her 'Southernness' adds, 'to know oneself is to know one's region' (O'Connor 35). And the transcendentalists would want to add: to know one's self, one's region, would be to necessarily have an insight into all regions, into all selves. Robinson does not conform to this perhaps morally dubious notion of universality, as is apparent in her writing of race as excavated in Chapters 2 and 3, but she does indeed share the conviction that writers and theologians must see the green of their own grass, as it were. To disparage the local and, by extension, the Ordinary is a human tendency Robinson and the American writers she admires seek to overturn.

The American Renaissance and *Housekeeping*

Ruth's narration displays a keen eye for what could be termed the more mundane elements of daily life. The sights and sounds of the Ordinary are documented with a Thoreauvian meticulousness. For example, snow is described as 'granular in the shade, and in the sun it turned soft and clung damply to whatever it covered', and she later records the sound of the Ordinary: 'the sky was dark blue, there was no wind at all, but everywhere an audible seep and trickle of melting' (Robinson 1980: 69). These passages are taken almost at random, a fact made possible by Ruth's persistent focus on the Ordinary make-up of a day or of a moment, and this focus has a deeply American connection. Robinson has directed her interpreters' attention, as noted earlier, to the American Renaissance when they approach her first novel. Her very apparent fascination with these writers is down to their self-conscious use of language and with the extremely high expectations they had of language's possibility. To begin reading *Housekeeping* and its metaphors, a working knowledge of the writing of Emerson, Thoreau, Hawthorne, Whitman and Dickinson is needed as it certainly helps unlock Robinson's subtlety and locate the intellectual landscape of her first novel. She speaks and writes often of these writers, noting that,

> Nothing in literature appeals to me more than the rigour with which they fasten on problems of language, of conciseness – bending form to their

purposes, ransacking ordinary speech and common experience [...] always, to borrow a phrase from Wallace Stevens, in the act of finding what will suffice. (Robinson, NYT)

Yet Robinson is not just attracted to these writers for their elevated and innovative use of language, but also for the foundational assumptions on which their writing is founded. And what these writers share is the conviction that the Ordinary is theologically revealing; that it, when given attention, whether in writing or in daily experience, the Ordinary can be seen to house transcendence-in-immanence, what Kearney calls the 'sacramental return to epiphanies of the everyday' (Kearney 2010: 85). In other words, the metaphors of Dickinson; the grand expectations of Whitman's 'Song of Myself'; the theological documentation of Thoreau, all betray the connection they each subscribe to the Ordinary and the divine. Examples abound, such is the centrality of the Ordinary–divine connection perceived by the American Renaissance writers. Whitman notes in his epic that he 'find[s] letters from God dropt in the street, and every one is sign'd by God's / name' and asks, 'Why should I wish to see God better than this day?' (Whitman 1995: 67). Thoreau similarly records, 'When I see [...] this luxuriant foliage, the creation of an hour, I am affected as if in a peculiar sense I stood in the laboratory of the Artist who made the world and me' (Thoreau 1983: 354). Emerson's famed 'embrace of the common' was not a straightforward turn to the natural world in search of inspiration, but rather an open armed embrace of immanence as the only theological show in town. And as the introduction to this book discussed, Robinson sees the term 'transcendentalist' to be something of a misnomer for a man so concerned with the everyday; in fact, one has the suspicion that if it didn't sound so clumsy, Robinson would opt for its opposite – 'immanentalist' – to more accurately capture Emerson and his theology. He goes to nature with full expectation that it is in the material world that God can be located. And this pantheistic impulse need not lead to actual pantheism, for it is surely the case for Emerson that God is met in the *experience* of encountering nature rather than a divine presence in an object itself. This takes us further into Robinson's love for these writers, for it is their positive appraisals of perception that has her attention. And it is not just the content of their work that pulls

Robinson to it, but also the style and rhythm of their writing. Ravits (1989) also observes how Robinson 'captures the resonances of traditional American poetry and prose in her writing, embracing both sides of the American inheritance in her efforts to retell the story of heroic selfhood – even as her version, in Pound's words, "makes it new" by making it female' (Ravits 1989: 644). The 'femaleness' of the text is crucial and critics have established the novel as a feminist American classic, one that troubles the patriarchal canon as it, to use Ravits' term, 'extends the American range'.

With this in mind, *Housekeeping* emerges as a literary critic's dream. The richness of the language and the nuance of its symbolism, coupled with the sheer number of metaphoric episodes, result in what is essentially an endlessly interpretable novel. Given the text began life as a series of experiments in extended metaphors – as Gardner has recorded, 'inspired by the great nineteenth century American writers Herman Melville, Emily Dickinson, and Henry David Thoreau' – it is perhaps running the risk of being detrimentally eisegetical to attempt a grand and unifying interpretation of Robinson's debut (Gardner 2006: 32). An interpretation that attempts to unite the many and pluralistically suggestive images under one hermeneutical banner seems inappropriate for such a densely symbolic novel. But it is clear for readers of *Housekeeping* who have a working knowledge of these classic American writers that Robinson picks up on sets of images first introduced in the continent's literature 140 years prior. Thoreau's writing of the train and the sounds of its whistle and its impact on time in America; *Walden*'s (1854) focus on water and on the lake; Emerson's play with the transparency of the individual in the natural world; Emily Dickinson's fly buzzing as she nears death (and her poem 'I Felt a Funeral' is, of course, name-checked in the novel itself); Hawthorne's darkening of the transcendentalist woods in tales like 'Young Goodman Brown' (1835); Edgar Allan Poe's writing of doubleness and doppelgängers: each of these writers and their distinctly American ideas are given a nod in Robinson's novel, and this is important to our reading of it. So instead of producing a systematic interpretation, I want to begin not with the precise contents of the novel's metaphors and images, but with the very blunt fact of their multiplicity and their rich *Americanness*. In lieu of a unifying thesis, then, I want, instead, to probe Robinson's use of metaphor, asking: *to what theological end is her use of symbol and metaphor?* In answering such a key question, we will have to delve into the American nineteenth-century writers Robinson so admires for whom metaphor was a very serious business, a crucial testing of the limits of the possibilities of what language could do. A point often overlooked is that it was Melville's *Moby Dick* (1851) that properly induced Robinson's famed love of Calvin. Given free rein on what to teach her graduate students at the Iowa Writer's Workshop, she opted to teach *Moby Dick*. As part of her preparation, Robinson sought to educate herself on Melville's intellectual background, on the landscape of ideas in which he was immersed. 'Of course it has to be Calvinism, because that's where he came from', she reasoned, and 'went to the library and got Calvin's *Institutes*, and – to my students' surprise – I taught an entire graduate seminar which was simply going back and forth between the *Institutes* and *Moby Dick*' (Larsen and Johnson 2019: 206). Discussing this in an interview, Robinson says that 'reading Calvin helped me read Melville, and reading Melville helped me read Calvin' (Larsen and Johnson 2019: 206). I think it is probably fair to suggest that the focus of the Robinson scholarship has taken the first part of Robinson's phrase more seriously than the second, despite *Housekeeping*'s opening line – 'My name is Ruth' – echoing so clearly Melville's American classic. Theologians are much more keen to read her novels as an inevitable result of Calvinism and have been less forthcoming in allowing her literary influences to, at least in part, account for her Calvinism. And if we are to take seriously Robinson's constant claiming of the American Renaissance, we should begin with her fascination with their metaphors and, in particular, with her debut novel's engagement with them.

Ruth, Robinson's first protagonist, is a metaphor maker. Granted access to her imaginings, we are presented with several extended symbolic passages: from seahorses in a timepiece; a praying parrot burned in a fire; a woman who saw ghost children. And as noted, it would be easy to try to unite these metaphorical episodes under a unifying interpretation, but to do so initially would be to ignore the peculiarity of their presence. Ravits lays bare the connection between Robinson and her literary influences on symbol, arguing that,

> Since the time of Emerson, Hawthorne, and Melville, our fiction has been replete with heavy symbolic representations. It is not surprising, therefore,

that Robinson's protagonist also should regard the sensible world not as an ultimate reality, but as a system of signs to be deciphered. (Ravits 1989: 650)

Ruth is not some Emersonian prototype, though, and that is not what Ravits would claim either. Instead, as will be established, Ruth is written in an Emersonian register in which the natural world is seen – without the need to establish or argue for this – as a symbol or metaphor of the mind. Robinson constructs a character who participates and shares in the foundational assumptions made by American Renaissance writers while also, as will be developed particularly in relation to Emerson, providing room for her to expand and critique the conclusions reached by some of its figureheads. To have a narrator freely engage in the extended metaphors noted above is itself an interesting point worth considering. And to consider it well, we need to do two things: first, we readers must keep in mind that Robinson herself regards *Housekeeping* as something of a theological novel and, second, given this and the metaphorical make-up of the novel require us to position it in relation to important theological work on metaphor. And for this second task we will eventually turn to Sallie McFague.

Mist and moonshine: *Housekeeping*, transparency and selfhood

To take just one overlap between the American Renaissance metaphors of Emerson, for example, and Robinson's first novel is to discover her self-conscious entry into nineteenth-century writing, but also to perceive Robinson's reinterpretation of the tradition. She is certainly no passive recipient of her favoured American writers, but consciously engages in the extension and problematization of their central ideas. A key example of this is *Housekeeping*'s use of the image of transparency. A central metaphor to Emerson's 'Nature', transparency is also taken up by Robinson's novel but its implications are darkened, as we will see. But before we turn to Robinson and Emerson's respective uses of the image, it will be useful to excavate the foundational reasons for their text's radically different treatments.

In American Renaissance writing, the woods are an important and significant location. Thoreau takes up the solitary task of documenting the natural world from his transcendentalist hermitage. He was given this land by Emerson, and certainly the inspiration for the *Walden* project came from the theological optimism of Emerson's writing. For Emerson, the woods are a special place and sits at the heart of his most well-known essay. The woods contain 'perpetual youth', and provide the setting for Emerson's jubilant return to nature (Emerson 2000: 6). This sense of youth is retained by Robinson in her invocation of the woods in *Housekeeping*, but the overall impression is darkened by her prose. As Ruth describes, 'we would walk among those great legs, hearing the enthralled and incessant murmurings far above our heads, like children at a funeral' (Robinson 1980: 98). Emerson's transfiguration to transparent eyeball transforms the woods from physical space to sacred site. The reverse is true for Ruth who admits, 'the woods themselves disturbed us' (Robinson 1980: 98). The divergence between Robinson's novel and the tradition she loves is connected to a radically different conception of transcendence held by the American Renaissance writers, on the one hand, and Ruth, the novel's narrator, on the other hand. Robinson's first novel has no real notion of transcendence, particularly as Christian theologians might speak of it. In this it stands in direct contrast to the *Gilead* novels that, at the very least, open themselves to the debate on a transcendent reality. One of the reasons for this difference is formal. As readers we are given only the mind of Ruth as the lens by which we see the world of the text. But this is just another way of saying the same thing, for the text is nothing outside of Ruth's mind, so is a reflection of the world view of its creator. And she is a protagonist with no real belief in transcendence. Where Ames talks of God and transcendence as a facet of reality, Ruth sees the Bible as a story among stories, a myth with no more veracity than tales of Sisyphus or Baal Hammon. Ruth's trajectory in the novel is not simply an uncomplicated outworking of Emerson's essays. Instead of a transparency produced by positive communion with nature, Ruth is lost in darkness.

Ruth's troubling response to nature and the woods is rendered intelligible by Emerson, who comments, 'the ruin or the blank that we see when we look at nature is in our own eye' (Emerson 2000: 38). For Emerson, nature exists as a kind of spiritual Rorschach test, reflecting back to the observer something of what exists internally. Ruth's fear of the woods is equal to her fear of herself; the forest contains a darkness that hides and conceals, and Ruth, too, knows something of concealment with her inability to deal with her mother's death. She and her mother are blurred together, a haunting feature of the novel that means Helen's absence is replicated in Ruth's transparency. Where Emerson merges with and becomes one with nature to declare 'I am nothing', Ruth finds that this nothingness is a constituent of her being. Robinson here negatively mirrors Whitman's declaration 'I contain multitudes' with Ruth's implicit cry 'I contain nothing' (Whitman 69). Indeed, in *Housekeeping* and 'Nature' there are two kinds of transparencies: Emerson's celebrated transparency as a spiritual achievement of unity with the universe, and Ruth's fearful realization that she does not feel like a distinct, real person. This is given metaphorical form in the text in Ruth's reflection-less image, in the many instances of reflective surfaces in the novel refusing to carry her image. Emerson's dissolving dichotomy of the ME/NOT ME relies, it seems, on 'me' having a defined and definable content. Ruth's existential situation has arisen from a total inability to positively set out on the work of identity creation. Her 'nothingness' is a direct result of this failure to self-create, linked as it is with her complete repression of her mother and her mother's death. This suppression is, in Ruth's case, synonymous with a repression of the self. The mirroring between them is so strong in the novel that individual identities begin to blur and merge to the extent that, if Helen is to be repressed, it necessarily follows that Ruth also represses her 'self' too. Ruth reveals something of the cause of her psychological anxiety in her comment, 'I was afraid to put out my hand, for fear it would touch nothing' (Robinson 1980: 70). She specifically chooses the phrase 'touch nothing' over 'not touch anything' indicating a struggle to come to terms with a seemingly inherited familial nihilism.

It would appear that Ruth is most afraid of the nothingness she finds when she is forced into an inward gaze. Her self-conception is one of minimal existence and she accepts her ontological transparency as an unalterable fact of her being. As she reveals, 'it was a relief to go to Latin class, where I had a familiar place in a human group, alphabetically assigned' (Robinson 1980: 136). Ruth's identity is formed passively. She does not, in Sartrean fashion, see nihilism as a basis for unlimited possibility in self-construction; rather, she attaches herself to others and assimilates herself into them. Two instances of this stand out: Ruth notes, 'we – in recollection I feel no reluctance to speak of Lucille and myself almost as a single consciousness' (Robinson 1980: 98); and, later, 'Sylvie and I (I think that night we were almost a single person)' (Robinson 1980: 209). Ruth's response to the realization that she, her 'self', is vacant, is to find identity through other people. This fact does not escape Lucille's notice who simply states, 'all you ever do is stand around like some stupid zombie' (Robinson 1980: 127). Like a zombie Ruth depends on the fully alive to sustain her 'minimal existence' and just as a zombie straddles boundaries of dead/undead, Ruth similarly finds herself caught in a kind of purgatorial limbo stretching between Lucille and Sylvie, reality and imagination, birth and death. And living in this liminal space, where existence itself is stretched thin enough to become transparent, Ruth reaches for language, as discussed later.

That Robinson situates the metaphors of her debut in nineteenth-century American writing ensures the 'Americanness' of the novel, and encourages her readers to identify the distinctly American anchorings of her writing of transparency. As readers of the transcendentalists are well aware, transparency has a rich American literary tradition, beginning with Emerson and Fuller. Transparency for both is the product of a satisfying and transfiguring communion with the natural world: when the division between the 'ME' and 'NOT ME' dissolves, or, to be more precise, reveals itself to have been artificially imposed the whole time. Robinson enters the American canon and problematizes Emerson's optimistic transparency with a much bleaker take on individual American religious possibility. The divinity implicit in transcendentalism is replaced in *Housekeeping* with a fundamental lack and loss, and the impact on the transparency metaphor is tangible. Robinson darkly mirrors Emerson's famed forest passage with *Housekeeping*'s basement scene.

The scene takes place during the Fingerbone flood and, having followed Sylvie down to the darkness with all candles having been extinguished by the fierce wind, Ruth begins to call out for Sylvie in the obscurity of the basement. Ruth depicts a dark solitude here: 'deprived of all perspective and horizon, I found myself reduced to an intuition, and my sister and aunt to something less than that' (Robinson 1980: 70). Here Ruth experiences a mode of existence that hardly qualifies for the term. Indeed, as she reveals, 'when we did not move or speak, there was no proof we were there at all' (Robinson 1980: 70). Robinson interrogates the very notion of 'being' here, questioning the parameters enclosing the murky term 'existence' and asks the question: As Ruthie fades out of the sensible world in the basement, can she really be said to exist at all? It is not merely left up to the reader to make sense of this question as Ruth is faced with it head on later in the text when she is told by Sylvie, 'you're so quiet, it's hard to know what you think' (Robinson 1980: 105). Ruth's reaction, 'I suppose I don't know what I think', termed by Robinson as a 'confession', 'was a source of both terror and comfort' as it compounded her realization that she 'often seemed invisible – incompletely and minimally existent' (Robinson 1980: 105). Ruth's unusual ambivalence here is striking: she feels both terror and comfort at her realization.

The famous passage from Emerson's most well-known essay marries interestingly with Robinson's basement scene. These words are at the heart of American literature, and reach across the decades to leave a mark on this novel: Emerson writes:

> In the woods we return to reason and faith. There I feel nothing can befall me in life – no disgrace, no calamity [. . .] which nature cannot repair. Standing on the bare ground – my head bathed by the blithe air and uplifted into infinite space – all mean egotism vanishes. I become a transparent eyeball; I am nothing. (Emerson 2000: 6)

The loss of the self, a theme common to both passages, is nonetheless treated very differently. Emerson's tone is one of joyful celebration; there is the distinct sense he is delighting in his experience when he declares 'I am nothing' (Emerson 2000: 6). While these passages are communicating the loss of the self, the language used to communicate the effect of the event is very different in *Housekeeping* and 'Nature'. Emerson finds the experience of being in nature, 'under a clouded sky, without having in my thoughts any occurrence of special good fortune', so fundamental and essential to his identity that he begins to blur the boundaries of self and world, of personal identity and divinity – 'I am part or parcel of God' (Emerson 2000: 6). For Emerson, as Richardson Jr.

notes, 'nature was [his] starting point for a new theology' (Parle and Morris 103). This new theology finds its genesis in nature and its *telos* in vision, as Emerson has it, 'I see all; the currents of the Universal Being circulate through me' (Emerson 2000: 6). Through this revelatory experience Emerson moves from being a keen observer of nature to a being inseparable from nature, from the ability to view nature from a limited perspective to viewing the world from nature's perspective, enabling him to enjoy an existential harmony with the natural world, an experience that qualitatively modifies his vision of the Ordinary.

What Ruthie experiences in the basement could properly be termed as 'solitude', an event that removes her from the community and cuts many of the ties that connect her to the external world. Solitude as a condition of existence is celebrated by Robinson in her non-fiction, commenting, 'I grew up with the confidence that the greatest privilege was to be alone and have all the time you wanted', and confessing, 'I'm a kind of solitary' (Fay, *Paris Review*). Robinson is well known for her positive attitude towards the experience of solitude and she and Ruth share solitude as a feature of their childhood and adolescence, as Robinson writes, 'I remember when I was a child at Coolin or Sagle or Talache, walking into the woods by myself and feeling the solitude around me build like electricity and pass through my body with a jolt that made my hair prickle' (Robinson 2012: 88). Where Robinson and Emerson celebrate their disappearance into the natural world, Ruth finds genuine solitude frightening. To be alone for Ruth is a physical revelation of what was always true, that to exist is to be entirely alone. This central Robinsonian truth is compounded by Ruth's minimal existence, the fact that she doesn't seem to be able to keep herself company. For Robinson it is clear that loneliness, solitude and silence are things to be sought out, welcomed and experienced as an unavoidable aspect of existence: she is a true Emersonian in this regard. Ruth's reaction to her experience in the basement runs contrary to this kind of thinking, however, and the tension resulting from reading this passage alongside Robinson's positive espousing of solitude in her essays and her general advocacy of Emersonian approaches to nature reveal Ruth to be something of an anomalous Robinson character, one trapped in loss and seeking escape in language. But the heightened attention to the Ordinary and the honouring of Ordinary detail in language connects her to the later *Gilead* characters, and puts her in more positive dialogue with the transcendentalist.

As one of Robinson's most obvious American influences, Emerson saw little difference between the language we use about the world and the world itself. As Gura observes, 'Nature is language too, providing man the symbols to speak about his innermost thoughts as well as to describe the world around him' (Gura 2007: 94–5). The material world and the material *of* the world are not incidental to language, according to Emerson, but actually condition and structure it. For this reason, there is a symmetry between our metaphor making and the world it is seeking to report on. For, at base, 'words are signs of natural facts' (Emerson 2000: 13). Language, for the transcendentalist, has come to us from an original, universal and pictorial language. The origins of our speech spring from a primitive poetry in which the natural world and words were as closely connected as could be imagined and Robinson, too, in a 1987 piece affirms this view, writing, 'I subscribe altogether to the idea that every word is a poem at root' (Robinson 1987). Granting this origin, metaphors emerge in Emerson as a special case of language: language self-conscious of its own history and birth, speaking in pictures to override the division between 'out there' and 'in here'. And so it is with Ruth. The lake, of which Robinson has said she considers *Housekeeping* to be about, takes on various metaphorical connotations for Ruth. At one and the same time, both womb and tomb, it is also the water of flood and Flood, a reminder of her grandfather and mother, and a metaphysical pointer to both impermanence and the seeming certainty of insidious change. This Emersonian correspondence, and recognition of this correspondence, between inner and outer, that is, between inward emotional states and the natural world, is itself our earliest language. And Ruth's relation to the natural world is both an example of this correspondence and a deepening of Emerson's original analysis. It is of no surprise then to have Robinson in 1987, seven years after the publication of *Housekeeping*, declare, 'I am an Emersonian. I think of language as the creature, and the genius of collective humankind' (Robinson 1987).

When Emerson's 'Nature' was published in 1836, it attracted harsh criticism from some for its supposedly abstracted treatment of language, beauty and God. As Gura puts it, 'it ['Nature'] was so unmistakably different, in language and in play, that many people simply did not know what to make of it and threw it off as so much transcendental mist and moonshine' (Gura 95). But Emerson, writing in the 1830s, generated a momentum and set in motion some key American ideas that would spark in the minds of Nathaniel Hawthorne, Emily Dickinson, Walt Whitman and Margaret Fuller. And these writers would, in turn, inform the writer of *Housekeeping*. And while Robinson's first novel is more trains and lake than it is mist and moonshine, American Renaissance writers have their fingerprints on it and in the metaphors of its narrator.

Emerson's philosophy of metaphor finds a home in Sallie McFague's theological analysis of language where she too notes that metaphor is not merely prevalent in language, but actually constitutes language itself. She writes, 'far from being an esoteric or ornamental rhetorical device superposed on ordinary language, metaphor *is* ordinary language. It is the *way* we think' (McFague 1982: 16). Ordinary language is metaphorical and it, to use McFague's helpful phrase, operates on the principle that a thing both 'is and is not' (McFague 1982: 13). The objects, sights and experiences of the world stir in us an inevitable cocktail of similarity and disunity – 'this event was like this but also not like it in one crucial way'. Metaphors, most obviously similes, are not one way of thinking among many, but in truth, metaphors reveal in their workings how we think all the time; they uncover the base of our thought patterns. A cup of water is never simply a cup of water. On a more literal level, it is a prism through which light passes; a source of life; a home for bacteria (the reader will note how I haven't even been able to avoid metaphor here, either, with 'prism', 'source' and 'home'). But it is also reminiscent of the return home from the long run; the smell of the river, or perhaps the ritual and sacrament of baptism. In *Housekeeping* every cup of water is the lake, every cup is a symbol of death and loss. It both is and is not the lake, and the cup of water is our way into how Ruth thinks generally – in metaphors, like everyone – but also how metaphors of and for loss are a way in to how *she* thinks particularly. We can use Emerson's correspondence theory, then, to 'reverse engineer' how we normally think of metaphor, and use the contents of Ruth's images to guide our reading of the psychology from which they came.

This is merely to say, then, that *Housekeeping* is told by a narrator who participates in and evidences the peculiarity of human language; this, at this stage, is to have said little more than that '*Housekeeping* is a novel that bears resemblance to the real world, and real people'. In other words, I have said nothing of particular interest to readers of Robinson in particular. But if we take this as a starting point – the inescapability of metaphor in thinking, speaking, acting, listening – then we can pay attention to this general truth's particular outworking. And this is where Robinson's debut begins to intersect satisfyingly and disruptively with theology. We shift focus now from *American* metaphors to American *metaphors*, examining the theological implications of Robinson's self-conscious turn to metaphor in her debut.

The naming of things: Protestant metaphors and Catholic poetics

Housekeeping is, above all, about loss. Ruth, as she says near the end of the text, understands her mother's death as an abandonment; and the metaphors and imaginative episodes that make up large parts of *Housekeeping* are, in some way, a response to a fundamental and substantial loss. At the close of the novel, Sylvie and Ruth are left to wander. They have been expelled from housekeeping, from the domestic security in which they never truly felt at home. The foundational maternal loss experienced by Ruth at an early age is replicated in even a house's refusal to claim her. In this way, Ruth and Sylvie's departure from home connects Robinson's first novel to the early biblical stories of loss and wandering. Adam was, as the story goes, given the task of naming the world and its creatures. The naming of things is, according to this creation myth, a primary task of people and Ruth's speech and her richly imaginative thinking emerge as her means of naming loss. The parrot burned in the fire; the sea horses preserved from time's passing; the woman who lost her children: these passages make it into Ruth's narration because in them she has a way of speaking about loss that is more acceptable than facing the notion of a maternal suicide directly. The first half of the text contains only one use of the word 'death' and it is used by Ruth to refer to a future event, the then 'yet-to-happen' death of her grandmother. As Ruthie notes, 'she always took some satisfaction in thinking ahead to the time when her simple private destiny would intersect with the great public processes of law and finance – that is, to the time of her death' (Robinson 1980: 27). Death here is spoken about as something still to come, an unrealized future. However, when discussing the event of death itself, as a blunt fact of unalterable history, Ruth refuses to use the 'd' word, preferring instead the use of euphemism to describe the event. For example, Ruthie's grandmother did not 'die', she 'eschewed awakening', or she 'did not awaken' (Robinson 1980: 29, 164). The finality of the word 'death' is avoided with this strategy and the metaphor of sleep ensures that awakening is always a possibility; indeed, as Ruth later notes, 'perhaps we all awaited a resurrection' (Robinson 1980: 96). By absorbing the permanence of death into the transient nature of sleep, Ruth can retain her hope of resurrection and avoid both the finality and trauma of death. And her non-literal linguistic strategies when discussing death reveal a faith in language to insulate from unbearable trauma.

McFague's work *Metaphorical Theology* (1982) is a stunning contribution to contemporary theology and was published two years after *Housekeeping*. It is of little surprise, then, given their historical proximity, the two writers share overlapping interests in language, story and metaphor, and dialogue with one another in interesting ways. McFague writes,

> Consciousness of the relativity and plurality of interpretations forces us to recognise that language is not just the halting attempts by 'Christians' to say something appropriate about God, but is the halting attempts by specific individuals: by Paul, a first-century convert from Judaism, who had great empathy with the problems of Jewish Christians but little sympathy for women or slave Christians; by Julian of Norwich, a medieval woman mystic, who spoke of 'our tender Mother Jesus'; by Reinhold Niebuhr, a twentieth-century preacher from Detroit, whose experience with American capitalism caused him to see human sinfulness as the basis for political 'realism'; by Mary Daly, a twentieth-century, Catholic-educated feminist, who sees the history of the world's religions as an exercise in misogyny. (McFague 1982: 3)

What McFague argues here is for a recognition among theologians of what has been clear and obvious to literary scholars and critical theorists for many decades: that our language is conditioned by experience, that what we 'see' is largely filtered by what we have experienced. And, by extension, this implies our metaphors are given their context and implication by our experience; and, crucially, the way we read, and the way we overlook text, too, shaped by our experience. To say that this is obvious to literary scholars and critical theorists is not to criticize the insights of McFague, a theologian, but merely to point out how reluctant theology has been to treat the Bible as a text. That McFague's assertion of authorial limits and biases should appear relatively anomalous within a theological tradition is testament to how the Bible has been kept from the kinds of reading that Shakespeare, Dickinson and Kafka have endured over the years. But buried in McFague's statement is the assumption that we write out of our experience and that to read well, we must read in the knowledge that writers, too, write out of experience and that experience implies perspective, and perspective in turn implies limitation.

In Chapter 3 we will look closely at Robinson's approach to substitutionary atonement. But leaving the finer theological points of this debate to one side for now, it is important at this point to note that she does not want to engage in an argument with those who 'find these understandings right and moving' (Robinson 2015: 194). That she includes the feeling of being moved here is crucial, as it signals something of Robinson's approach to scripture. To be moved is to have found meaning, and Robinson wants to take no issue with an interpretation in which Christians have found meaning. Even the word 'right' does not necessarily imply 'correct' or 'true', for it is surely possible to have an interpretation feel 'right' without ever being able to prove its truthfulness. 'Right' is also, then, a word that signifies the discovery of meaning. And this is a wider point for Robinson's theology: to read the Bible is to read for meaning, not necessarily truth. This is not to place meaning and truth at opposite sides of a chasm, as if one does not imply the other, but rather to correctly order the priorities of a reader. For Robinson, meaning precedes truth, and her struggles with scripture in her essays are always much more concerned with the meaningfulness of an interpretation much more than with the correctness of their findings. This is, of course, to define truth in the very narrow way of the logical positivists that Robinson so despises. But if we are to expand the definition of truth past 'fact', then meaning and truth may well eventually become synonyms. And this would not be much of a problem for Robinson. In fact, it is much more true to the human experience of reading a text.

To return to *Housekeeping* and McFague's insistence on the limits of biblical writers, it becomes very clear that to read Ruth's narration is to be introduced to the experience-structured mind of its creator. McFague argues, 'feminists generally agree that whoever names the world owns the world. The Genesis story, according to the traditional, patriarchal interpretation, sees Adam naming the world without consulting Eve' (McFague 1982: 8). In some ways, *Housekeeping* is a revision of this origin myth. Robinson deliberately and literally submerges her main male character within the first few pages, and the names given to things in this novel are given by women. Early on, Ruth recounts a day in her grandmother's life following Edmund, her husband's, death. It is worth quoting in full.

> One day my grandmother must have carried out a basket of sheets to hand in the spring sunlight, wearing her widow's black, performing the rituals of the ordinary as an act of faith. Say there were two or three inches of hard old snow on the ground, with earth here and there oozing through the broken places, and that there was warmth in the sunlight, when the wind did not blow it all away, and say she stooped breathlessly in her corset to lift up a sodden sheet by its hems, and say that when she had pinned three corners to the lines it began to billow and leap in her hands, to flutter and tremble, and to glare with the light, and the throes of the thing were as gleeful and strong as if a spirit were dancing in cerements. (Robinson 1980: 16)

The passage shimmers with a paradoxical blend of anticipation and presentness; and it finishes with the both 'is and is not' of McFague's analysis of metaphor. This, among other similar passages, reflects the effect of a substantial loss on perception of the Ordinary. Grief here gives way to presentness, and makes strange the given, or, perhaps more accurately, intensifies the experience of the given so that its inherent strangeness is palpable. 'And every evening would bring its familiar strangeness', Ruth goes on to record, and this familiar strangeness is a phrase that efficiently captures what Robinson's novels, in part, seek to remind their readers of. John O'Donahue opens his *Anam Cara* – a meditation on Celtic Christianity – with the phrase 'it is strange to be here, the mystery never leaves you alone', which could be taken as a gloss on Robinson's fiction as a whole, and this passage in *Housekeeping* specifically (O'Donahue 1997: 3).

Ruth names this experience of grief-sharpened experience, gives it a language and a metaphor in the term 'resurrection of the Ordinary'. In this way she participates in that prelapsarian command, the Edenic task to give things names, speaking in a kind of voice not given a hearing in the original creation myth. She creatively pens her own family's history, giving her present a past, and giving names to experiences she never had. 'So the wind that billowed her sheets announced to her the resurrection of the ordinary. Soon the skunk cabbage would come up, and the cidery smell would rise in the orchard', writes Ruth, and this resurrection operates as a metaphor for attention. A page or so from this passage, Ruth once again recounts an evening in which her grandmother goes out to the garden. This scene, filtered through Ruth, is full of metaphor and full of the Ordinary.

> What was it like. One evening one summer she went out to the garden. The earth in the rows was light and soft as cinders, pale clay yellow, and the trees and plants were ripe, ordinary green and full of comfortable rustlings. And above the pale earth and bright trees the sky was the dark blue of ashes. (Robinson 1980: 19)

This is the resurrection of the Ordinary, or, to use another theological term, the 'transfiguration of perception'. Sylvia asks herself, 'What have I seen, what have I seen. The earth and the sky and the garden, not as they always are' (Robinson 1980: 19). And the answer is, of course, that she has seen these things exactly as they are. Ruth notes earlier that her grandmother 'distrusted the idea of transfiguration', and in a novel that sustains a caution with regard to change and transformation, it is important to note that it is not the Ordinary that is transfigured in this resurrection, but perception *of* the Ordinary (Robinson 1980: 10). And Ruth's imagining of this scenario exhibits the heightened attention of her grandmother's presence here through metaphor. In the passage, Ruth uses at least three metaphors, and it is clear that for Ruth, the resurrection of the Ordinary is best served in the reaching for the metaphor. The metaphors of *Housekeeping* are the means by which its narrator has to name experience. Ruth's participation in the primal command to give things names implicates her in the taxonomic task of giving loss a set of images adequate to experience. The text, read in this light, becomes a search for supple language to name and respond to loss.

The American poet, Marie Howe (1950–) released her collection *Magdalene* (2017) thirty-seven years after Robinson's debut; yet despite the time lapse, the two books intersect beautifully. In particular, Howe's poem 'The Teacher' stands out as a remarkable conversation partner for *Housekeeping*. The collection's speaker – the constantly shifting voice of the biblical character, Mary Magdalene – tells in this poem of living in the afterglow of encounters with The Teacher – Jesus.

> It wasn't that I saw something new – or saw suddenly into him, / not that, not ever / but that the room itself, whatever room we might be standing in, / assumed an astonishing clarity: / and the things in the room: a table, a cup, a meowing cat. (Howe 2017: 43)

Howe's speaker experiences at the poem's close what Ruth terms a 'resurrection of the Ordinary', what I am terming a 'transfiguring of perception'. And Howe is just as clear as Robinson that the Ordinary stays Ordinary in this experience – it is perception that adapts to honour and accommodates the Ordinary itself. I have written elsewhere on how this poem of Howe's interacts with and problematizes the largely Protestant tradition of American writing I identified earlier as the American Ordinary tradition (Cunning 2019). Howe's Catholic poetics eschews the Emersonian conviction that metaphor is necessary for full participation in divinity. For her, the transcendence implicit in transcendentalism implies a vertical set of metaphors tempting us always to lift our heads from the thing itself. In her work she offers an eye-level immanence, a distinctly Catholic approach to metaphor and the Ordinary. For Howe, metaphors are to make a thing more here than there, and their purposes never enrol the Ordinary as a means to an end.

I bring in Howe here to provide a contrasting, but equally rich, voice to balance Robinson's Ruth. And this contrast is given theological foundation in McFague's distinction between symbolical and metaphorical language. 'The Protestant tradition is, I would suggest, "metaphorical", the Catholic "symbolical"', argues McFague, adding that the Protestant tradition 'tends to see dissimilarity, distinction, tension and hence to be skeptical and secular, stressing the transcendence of God and finitude of creation', where the Catholic tradition, 'tends to see similarity, connection, harmony and hence, to be believing and religious, stressing the continuity between God and creation' (McFague 1982: 13). Now McFague is clear that these distinctions are not strong and stable, and are 'not meant to be directly related to the Protestant and Catholic ecclesiastical institutions' (McFague 1982: 13). In fact, she goes on to add that 'not only are many Protestants "catholic" and many Catholics "protestant", but it is obvious that either tendency without the other would be insupportable. They are complimentary' (McFague 1982: 13). So the distinctions McFague makes between broadly Protestant and Catholic approaches to religious language are in no way meant to put up neat walls, but simply to begin to frame a useful conversation on the meaningful ways people have found to speak of their experience. She glosses David Tracey's work *The Analogical Imagination* (1981) to put this distinction another way: 'there are characteristic differences in the Christian community between those for whom experience in the world engenders primarily a sense of wonder and trust and those for whom it engenders primarily a need for healing and transformation' (McFague 1982: 14). The former 'moves from unawareness of harmony, taking the negatives into account, while the second moves from an awareness of the negatives, reaching toward a future harmony' (McFague 1982: 14). This latter way of seeing and experiencing is, to use McFague's classifications, a Protestant engagement with the world. And within Robinson's fiction there is undoubtedly a shift between *Housekeeping* and *Gilead* in how the narrators see their world. Ames' approach is nicely summarized in the first way, in that he has a base sense of wonder at the world as it is, and approaches the problems of his community and family from a prior assumption of wholeness and unity. He is, like Robinson, then, when she notes 'my Christology has awe as its first principle. It is a very generalised awe, since Creation is full of the glory of God' (Robinson 2015: 195).

Ruth's way of seeing certainly belongs to the more distinctly Protestant tradition of speaking of the world. The natural world, for example, is not so much evidence of the general glory of God for her, but is rather made up of substances yearning for completion, return and reconciliation. And her enrolling of extended metaphors to describe this world substitutes a this for a that, a distinctly Protestant approach to both language and reality. So it is the case that the pages of *Housekeeping* glisten with not merely the hope of reconstitution, but the expectation of it. Ruth muses, for example:

> For when does a berry break upon the tongue as sweetly as when one longs to taste it, and when is the taste refracted into so many hues and savers of ripeness and earth, and when do our senses know any thing so utterly as when we lack it? And here again is a foreshadowing – the world will be made whole. (Robinson 1980: 152)

Ruth's sense of a law of completion that will knit the world together is gleaned from observation. 'Every winter', she observes, 'the orchard is flooded with snow, and every spring the waters are parted, death is undone, and every Lazarus rises', and earlier she observes how 'in a month those flowers would bloom' (Robinson 1980: 124, 16). The pattern of the seasons and the floods and receding of floods are read like a text by Ruth, and she finds there a natural theology of completion for, 'what are all these fragments for, if not to be knit up finally?' (Robinson 1980: 92). But even before considering this notion of completion, it is important to pause and reflect on the foundations of such a belief. If restoration is expected, then implication is its necessity. And this is fundamental for Ruth; it is a primary assumption. Indeed, the Ordinary for Ruth needs healing and transformation, just as she sees in her imaginings of her grandmother in which 'the dear ordinary had healed as seamlessly as an image on water' (Robinson 1980: 15). The Ordinary in *Housekeeping* is seen and experienced by a young woman who lost her mother to suicide, so it is necessarily experienced in and through grief. Ruth dreams of the lake and in the dream it is 'knit up of hands and upturned faces' (Robinson 1980: 41). As noted earlier, the woods – that site of spiritual optimism in the American 1830s – terrify her too. The loss of Helen, the death of her grandmother and fleeing of her sister are all bereavements that endow the Ordinary itself – always operating symbolically anyway – with loss and with death. Ruth's language, then, is built on the fracture of metaphor, and their content amplifies this basic truth of experience: loss is pervasive and resurrection is required. So when Ruth uses the language of completion and restoration, she reveals her desire for this world, a place of loss and contingency, to be reconstituted. As Ravits puts it, 'Ruth is a visionary whose unassuaged longing causes her to imagine possibilities of restoration in terms reminiscent of Emerson's "law of compensation"' (Ravits 1989: 651). For Emerson, as it is with Ruth, this law of compensation – the belief that the world will made whole – is not a theology but a philosophy read from nature itself. Nature is built on balance and equilibrium, 'every excess causes a defect; every defect an excess', as Emerson puts it (Emerson 2000: 157). And Ruth's experience is of imbalance and excessive tragedy, so the restoration she hopes for is the compensation she feels she is due. Her turn to metaphor, then, classifies her as something of a Protestant thinker. Implicit within metaphor is distance, dissimilarity and tension. In her desire to speak of the world of experience in metaphor, Ruth subtly hints towards a conception of the world as incomplete, imperfect and tinged with loss. The micro-transaction of metaphor – saying one thing in terms of another – is a stepping stone and blueprint for Ruth's thinking more broadly. Like the object of a metaphor, Ruth's world will, ultimately, she hopes, be traded. And we only know what loss is because of an inherent intuition of a world in which loss is impossible. Earlier it was noted that Ruth has no real notion of transcendence and no evangelical or dogmatic belief in God; so when she imagines a reconstituted world of returned things, she does so from without the conventional limits of Christian orthodoxy. And this comes in to sharp focus when she turns to the Bible.

Housekeeping and the Bible: Stories among stories

While it would be in the gap between *Housekeeping* and *Gilead* that Robinson would truly immerse herself in Calvin and Calvinism, it is an unavoidable fact that this 'pre-Calvin' novel is fascinated with the Bible, and most particularly the Old Testament. And without the theological acumen Robinson would go on to develop, *Housekeeping* is, paradoxically, just as theologically interesting as the *Gilead* novels. Because in the absence of knowledge of centuries-old debates on prevenient grace or limited atonement, Robinson is free to engage literarily with Bible stories and characters where she will later write typologically. It is undoubtedly true that the Bible becomes increasingly important for Robinson, from the writing of the agnostic Ruth to her second female orphan figure, Lila, who discovers herself in the pages of Ezekiel. However, this is not to say that *Housekeeping* is not valuable in its treatment of scripture, but merely to note that its underlying assumptions about scriptural authority are simply different.

Housekeeping, published right at the beginning of the 1980s, reminds its readers of the importance of interesting language in American culture. In 1987 Robinson, in strong terms, critiques the 'dumbing down' of public language (something she continues to address in each of her subsequent essay collections) and the implicit notion that the average intelligence of the average American person will not tolerate complexity, or even beauty, in language. Her novels are, without exception, 'slow' or, as James Woods puts it with reference to *Gilead*, Robinson writes so that 'we might slow down to walk at its own processional pace'. Her novels insist on the way they are to be read, and make no accommodation for the busy mind or the fast reader. They cannot be read for information or even really for plot. Language and the belief that careful, considered and beautiful language can invigorate a culture is a key Robinsonian conviction.

When Ruth turns to scripture, she does so with the full intention of interpreting it. The novel wears the subjective nature of its reading of the Bible lightly, and in doing so, stands as a quiet critique of certain Christian approaches to Bible texts. In Chapter 4 we will consider Robinson's rejection of academic literary theory in terms of poetry and novels, but for now we can note this rejection and reflect on its implications for Bible reading. Robinson's suspicion of 'theory' is not a rejection of its assertions on the subjectivity of reading, but a reaction against its impact on how texts are seen and considered in themselves. To read a text with a theory in mind is to reduce literature to the level of data or information. This runs contrary to what literature – and the Bible – is and does. To think of great art and scripture in the necessarily reduced terms of an 'issue' or idea or even a specific theology is to restrict the possibilities that can occur in an individual encounter with a text. Robinson would have no trouble with a reader reaching a 'feminist' or 'socialist' interpretation of a passage, but she does object to the notion of feeding verses of a text into an almost mechanized theory. To do so is to do violence to meaning. And with Robinson's strong convictions on the necessity of open engagement with the Bible in mind, Ruth emerges as a character whose reading is guided not by theory, but is filtered through experience.

The close of *Housekeeping* takes its reader on a tour of the Bible, from Creation to crucifixion, and this brief section is fascinating when read in light of what was still to come from Robinson many years later. Ruth's reading of biblical text hones in specifically on death. The murder of Abel; Job's children; King David and Absalom: these narratives are tales of mourning, death and grief. 'The force behind the movement of time is a mourning that will not be comforted', concludes Ruth, which really is an inevitable conclusion given by her Old Testament sources (Robinson 1980: 192). Ruth's finely honed attention is not attracted to, say, the construction of the Temple; or the Exodus narrative; or the more joyous of the Psalms. Her focus is claimed by the narratives of loss that populate the Hebrew scriptures, and this of course evidences that basic fact discussed earlier – that what we see and what we choose to emphasize is conditioned and generated by our experience. Ruth goes on to interpret the story of Cain's murder from the perspective of God, who, 'in the newness of the world' was a 'young man', scandalized over 'the slightest things' (Robinson 1980: 192–3). This reading demonstrates a liberated relationship with text that simply may not be possible for the more formally theologically educated. Robinson returns to a Ruth-like character in *Lila*, and uses her to demonstrate just how theologically insightful the 'unchurched' can be – because of, not in spite of, their lack of induction into orthodoxy.

Ruth's reading of the effects of this primal murder is beautiful, and so different to that which a more conservative theologian could produce. For her, the first murder was really a second creation, an act that made the earth absorb the blood spilled and the grief caused, and had just as crucial a role in shaping the world she has inherited as the original Creation did. The generations flowing from Cain all 'remembered that there had been a second creation, that the earth had run with blood and sorrow', records Ruth, and the Flood was made necessary by these rivers of blood (Robinson 1980: 193). But, as Ruth rightly observes, the Flood took more humans than Cain ever did. So, even now, there is 'a certain pungency and saver in the water, and in the breath of creeks and lakes, which however sad and wild, are clearly human' (Robinson 1980:

193). Ruth moves from this Old Testament of loss and reveals an almost latent Christian hope of restoration founded on the stories of the New Testament. For Ruth, the incarnation was made necessary and possible by humans, by the 'vortex we made when we fell', and Jesus' life was spent repairing, stitching and completing (Robinson 1980: 194). This reading of Jesus' life is, to Ruth, 'a fact that allows us to hope the resurrection will reflect a considerable attention to detail' (Robinson 1980: 194). At the close of the novel, Ruth gets within arm's reach of orthodoxy, with talk of incarnation and resurrection. But in the very next paragraph, she once again returns to metaphor and symbol, interpreting Jesus' resurrection as a metaphor for how grief was experienced by those closest to him. And Ruth's keen turn to metaphorical readings of scripture lead us, finally, to one more consideration of *Housekeeping*, one that positions it in relation to a more radical theology than Robinson would ever go on to claim.

Housekeeping and the death of God

The text of *Housekeeping* belongs, in some senses, less to the Calvinist and positive theological influencers Robinson will later go on to recommend, and more to the death-of-God theologies of Nietzsche, Altizer and Mark C. Taylor. And while Robinson would no doubt resist the connections between her debut and the 1960s death-of-God theologians, it has to be conceded that *Housekeeping* is simply not deployed in the same theological register as the novels that follow it over twenty years later. Ruth is, according to her author, to be seen as a theologian. 'I've been interested in theology for as long as I've known there was theology. It is an absolute habit of mine to make my characters into theologians, I realise that. Every one of them', says Robinson (Chapter 5). So it would seem impossible to avoid the theological implications of *Housekeeping*; but that need not necessarily lead us to the intellectual landscape of the later *Gilead* trilogy. Instead of attempting a homogenizing unification of Robinson's novels, it is key to accept the radically different theologies of *Housekeeping* and the *Gilead* novels; in fact, it is crucial that we begin with the fact of the disparity, for there may well be a theological reading of Robinson's intratextual shift from her debut to *Gilead* that sheds some light on her development as a theologian. So where Calvin and Barth can be seen to be lurking in the background of Robinson's later novels, it is the contention of this chapter that *Housekeeping* rather negatively shadows what will become the positive theology of the *Gilead* trilogy. And in order to highlight this development, it is fruitful to expose this debut novel to some theologies not immediately identifiable as inherently 'Robinsonian'. In what follows I want to avoid asserting that *Housekeeping* is simply a 'death-of-God novel' (whatever that may be said to be), and instead seek to make the novel speak its theological implications in conversation with what may seem to be radical dialogue partners. And one of the most interesting and persuasive reasons to look to, say, Mark C. Taylor's theology, is the explicit connection made between the death of God and a resultant privileging of language.

The text of *Housekeeping* is a product of Ruth's mind. That is, a reader is privy to no other source of information, judgement or reality than that which is given by her as narrator. This is, of course, true of many novels written in the first person, but in a text that bears the marks of the death of God as subtly as *Housekeeping*, it is of particular interest. The link between the absence of God and the centrality of language as it is presented in the novel is read here as causal. Indeed the connection between the death of God and the subsequent privileging of language is one made by contemporary radical theologians, as Taylor argues, 'the death of God, the disappearance of the Father, is the birth of the Son, the appearance of the Word – the appearance of language as Sovereign' (Taylor 1982: 91). As a diagnostician of the condition of language post-God, Taylor asserts the primacy of the Word when the transcendent foundation once provided by God is no longer a given. In other words, post-Nietzsche and post-Freud, language ceases to reach for the ineffable nature of the divine and becomes sovereign in and of itself. As Taylor puts it, the death of God meant 'the narrative thread [of the world] unravelled leaving a text to be interpreted in place of a story to be uncovered' (Taylor 90). There is no transcendent reality for language to report to, instead language designates the limits of its own inquiry. This shift from the divine Word to 'words' is evident in the operation of diverse fields of thought, including Nietzschean aesthetics, contemporary radical theologies, psychoanalysis and Derridean deconstruction. This shift is also exactly what is found in Robinson's first novel. Ruth becomes a poet of her own history, an imaginative writer of memory, event and narrative and a creative interpreter of text, scripture and story. If the death of God implies the birth of language as replacement source of redemption, Ruth responds to this in her distinctly literary approach to her own existence. With no transcendent reality anchoring a 'true' or 'truthful' relation between speech and the external world, the individual becomes an imaginative co-conspirator in the creation of meaning. Taylor comments, 'since the world text no longer had an authoritative author who established its intrinsic intelligibility, interpretation by necessity became creative rather than imitative' (Taylor 90). The death of God inaugurates a hermeneutic imperative; where once the world had meaning inscribed by a divine author, it now exists as a text waiting to be both interpreted and written. In theological language, the absence of the Johannine Word become flesh means the task of every individual interpreter is to ensure the enfleshment of words by themselves, for themselves. In this way meaning is to be invented, extracted and shaped from the otherwise nihilistic raw materials of a godless cosmos.

Thomas Gardner's insightful piece, 'Enlarging Loneliness', makes a compelling case that Ruth 'picks up on a set of images first put into play by Emily Dickinson and unfolds them in a new situation, examining the world they make visible' (Gardner 2006: 11). Gardner suggests that in adopting a truly poetic approach to the interpretation of reality, Ruth becomes an active participant in the business of perception rather than a passive observer. Robinson herself declares, 'I think it is past time to put aside other business and turn our energies to the remystification of virtually everything' (Robinson 1987). Here Robinson voices a conviction close to what Ruth actually does in the course of the novel. Robinson is not calling for an unchecked inventiveness in language, but a 'freeing up' of constraints put on language that designate what it can and cannot do. Reacting directly against a positivist approach to the utility of language, Robinson is arguing that language is, paradoxically, more adequate to experience when its user lets go of prescriptive and reduced notions of veracity or accuracy. She writes,

> We cannot in good faith sketch serpents in where the cartography of our understanding frays. But perhaps we can develop language that will

acknowledge that it does fray, and where it does, and that those things we do not understand are not mere gaps to be closed by extensions of existing ways of thinking, but are sphinxes, riddles, their solutions likely to be astonishing and full of implication. (Robinson 1987)

Ruth, conscious of the manner in which language shapes reality, engages both in the interpretation of her experience and the creative additions to what she knows. As noted earlier, Ruth struggles to make any clear distinctions between reality and dreams, between empirical fact and imagination, and this blurred division – which is really no division at all – is revealed in her apparent omniscience in recounting her family history. Ruth records events she surely would have had no knowledge of, describing them with the confidence of a poet and depicting the emotional states of her grandmother with a surprising certainty. For example, Ruth's imaginative omniscience extends far into the past preceding her birth, of the lives of her mum and aunts and grandmother: 'after their father's death, the girls hovered around her, watched everything she did, followed her through the house, got in her way' (Robinson 1980: 10). She records poetically the quality of an experience she never had, noting, 'time and space and light grew still again and nothing seemed to tremble, and nothing seemed to lean' (Robinson 1980: 15). In the 'resurrection of the ordinary' passage, Ruth seems to enter the mind of her grandmother, recalling the sensual features of the event, the feel of the wind, the smell of flowers and simply *knows* the impact the experience had on Sylvia. And where Ruth's imaginative inventions are there for all to see, it is Ruth herself, noted above, too, that seems to have less tangible existence than her poetic visualizations.

From Lacan to language: Reflections

Robinson's interaction with the American Renaissance tradition, explored earlier, gave us a useful lens by which to view her writing of transparency in *Housekeeping*. But Emersonian transcendentalism is not the only productive set of ideas with and against which Robinson's novel can be read. Indeed, transparency as an image of a troubled sense of identity is also implicit within certain psychoanalytical approaches to selfhood. Robinson sets up the crisis of selfhood in the text as one of ontological transparency. Beginning from a seemingly confident statement of self-assertion – 'my name is Ruth' – the narrator goes on to describe her existence as one that barely qualifies for the term, a pervasive limpidity leaking into every self-conception (Robinson 1980: 3). As the text develops, Ruth's self-conception (or lack of) becomes clear, literally, as a transparent self. Imagining what her aunt thinks of her, Ruth writes, 'she did not wish to remember me. She much preferred my simple, ordinary presence, silent and ungainly though I might be [. . .] She could forget I was in the room' (195). The 'reduced' Ruth is described in the text as possessing a complete lack of self-reflection, literal as well as psychological. The novel itself is full of reflective surfaces: the lake itself, evening darkened windows and a number of actual mirrors. Ruth imagines herself looking through windows from the outside, staring in at a family scene absent from her own history or experience. When she cannot look through a blackened window, she equally cannot see her own reflection, the mirror-like surface becoming 'warped and bubbled', or 'warped as water' (Robinson 1980: 188, 86). While it is unclear whether it is the windows themselves that are distorted or if it is Ruth's self-perception, she cannot get a glimpse of herself. With this in mind, Lacan's concept of the 'mirror stage' marries interestingly with Robinson's novel. As he would have it, the sight of oneself in the reflection in a mirror is a symbolic event that begins the movement towards owning an individual identity for a child, distinct from mother, the self seen for the first time as an integrated whole. Of course this is precisely the opposite of what occurs in Ruth's experience, the uncanny tripling of Helen onto Sylvie and onto Ruth means that to look at either woman necessarily means looking at Helen. Reflection as a means to separate oneself from maternal possession, then, is not possible for Ruth, her mind and self-conception being so bound up with her mother, her suicide and her absence that any notion of self distinct from her is an impossibility. The absence of Helen necessitates the absence of self for Ruth and her ontological transparency is the product of her tendency to conflate her identity with that of her mother, her sister and, as the text progresses, her aunt Sylvie. Rather than actively set upon the task of self-creation, Ruth passively assimilates herself into those she finds herself closest to, revealing, 'I feel no reluctance to speak of Lucille and myself almost as a single consciousness', and later, 'Sylvie and I

(I think that at night we were almost a single person)' (Robinson 1980: 98, 209). The reader is confronted with a narrator who is aware of her own emptiness, has no notion of God and cannot conceive of her 'self' apart from a history of absence and defection. With no transcendent reality operating above Ruth's mind, she turns, within the text of the novel, to language as a replacement source of selfhood.

Where *Gilead* presents a conception of self that is rooted firmly in the theological, *Housekeeping* instead posits language as the alternative foundation for self. Ruth's poetic sketching of reality is in itself revealing of her faith in language to hold and create meaning, and ultimately, in the absence of a divine grace that safeguards identity through time, Ruth looks to language as a source of reflection. Indeed, where the reflective surfaces of Fingerbone refuse to carry Ruth's image, language itself, its images and metaphors, become the replacement mirror, a means for Ruth to construct a sense of self that she can 'see'. Language functions in the text of *Housekeeping* as the solution to ontological transparency. As Arendt writes, 'implicit in the urge to speak is the quest for meaning, not necessarily the quest for truth' and this is precisely the case for Ruth in her building of a world and a set of memories that are in dubious relation to actuality (Arendt 1971: 99). Gardner, in reading Ruth's use of imagery as a Dickinsonian experiment, concludes that, 'as Ruth inhabits and gives voice to analogies, she both builds a world for herself in a place of abandonment and extends, by reenacting the manner of speaking, a conversation Dickinson had begun' (Gardner 31).

The divine absence – relative to *Gilead*, *Home* and *Lila* – necessarily impacts Ruth's reading of scripture. Allowing no reality beyond that which can be constructed in language leaves no room for revelation, and this is one of the most profound differences between Ruth and Ames. *Gilead* exhibits, as the next chapter will make clear, an awareness of that which exists beyond it as text – both in terms of what Ames does not say due to conscious self-editing and in terms of what he cannot say because of the ineffable nature of God and grace. Ames approaches scripture as a site of revelation, as a place of communion between divine truth and human interpretation. Ruth, on the other hand, treats biblical narrative as a story among stories, and certainly the notion of a transcendent truth emerging from the text is alien to her. When Ruth makes use of the Bible, it is inevitably reshaped and retold in ways that reflect her own psyche. Indeed, Ruth engages with scripture as an existentially symbolic text that speaks to her own experience of absence, not as a source of theological truth. This is not to suggest that Ruth's approach to scripture is necessarily wrong for Robinson, for, Lila, too, finds language equal to her experience in the book of Ezekiel. Of course *eisegesis* is inevitable, but the question operating behind all this is: 'when a character interacts with the Bible, what is implicitly thought to be ultimate'? In other words, is there anything beyond the *text*. For Ruth, the notion of a divine reality operating beyond the religious narratives she employs in *Housekeeping* is unthinkable.

As noted, the close of Robinson's debut novel does not present much in the way of hope for its narrator. By the end Ruth has fully entered transience and has become utterly other to those around her. It is difficult to read the crossing of the bridge scene as anything but a death for Ruth; either a suicidal jump with her aunt, or an accident that caused them to fall. In either version, Robinson's novel closes with a ghostly Ruth, a character totally submissive to her transparency. In the absence of the divine Word, mere words are simply not enough. Language, although conceived of as an alternative source of selfhood, ultimately fails Ruth, simply because there is nothing anchoring its use except the mind of its user and, as noted, this is a mind profoundly fractured by loss, grief and trauma. It is no accident then, that when Robinson turns to the more explicitly theological, in *Gilead*, language returns as a central theme of the text and, as will be developed, its function is profoundly altered by the assumption of the ineffable residing beyond its reach. Negatively implied here is the positive task *Gilead* sets for itself: a reinvestigation of language rejuvenated by a horizontal transcendent reality. Words now participate – just like any Ordinary phenomena – in a grander reality that enriches them and grants them their power. Unanchored from the transcendent, *Housekeeping* ultimately highlights the huge difference a belief in God can make to our underlying assumptions about the utility and reach of language.

Robinson's importance as a positive and constructive theologian is very much in preparation in this initial novel.

2

Gilead and the intersection of language

Theology: Robinson, Ames and the trouble of language

Ames, commenting on the huge collection of sermons he has read and amassed over his life, confesses, 'I wrote almost all of it in the deepest hope and conviction. Sifting my thoughts and choosing my words. Trying to say what was true. And I'll tell you frankly, that was wonderful' (Robinson 2004: 22). Ames states clearly both the task of the preacher and the role of theological language: trying to say what is true. Indeed one of the central ironies of *Gilead* is that, as Ames experiences proximity to God, he simultaneously feels powerless to articulate the contents of his experience, a closer relation to God paradoxically bespeaking an inarticulation, his own entry into a 'cloud of unknowing'. He writes, 'I feel sometimes as if I were a child who opens its eyes on the world once and sees amazing things it will never know any names for and then has to close its eyes again' (Robinson 2004: 64). Ames is, as a preacher, a man whose life has been characterized by a commitment to language, his vocation existing as an implicit statement of a confidence in the power of words for the task of truth-telling. One of the text's central dramas, then, is Ames' struggle with his faith in words as their incapacity to grasp the reality he intuits becomes painfully conscious. He describes how 'so often I have known, right there in the pulpit, even as I read the words, how far they fell short of any hope I had for them. And they were the major work of my life, from a certain point of view. I have to wonder how I have lived with that' (Robinson 2004: 79). He knows more than he has words for and frequently encounters the limits of language generally, and the frailty of *his* language specifically. For Robinson, pursuing the frayed edges of communicability is not only the role of the theologian but also an imperative for the author of fiction.

> The unnamed is overwhelmingly present and real for me. And this is truer because the moment it stops being a standard for what I do say is the moment my language goes slack and my imagination disengages itself. I would almost say it is the moment in which my language becomes false. (Robinson 2012: 20)

This passage is of central importance, principally because it states how Robinson views her own task as a writer. Implicit within this admission is the fact that Robinson, in writing fiction, like Ames in his sermons, is 'trying to say what is true'. Crucially, she reveals that it is the subtle and pervasive presence of the apophatic, which she defines as 'reality that eludes words', that keeps her imagination engaged and, by association it would seem, the truthfulness of her language intact (Robinson 2012: 19). Indeed language, whether in fiction or in theology, that does not acknowledge the meaning that exists beyond its conceptual reach, is fundamentally *untrue* for Robinson, rendering itself disingenuous in the face of the pervasive presence of the apophatic. As *Gilead* wrestles with both the necessity of words and their inevitable failure, Robinson develops a distinctive solution to the failure of language, through Ames and his relationship with Jack.

Ames and Robinson share some key ideas and assumptions about theology, meaning and truth. Robinson writes: 'it [theology] earns its authority by winning assent and recognition, in the manner of poetry but with the difference that the assent seems to be ultimate truth, however oblique or fragmentary the suggestion of it' (Robinson 1998: 117). For Robinson, theology is more like poetry than philosophy, more like a human voice than a logical proposition. Theological truth is not argued to or deduced from a set of facts; rather, it becomes true for the individual when it acknowledges, expresses and energizes something intuitive, something that the imagination recognizes, works with and expands. Theology is true when it grants its recipient a set of images, words or ideas that enlarge his or her vision of reality of what is possible or what might be. Crucially, it builds on what is already present in the mind of the believer, as Robinson comments, 'I seem to know by intuition a great deal that I cannot find words for' and it is the role of theology to find these expressions (Robinson 2012: 20). Importantly however, it is essential for Robinson that theology is never 'done'. Speaking of scripture she comments, 'for me, at least, the text itself always remains entirely elusive. So I must come back to hear it again, in the old phrase, to have it opened for me again' (Robinson 1998: 231). Since theology works with the texts Robinson is speaking of, it is true to say that theological reflection will never reach the point of having exhausted the riches of its sources. This is certainly true in her own experience of church, the institution theology is meant to serve: 'only [there] did I hear experience like mine acknowledged, in all those strange narratives, read and expounded and, for all that, opaque as figures painted on gold' (Robinson 1998: 229).

It would be easy to see Robinson's conception of theology as it has been laid out thus far as akin to Qoheleth's wind-chasing, a fruitless endeavour that goes on indefinitely, achieving nothing in the process. Indeed the opacity of scripture could easily be seen as a barrier to genuine engagement in its theological meaning. However, for Robinson, it is precisely this elusiveness that makes theology worth pursuing. Indeed, as Robinson repeatedly emphasizes, it is the role of art, of theology and of fiction to continually make inroads on what cannot be said, even though such an advance would likely open a door to yet more unnameable reality. In this way theology is adequate to experience for, as Robinson insists, strangeness is a constant of existence: 'what isn't strange, when you think about it', notes Lila in a typical Robinsonian observation (Robinson 2014: 82). Theology encounters the apophatic, in Robinson's terms, in order to generate further language, image and metaphor, evoking 'sermon, sacrament, and liturgy, and of course, Scripture itself, with all its echoes of song and legend and prayer' (Robinson 1998: 117). In its unfinishability, theology is a landscape in which individuals pursue understanding, not in any kind of complete sense, but always opening onto fresh potentials for (re)new(ed) meaning. Robinson's theology, as Ploeg notes, focuses 'squarely upon divinity and humankind's participation in it, upon that which the human mind cannot fully imagine and which language cannot adequately articulate' (Ploeg 2016: 5). Theology, in this conception, beckons its listener, its reader, to return again and again to its sources and the ideas that are generated from them and 'is never finally anything but theology, words about God, proceeding from the assumptions that God exists and that we know him in a way that allows us to speak about him' (Robinson 1998: 117). This 'speaking of God' implicitly assumes the understanding of those who participate in theological language and Rowan Williams, following Wittgenstein, makes the argument that 'understanding', specifically the understanding of utterances or language, is best seen as 'a matter of knowing what to do or say next [. . .] rather than being a matter of gaining insight into a timeless mental content "behind" or "within" what is said, it is being able to exhibit the next step in a continuing pattern' (Williams 2014a: 68). For Williams, understanding is not merely the destination of thinking, it is also the terminal from which a new utterance, one that is coherent with what has come before, can be articulated.

This mirrors what Robinson speaks of when she discusses the operation of theology. For Robinson theology is 'written for the small community of those who would think of reading it', and its continuation and development is dependent on the confidence of its readers to 'understand' in the sense that Williams defines it, the confidence to 'go on' and venture the next move (Robinson 1998: 117). Theology is not a set of arguments laid out to convince the reader of its truth, it is written instead for this who 'know the tale already [. . .] and who attend to its retelling with a special alertness' (Robinson 1998: 117). What Williams writes about the reading of a text is pertinent to Robinson's view of the function of theology,

> The search for meaning – that is, the search to understand what is said, written, depicted, the search to 'make sense' of it as something to which I can respond, the search to grasp it as part of a practice in which I can find my own human place – is always a search for the next thing to say. (Williams 2014: 91)

For Robinson, the reading of theology will always enhance a sense of the unsayable and of wonder; of scripture she asks, 'what can these strange stories mean? After so much time and event and so much revelation, the mystery is only compounded' (Robinson 1998: 243). Theology, then, begins in mystery, seeks to 'go on', inevitably opening up on yet more mystery, leaving its reader to attempt the next utterance. She writes, 'the mystery that compels science and the mystery that elevates religion seem very like one another. In neither case is there a reason to suppose that mystery will be exhausted or dispelled' (Robinson 2015: 152). Robinson is acutely aware of the paradox at the heart of language here: the simultaneous impossibility of theological language and the power it has, at its best, to evoke that which resides outside its reach. Commenting on hypothetical scientific articles that might be titled 'Learned Ignorance' or 'The Cloud of Unknowing', she notes that, despite their titular admission of the incapacity of language, they are also 'demonstrations of the extraordinary power of language to evoke a reality beyond its grasp, to evoke a sense of what cannot be said' (Robinson 2012: 19).

Robinson's conception of theology is not of a discipline saturated with certainties and propositions, rather, she writes,

> I study theology as one would watch a solar eclipse in a shadow. In church, the devout old custom persists of merely repeating verses, one or another luminous fragment, a hymn before and a hymn afterword. By grace of my abiding ignorance, it is always new to me. I am never not instructed. (Robinson 1998: 230)

This is the essence of theological thinking for Robinson. Theology is never an exercise in the purely abstract, as Ames comments in a repudiation of a philosophical text he has encountered, 'I can't quite see the meaning of a statement so purely hypothetical as this' (Robinson 2004: 54). It is a journey through mystery, always as an attempt to put a name to the ineffable for the benefit of its participants. Robinson's fiction, most particularly *Gilead*, constructs a theology through a careful layering of confidence and uncertainty. This is a dialectical move in which Robinson allows Ames' kataphasis to sit alongside his more apophatic impulse which in turn leads him on to a much deeper theological territory. As will be developed, Robinson consciously imbricates the theology of Ames, texturing simple statements with a complexity linked to the ineffability at the centre of all theological reflection.

While Ames shares Robinson's view of theology as an exploration of mystery, he also meets the often painful incapacity of language head on in the text of

Gilead.[1] As the narrative unfolds, two specific theological problems arise for Ames with respect to language. The first is the vertical relationship between self and God, specifically how the mind can generate a language capacious enough to grasp the reality it intuits. The second problem, mirrored by the first, is the issue of language's incapacity to reach across the figured distance existing between human persons. These issues surrounding language explored by Robinson in the text, through Ames, are subtly different though; he is a man that finds it easy to speak *to* God (prayer) yet nearly impossible to speak *of* God (theological language) and conversely, he finds it easy to speak *of* other persons yet nearly impossible to speak *to* them in any meaningful sense. These crises of meaning and of truth and how they might co-mingle in human language tend to run parallel to one another throughout the text as somewhat separate issues. However, in the figure of Jack, Rev. Ames finds a man he simply cannot speak to properly and, most acutely, cannot speak of God to. For Ames, Jack is where his two struggles with language meet and intersect. His conversation with him on predestination and the sermon he gives in his presence reveal how excruciatingly inadequate language can feel when it is aimed towards Truth in his presence.

Exploring how Ames experiences and deals with these crises reveals much about his, and by association, Robinson's, theology of language. To begin with it will be instructive to look at the two issues separately, Ames' struggle to speak of God and his difficulty in communicating meaningfully with others, in order to expose the strategies he employs to counteract the failure of his words. However, as will be argued, Ames ultimately finds a solution to the frailty to language, in both the vertical and horizontal senses, theologically through his reading of incarnation and, flowing from this, through the act of physical blessing: the physical performance/embodiment of a reality that has eluded his words throughout the text. By examining the relationship between kataphatic and apophatic elements in Ames' theology, the central importance of blessing becomes clear as a means to transcend the limits of language and bridge chasms that would otherwise remain fixed.

---

[1] Both agree on the fundamental importance of maintaining 'mystery' as a category in theology, however, as Chapter 3 demonstrates, there is a fundamental and ethical division between the two when it comes to their respective use of the term 'mystery'.

Feuerbach: The perils of vertical language

Much of Ames' waking life is spent in prayer. It is the psychic space to which he retreats in order to wrestle with his moral obligations and his ethical shortcomings; it coming easily to him, whether he is praying for his congregation, imagining 'peace they didn't expect and couldn't account for descending on their illness or their quarrelling or their dreams', or struggling with his mortal insufficiency, usually to do with something Jack has brought to the surface of his mind (Robinson 2004: 81). Indeed, Ames experiences prayer as something essential and necessary, as natural as any kind of communication. He notes, 'for me writing has always felt like praying, even when I wasn't writing prayers' (Robinson 2004: 21). Despite his impulse towards prayer, Ames finds speaking about God highly problematic and it is certainly surprising how few positive statements Ames makes about theology, doctrine or God in the course of his letter, instead admitting, 'I do try to write the way I think. But of course that all changes as soon as I put it into words' (Robinson 2004: 33). There are elements of thought, even though thoughts must happen in words, that resist expression for Ames. It is not that he lacks a wide enough vocabulary to fit his experience; rather, the suggestion is that words are fallible vessels for the journey between thought and expression. Robinson herself, in a review of Harold Bloom's *American Religious Poems: An Anthology* (2006), notes similarly, 'any writer who has wearied of words knows the feeling of being limited by the very things that enable' (Robinson review of Bloom). This kind of problem, the cleft between what is known and what can be spoken, is compounded further when thoughts that go beyond thinking, ideas of God and Reality, are tentatively given voice. Indeed when Boughton and Jack refer to Ames as 'cagey' in their conversation about predestination and divine grace, his outrage is only partial and reveals much about his attitude to theology, responding, 'I'm not going to force some theory on a mystery and make foolishness of it' (Robinson 2004: 173). For Ames, as for Robinson, theology is always an exploration in and of mystery. With an appreciation of the mysterious nature of theological enquiry, Ames tends to eschew dogmatism in favour of admitting there are things operating beyond his comprehension, as he states, summing up his feelings on language and theology, 'I'm just trying to find a slightly useful way of saying there are things I don't understand' (Robinson 2004: 173). Ames, then, finds it easy to talk *to* God in prayer yet finds it very difficult to speak *of* God in conversation or sermon.

While Robinson reserves her fiercest criticisms for Freud and Nietzsche, her protagonist in *Gilead* espouses a real admiration for the thinker that prepared the ground for much of their thought. Ludwig Feuerbach's *The Essence of Christianity* (1841), given to Ames as a present by his atheistic older brother, Edward, receives genuine praise from the preacher, despite its highly influential critiques of the contents of religious belief. Among the reasons Ames has for celebrating the book, it is worth noting that it, in Ames' mind, reads as a joyous exploration of the limits of reason and exposes the necessary incapacities of language and the imagination: 'that first chapter of Feuerbach, which is really about the awkwardness of language, not about religion at all' (Robinson 2004: 162). For Ames, Feuerbach makes only one mistake in his thinking, he 'doesn't imagine the possibility of an existence beyond this one' (Robinson 2004: 162). For Feuerbach 'the understanding is to itself the criterion of all reality', a philosophic move that rules out the possibility of a reality beyond comprehension in one fell swoop (Feuerbach 2008: 33). Granting Ames' assertion that this is an error on Feuerbach's part, the philosopher's text then becomes an attempt to find words for why humans feel an impulse towards the apophatic, why they have a desire to extend their understanding beyond themselves, upward and outward. For Ames the answer is simply because there *is* a reality 'embracing this one but exceeding it', a truth he experiences intuitively (Robinson 2004: 162).

In exploring the radical otherness of God and the supra linguistic nature of ultimate reality, Robinson is by no means breaking new ground. When Ames comments, 'creating proofs from experience of any sort is like building a ladder to the moon. It seems that it should be possible, until you stop to consider the nature of the problem', he is vocalizing an issue that has reverberated through the history of Christian theology, from the writers of the Hebrew Bible to contemporary radical theologians (Robinson 2004: 204). In her essay on Bonhoeffer, Robinson writes of religiosity, which is, she claims, '[a] transgression against God's otherness' (Robinson 1998: 112). Following

Barth, Robinson notes that 'falseness of some kind is a universal phenomenon of religious consciousness' and, granting this, kataphatic theology unchecked will necessarily exacerbate this falseness, the certainty of its language masking the ineffable core of theological reflection (Robinson 1998: 112). Kataphasis must open onto the apophatic, given the infinite otherness of its subject. Negative theology 'assumes that because 'God', being inexpressible and incomprehensible, is beyond naming and knowing, in terms of all the categories of human thought and knowledge, to 'know' God we must go beyond knowing to unknowing' (Lichtman 1998: 217). This unknowing, what Ames calls 'the limits of my understanding [. . .] that Horeb, that Kansas', is a creative silence in which a new utterance, deepened by the realization of its inevitable partiality, can be made (Robinson 2004: 217), as Lichtman puts it: 'as a moment in a dialectical relation to affirmative theology, it [unknowing] negates what can be said and known of God in order to leave the way open for deeper affirmations' (Lichtman 1998: 217). Ames' unknowing and struggle with theological language places him in the tradition of Paul who famously saw 'through a glass, darkly', but Robinson does not conclude with negative theology and she does not see language's fated failure as a necessary cause to give up theological exploration (1 Cor. 13.12). Rather, as is made clear in *Gilead*, the existence of the ineffable is to be seen as encouragement to engage the imagination in theological thinking and, when viewed in this way, theology in Robinson's work begins to look more like art than analytic philosophy. Ploeg makes a similar point with regard to Ames, noting that 'the inadequacy of language is not cause for spiritual doubt or existential despair, but is rather an opportunity to deepen his faith in the enduring nature of truth' (Ploeg 2016: 76). Ames, in terms of his approach to theological language, is very much Robinson's mouthpiece, voicing her firm conviction that while the divine necessarily eludes language, it is nonetheless accessible *through* words, in however limited a capacity.

'Every spirit builds itself a house, and beyond its house, a world; and beyond its world, a heaven', writes Emerson, providing a poetic expression for the trajectory of the human imagination from local to cosmological (Emerson 2000: 39). While Ames readily accepts that there are things he does not understand and the boundless mystery behind every thought, these admissions do not preclude him from engaging in an imaginative exploration of theology. Indeed, it should be said that it is precisely the existence of such pervasive ineffability that he, like Robinson, feels compelled to traverse the darkness of his comprehension through use of the imagination or, as he puts it, 'I am trying to describe what I have never before attempted to put into words. I have made myself a little weary in the struggle' (Robinson 2004: 51). Ames is a true Emersonian in his pursuit of original language, in his genuine attempts to pin down the spiritual meaning of the natural world; just as Emerson calls for an original relation to the world, Ames seeks to explore the limits of language, to excavate language itself for words evocative enough to hold experience itself. Just before this Ames describes his love for listening and imagining along with baseball games on the radio. Even though the static makes it hard to hear the action, perhaps even because of this, he loves spending his time this way, explaining, 'it felt good for me to imagine it, like working out some intricate riddle in my mind, planetary motion' (Robinson 2004: 50). Ames' delight in the half-heard baseball commentary reveals his preference for imaginative interpretation over a concrete detailing that leaves nothing unsaid. He comments, 'we have television now, a gift from the congregation with the specific intent of letting me watch baseball, and I will. But it seems quite two dimensional beside radio' (Robinson 2004: 143). This whole episode is figurative of Ames' approach to theology, ministry and prayer. Earlier it was noted that Ames prays for his congregation by imagining the results of his prayer descending on them. Equally, near the end of the novel he imagines an eschatological vision of his old friend Boughton, restored to himself as a father who would 'protect [Jack] as a father cannot, defend him with a strength he does not have, sustain him with a bounty beyond any resource he could ever dream of having [...] He would be that extravagant' (Robinson 2004: 271). This vision, a personification of grace itself, while not strictly scriptural, is born out of a life lived in the attempt to *imagine* what grace might look like. Following this hypothetical description Ames writes, '[t]here is no justice in love, no proportion in it, and there need not be, because in any specific instance it is only a glimpse or parable of an embracing, incomprehensible reality' (Robinson 2004: 272). The incomprehensibility of love does not render Ames speechless; rather, it encourages him to engage his imagination as a way of ensuring that the ineffable does not remain unexplored. This imaginative engagement with mystery is a feature of Ames' theological reflection and is a strategy he employs frequently in an effort to make himself useful in the face of the incomprehensible. It should be noted that in his imaginative engagement with theological truths, Ames tends always to favour images over rationalized theological statements, which is not to say that he does not value truth, but merely to highlight his implicit belief that theological truth is more faithfully served through image and metaphor than reductionist doctrinal statement. For this reason, Ames turns to the poets.

Where the language of theological and philosophical texts tend to discuss theological truth in a manner that disjoins it from quotidian experience, poetry, for Ames, fares better in its evocation of meaning beyond its mere words. Where theology has a tendency to, as Latz has put it, 'slip away from the concrete toward the abstract' (Latz 2011: 284), poetry, as McGowan argues, 'seeks a recurrent reinvention of language and consequently of the uses to which language can be put and the meanings that it can form' (McGowan 2013: 381). Poetry has a radical adaptability that renders it ideal for the imaginative approach to the theological that Ames favours. 'The poem', McGowan continues, 'occupies a tangible space in the world that speaks the silent unsayable that defines the core of the poet's lifelong task', and it is in this ability to speak the silent unsayable that the poem offers the narrator of *Gilead*, a means to transcend the limitations of normal theological language (McGowan 2013: 384). Just as for Emerson words bear a relation to spiritual facts, Ames sees a similar exchange between the natural world and the theological. He comments, 'the moon looks wonderful in this warm evening light, just as a candle flame looks beautiful in the light of morning. Light within light. It seems like a metaphor for something. So much does' (Robinson 2004: 136). Ames experiences the truth of Robinson's own assertion that 'reality is something that is available to us to know and to sense, and on the other hand it is emblematically meaningful – how it appears also communicates' (Gardner 2006: 49). Nature is emblematic to Ames, as it was to Emerson, and the implication is not that the natural is subordinate to the spiritual, but that reality is so inherently meaningful that, due to the limits of human comprehension, the divide naturally arises. Robinson seeks to bring the two together, not to create anything new, but to acknowledge what was always true.

For Ames this metaphor of light within light extends far and wide and reveals his view of language's relation to theology. He writes, 'it seems to me to be a metaphor for the human soul, the singular light within the great general light of existence. Or it seems like poetry within language. Perhaps wisdom within experience. Or marriage within friendship and love' (Robinson 2004: 136). It is interesting that Ames chooses poetry within language as an example of this metaphor at play. This image is about a specific and concentrated instance of a phenomenon within the phenomenon itself. The existence of a soul within existence itself, the soul being for Robinson, as well as for Emily Dickinson, the locus of all perception. Poetry exists in language then, for Ames, like the soul exists within existence, as the highest form of the thing itself. The soul is aware of its own existence in a similar way that poetry is aware of language: both are self-conscious and aware simultaneously of the frailty and sacredness of their condition. In the Christian imagination, marriage is a making sacred of love and friendship, a sacramental act intended to set apart and lift up a relationship. In the same way, the act of poetry is a setting apart of language with the intention of blessing it as somehow particular and worthy of dignity within language itself.

For Ames, poetry exists as a holy, that is 'set apart', collection of words, images and ideas that put a name on an experience of truth that tends to float above the reach of normal language. In trying to decide which books to reach for should he feel close to death, Ames considers Herbert and Donne alongside Barth and Calvin, poets alongside theologians. The commingling of language and imagination is fundamental to Ames' understanding of reality and of theology and he is always searching for a phrase or verse that opens up reality to him, that names it adequately; indeed, it should be noted that in the course of his letter he turns to memorized fragments of poetry as often as he quotes the Bible. In the process of admitting 'I have always wondered what relationship this present reality bears to an ultimate reality', a couple of lines from Isaac Watts come to him, 'A thousand ages in Thy sight / Are like an evening gone' to which he simply adds, 'no doubt that is true' (Robinson 2004: 118). In this specific instance the poem may be said to be about God's radical otherness, his omniscience, his atemporality, for example; however, the key point is that it wins Ames' assent, not through logic or reason, but through an imaginatively striking comparison. Guite argues 'in order to describe some aspects of our being human, an "inexactitude" may be, paradoxically, more adequate – indeed, more *exact* – than a supposedly exact expression' (Guite 2012: 6). While Watts' poem is about God, it is the finite 'inexactitude' of his comparison (one thousand ages being equal to an evening can hardly be said to be a statement of intended accuracy) that causes its sudden appearance in Ames' mind and how, in its inexactitude, the poem reflects the limits of human language without recourse to simple resolution. 'Poetry registers its own resistance to its very possibility', notes McGowan, and 'must bridge [...] realms of meaning, silence, and the unsayable in words that, however, are forever destined to signal their own inherent failure to meet the demands of the task' (McGowan 2013: 385). The self-conscious failure of poetic language does not render it useless however, and for Ames poetry has the power to hold the contradictions and difficulties that theological language gets into without need of tidy conclusions. In a paradoxical sense, the mysterious heart of theological reflection is more faithfully presented in the articulate inarticulacy of poetry than in the rigorous and reasoned language of philosophy or theology.

When Ames turns his thoughts to heaven, the theological problem of language and his method of solving it are laid bare. Heaven is, by definition for Ames, unthinkable, existing within the reality that exceeds the nameable universe. He admits, 'this morning I have been trying to think about heaven, but without much success. I don't know why I should expect to have any idea of heaven. I could never have imagined this world if I hadn't spent almost eight decades walking around in it' (Robinson 2004: 75). Ames encounters the world with perpetual amazement. For him then, if the nameable world contains such a superfluity of experience and meaning, it follows that heaven should confound any attempt at linguistic mastery. But by linking the two, heaven and the world, Ames gives himself an imaginative way to conceptualize what would otherwise remain utterly hidden. By extrapolating from the experience of the world upwards, Ames can land at a conception of heaven that he can hold in his mind while retaining the utter ineffability of the reality. He describes, 'if I were to multiply the splendours of the world by two – the splendours as I feel them – I would arrive at an idea of heaven very unlike anything you see in the old paintings' (Robinson 2004:169). This method avoids theological conjecture, something Ames is totally opposed to, noting 'we know nothing about heaven, or very little, and I think Calvin is right to discourage curious speculations on things the Lord has not seen fit to reveal to us' (Robinson 2004: 189). Beginning from the experienced, the seen and heard of the actual world, Ames meditates on what a reality beyond this one *might* mean. For an analogous reason he turns to poetry, a medium that deals in the very stuff it seeks to transcend, namely language. Kearney writes,

> If transcendence is indeed a *surplus* of meaning, it requires a process of endless interpretation. The more strange God is to our familiar ways, the more multiple our readings of this strangeness. If divinity is unknowable, humanity must imagine it in many ways. The absolute requires pluralism to avoid absolutism. (Kearney 2010: xiv)

While Ames would not use this sort of language to express the otherness of God, he does engage in Kearney's 'endless interpretation'. Ames' thousands of sermons, his memorization of poetry and his interaction with the natural world are all attempts to interpret the divine and to render it somehow communicable in language, however partial the result may be. The currency of poetry is the referential language of common life, a fact that explains Ames' attraction to its theological potential. When Ames reaches for Watts or Donne, he reveals a faith in the power of words to refer to what they cannot, to somehow house the unspoken. Poetry bridges the gap for Ames between an incapacitated language and a reality that must forever elude expression, between the world apparent and the reality he imagines. By maintaining a link between what can be said and what cannot, binding kataphatic and apophatic impulses together, Ames rescues his theology from both a cerebral silence or a dogmatic certainty. He writes,

> I can't believe that, when we have all been changed and put on incorruptibility we will forget our fantastic condition of mortality and impermanence, the great bright dream of procreating and perishing that meant the whole world to us. In eternity this world will be Troy, I believe, and all that is passed here will be the epic of the universe, the ballad they sing in the streets. Because I

don't imagine any reality putting this one in the shade entirely, and I think piety forbids me to try. (Robinson 2004: 65)

Ames struggles to speak meaningfully of God, and this struggle is made apparent in the very methods he uses to circumvent it. His emphasis on the imagination in theology reveals his awareness of the impotency of simple certainties and logical reasoning, and lays bare his preference for poetry, metaphor and symbolism as a means to gain theological insight. Faced with the incomprehensible reality of God, heaven and grace, Ames employs the imagination as a means to transcend the limits of mere language and instead explore the creative failure of language itself, the frontiers on which language loses its power and, in its collapse, reveals more than it ever could in its certainty.

The horizon: Horizontal collapses

One of the central concerns of Robinson's fiction is the distance that exists between persons, particularly between individuals who are otherwise bound together by family ties and loyalty. Robinson's novels explore this space, setting off from the assumption that this remoteness is universal and pervasive. It is certainly a feature of Ames' life, a fact that haunts him throughout the narrative, making him realize, 'I've shepherded a good many people through their lives, I've baptised babies by the hundred, and all that time I have felt as though a great part of life was closed to me' (Robinson 2004: 62). At the beginning of the text Ames' separateness is figured in his reports of struggling to hear Lila and Robbie from another room, noting, 'it's not the words I hear, just the sounds of your voices' (Robinson 2004: 5). When a couple of pages later Ames quotes 'hear and hear but do not understand' in terms of his relationship with his father, he may as well be talking about his marriage to Lila or indeed any of his relationships (Robinson 2004: 8). 'A man can know his father, or his son, and there might still be nothing between them but loyalty and love and mutual incomprehension', he notes, speaking specifically of the paternal relationships in his history but with a sentiment that applies to every protagonist in Robinson's fiction (Robinson 2004: 8). The beginning of the novel problematizes proximity in terms of language's capacity to bridge the distance between people. Similarly, later in the text, Robbie comes to Ames, who is just finishing reading an article and asks him to look at the picture he has made. Ames, in relaying Lila's response, highlights the level of disconnection he feels himself to be, and, even more poignantly, how removed he must appear to his wife: 'your mother said, in the kindest, saddest voice, "He doesn't hear you." Not "He didn't" but "He doesn't"' (Robinson 2004).

Earlier it was noted that Ames eschews dogma and tries to avoid prioritizing doctrine above imagination. One of the ways he does this, he reveals, is by imagining his late daughter, 'coming back from a place where everything is known, and hearing my hopes and my speculations the way someone who has seen the truth face-to-face and would know the full measure of my incomprehension' (Robinson 2004: 23). He admits, 'that was a sort of trick I played on myself, to keep from taking doctrines and controversies too much to heart' (Robinson 2004: 23). Of course, while this method relies on the hypothetical, the imagined Rebecca returning to him, when Lila enters Ames' church on that first Sunday, his imagined scenario becomes a reality. Ames figures Lila as a kind of omniscient other, returning from total comprehension to visit an old man struggling with the complexities of the unsayable. When Lila first enters the church, Ames imagines her saying 'I came here from whatever unspeakable distance and from whatever unimaginable otherness just to oblige your prayers. Now say something with a little meaning in it' (Robinson 2015: 24). The space Lila inhabits in the Amesian imagination is the point at which the futility of theological language is felt most acutely,[2] both as a tool to reach upwards to God and outwards towards the other. He reveals, 'there is something in her face I have always felt I must be sufficient to, as if there is a truth in it that tests the meaning of what I say' (Robinson 2004: 156). The horizontal failure of language is seen clearly in Ames' first attempts to speak in Lila's presence, a striking example of a pervasive phenomenon that haunts Robinson's protagonist constantly.

---

[2] The name 'Lila' comes from the Arabic word for 'night', a connection that symbolizes nicely the darkness of Ames incomprehension in her presence.

Ironically, Lila's first visit to Ames' church happens on Pentecost Sunday, a celebration of the gift of the Holy Spirit to the first apostles and a remembrance of the miraculous gift of tongues which enabled them to speak to the gathered masses in their own languages. In direct contrast to this is Ames' own sermon that 'felt like ashes on my tongue'; it fails to say anything of meaning, or so he subsequently imagines (Robinson 2004: 24). Ames uses words like 'unimaginable' and 'unspeakable' when speaking of Lila, descriptors that emphasize her otherness and her strangeness; for Ames, Lila presents the sternest test of his effectiveness as a communicator just as Jack presents the sternest test of his moral character. The distance between people exists due to the strangeness of the other, a notion that is perpetually on the mind both of Ames in his letter and Robinson in each of her works. 'In every important way we are secrets from each other', says Ames, 'and I do believe that there is a separate language in each of us' (Robinson 2004: 224). Indeed, a life spent in the business of trying to say what is true has led Ames to the conclusion that genuinely meaningful dialogue is incredibly difficult, for the simple reason that 'we take fortuitous resemblances among us to be actual likenesses' (Robinson 2004: 225). For Ames, we get by with the illusion of genuine community, of a shared value and moral system, 'but all that really just allows us to coexist with the inviolable, untraversable, and utterly vast spaces between us' (Robinson 2004: 225).

Robinson's fictions, then, explore the spaces in which meaning and language collapse. Specifically, these collapses take place in the chasms that exist between self and other and self and God. However, while emphasizing the separation between individuals, Robinson does not imply that the idea of an interchange or meaningful exchange is impossible or indeed hopeless. The implicit theology of *Gilead*, as will be developed with reference to Ames' relationship with Jack, is that the very attempt to traverse these gulfs is itself holy. This is all figured in the literal journey Ames and his father make to visit his grandfather's grave: a long and dangerous trek across wilderness, through drought and occasional gunfire. As was noted, the relationships between fathers and sons in the text are always problematic. In the case of Ames' father and grandfather, the failure of language to carry anything of meaning between the two is obvious. Being vocational preachers, men with a deep commitment to writing and speaking what they believe to be true and meaningful, their inability to transfer this skill to their relationship with one another is all the more noticeable by the contrast. Their differing views on the use of violence and their race politics create a vast separateness that can never be crossed in language, the strangeness of one man's world view to the other rendering language utterly powerless. In setting up this problem of language though, Robinson provides something of a solution, as she does throughout the text, through the physical. Specifically in this instance, the literal pilgrimage to Ames' grandfather's grave, which implies the conclusion: where language fails, a physical response fares better. Upon arriving at the grave, Ames and his father find themselves in a landscape utterly transfigured by the appearance of the sun and moon on the horizon. That nature conspires in beauty at the point at which their journey reaches its destination is no accident and Robinson's point is clear. Ames' father comments on the way back from the experience, 'you know, everybody in Kansas saw the same thing we saw', in a futile attempt to distance himself from any kind of mystical interpretation of what he had seen (Robinson 2004: 55). However, as Ames reports, 'despite what he said, I could see that my father was a little shaken. He had to stop and wipe his eyes' (Robinson 2004: 56).

'The health of the eye seems to demand a horizon', writes Emerson, and in Robinson's novel, the horizon comes to represent an instance of divine beauty following an arduous journey towards another person (Emerson 2000: 9). The undertaking of a physical journey succeeds in overcoming spiritual and emotional distance, reaching the other in a way language could never achieve. Smith argues 'the visible horizon is not a boundary, but a symbol for the bonds of fatherhood shared between God and every human individual': while this statement largely overstates the potential in Robinson's fiction of 'shared bonds', it rightly notes the horizon's potency as an image of divine communion (Smith IJAS). In *Gilead*, the vision of the horizon is the reward for traversing the horizontal gulfs that separate individuals. This emphasis on physicality as a means to transcend the problems of language is a feature of the novel and by introducing this notion early in the text, Robinson structurally prepares her reader for the ending, building in a theology of embodiment that leads ultimately to the blessing of Jack.

Jack: Language and incarnation at the intersection

Jack is a solitary figure. And Robinson's characters are generally solitary figures: they find themselves alone with solitude as the general condition of their existence. Examples of this populate Robinson's fictions: Ruth's inwardness, Lila's mistrust of the world, Glory's homelessness and Ames' loneliness all coalesce in the overarching sense that, in Robinson's constructed worlds, to exist is necessarily to be alone. On this Robinson comments,

> One of the things that is most mysterious about consciousness is that we don't know what's in there. You can know someone, but they're so complex that even while you apprehend them, even while you appreciate them, it's as if there is a very dense centre of being that you never really know. (Gardner 2006: 60)

Robinson's fiction functions largely as an exploration of this conviction, in turn echoing Levinas' assertion that 'one can exchange everything between beings except existing. In this sense, to be is to be isolated by existing' (Levinas 1961: 42). For Robinson and for Levinas, existing *entails* isolation. He goes on: 'solitude lies in the very fact that there are existents. To conceive a situation wherein solitude is overcome is to test the very principle of the tie between the existent and its existing' (Levinas 1961: 43). For Levinas an encounter with another person is necessarily a confrontation with the absolutely other, an individual that possesses an existence that is wholly theirs and wholly not his, an unexchangeable core that resists translation. Ames expresses a sentiment close to this throughout the text, explaining,

> When people come to speak to me, whatever they say, I am struck by a kind of incandescence in them, the 'I' whose predicate can be 'love' or 'fear' or 'want', and whose object can be 'someone' or 'nothing' and it won't really matter, because the loveliness is just in that presence, shaped around 'I' like a flame on a wick, emanating itself in grief and guilt and joy and whatever else. (Robinson 2004: 51)

Language necessarily gets into difficulty when it is aimed towards grasping the other, the Feuerbachian god existing at the contours of sense and cognitive capacity. In line with Levinas' conception of individuality, language equally fails in horizontal reaches precisely because the other is just as untouchable as the divine. Ames and Levinas are in agreement on the solitary nature of the self and nowhere in the text does Ames feel this more acutely than when he encounters the impulse to understand and speak properly to his godson, Jack. In Jack, Robinson has the means to explore the conceptual space between persons and the intersection between the vertical and horizontal collapses in meaningful language.

On several occasions throughout the text, Ames and Jack experience the problem of language head on. Between them a chasm has been fixed across which words do not seem to cross. Ames' history with Jack is one tinged with unspoken hostility, littered with petty annoyances and thefts. At the centre of the separation, however, is Jack's abandonment of a young girl and the baby he had with her. In itself a moral low point for Jack, the act has particular poignancy when viewed through Ames' eyes, the loss of a wife and child a reality forced on him through their premature death. Jack, intended to be a son of sorts for the childless Ames, was never truly claimed by his godfather, a fact evidenced by Ames' memory of Jack's baptism: 'my heart froze in me and I thought, This is *not* my child – which I truly had never thought of any child before' (Robinson 214). The relationship between Jack and his godfather represents a particularly powerful example of a pervasive distance between the persons that populate Robinson's novels. Indeed, their difficult past merely exacerbates the deeper truth that both men stand at either side of a gulf, and would have done regardless of how their relationship played out. Jack's difficult behaviour and problematic abandonment of the girl and child raise to the level of consciousness the incapacity of language to reach another person. This 'speechlessness' is lamented by Jack in a conversation with Ames at the end of the novel: 'does it seem right to you, [. . .] That there should be no common language between us?' (Robinson 194). The feeling is absolutely mutual, Ames' letter gradually becoming preoccupied with Jack and the lack of understanding the two seem to share.

Taking Robinson seriously as a theologian necessities a reading of *Gilead* that is attentive to the absolute centrality of blessing, both for the text itself and for Robinson's theology more widely. 'I wish I could place my hand on his brow and calm away all the guilt and regret that is exaggerated or misplaced, or beyond rectification in the terms of this world. Then I could see what I'm actually dealing with. Theologically, that is a completely unacceptable notion' (Robinson 2004: 229). Over the course of his letter, though, it becomes clear that this isn't an unacceptable notion to Ames, despite his protestations. For the preacher the placing of a hand on a brow is a gesture that is more theologically significant than he grants in this passage, a fact evidenced by his remembrances of past baptisms, about which he recognizes, 'there is a reality in blessing, which I take baptism to be, primarily. It doesn't enhance sacredness, but it acknowledges it, and there is a power in that. I have felt it pass through me, so to speak' (Robinson 2004: 26). The phrase 'reality in blessing' is telling and, in typical Robinson fashion, multivalent. The word 'reality' points forward to Ames' musings on Feuerbach and the 'exceeding reality' the philosopher rules out. The use of reality here functions by bringing the actual and the unseen together. In blessing, Ames feels the gulf between God and self, and between self and other, close. He comments, 'the sensation is of really knowing a creature, I mean really feeling its mysterious life and your own mysterious life at the same time' and at no point in the text is Ames more positive about the prospect of knowing another person than here in his discussion of blessing (Robinson 2004: 26).

As the gap between individuals closes in the act of baptism, mystery is not somehow dispelled; indeed, as the other comes into proximity in this way, it is the very mysterious nature of their existence that strikes Ames. In this way, blessing operates analogously to Robinson's vision of theology discussed at the beginning of this chapter. Just as theology is an exploration of the ultimately apophatic, blessing operates as an acknowledgement of a wordless reality and functions as a means of *doing something* in the face of a pervasive incomprehensibility. Ames' recollection of his blessing of Lila reveals the truth of this, his account emphasizing the absolute mystery of the act itself and the reality to which it points. He notes he 'felt like asking her, "What have I done? What does it mean?" That was a question that came to me often, not because I felt less certain I had done something, but because no matter how much I thought and prayed, I felt outside the mystery of it' (Robinson 2004: 24). The blessing of Lila is a particularly poignant example of the phenomenon of blessing itself, just as blessing stands as a concentrated example of encounter within relationship in the text.

The solution to the deficit in meaning in theological language is solved for Ames through an imaginative reinterpretation of a doctrine that continually recurs in his letter: the incarnation. He writes: 'I realise there is nothing more astonishing than a human face [. . .] It has something to do with incarnation', and in his writing of the other through the lens of incarnation, Ames evokes both Calvin's theology of the stranger and Levinas' philosophy of the face, a blend that implies, as will be seen, the necessity of physical blessing (Robinson 2004: 75). Incarnation is a doctrine that resides at the point at which the vertical and horizontal meet and intersect, the idea of God become human brings the divine into dialogue with the finite and suggests that the flesh and blood of Ordinary human bodies is profoundly sacred, for it was seen fit to house God. For Robinson, 'a high Christology implies a high anthropology' and 'to properly value this pledge of fervent love, the incarnation, we must try to see the world as deserving of it' (Robinson 2015: 201). The incarnation, in Robinson's theology, is not seen as simply a means to an end, a doctrine made necessary to ensure salvation: it is a revelation, a 'making known' of the reality of the human self. Tentatively expressed in *The Givenness of Things*, Robinson makes a crucial connection between incarnation and the human self:

> But what *is* man? What does it mean to say, as the Gospel writers say and insist, that Jesus was indeed a human being? What we are remains a very open question. Perhaps some part of the divine purpose in the Incarnation of this Son of Man was and is to help us to a true definition. (Robinson 2015: 257)

Robinson does not outline in any detail what the nature of the link between the incarnation and the definition of human nature might be, an absence that is instructive in itself. The incarnation is, for Robinson, too theologically rich, too existentially meaningful to attempt a definition. She admits, 'I was slow at arriving at a Christology, at least in articulating one, because any account of Christ always seemed to me too narrow – however true in part, still false for all it excluded' (Robinson 2015: 209). Reluctant to 'force some theory on a mystery and make foolishness of it', Robinson, like Ames, merely suggests the existence of a connection between Christ and human other, and creates the space in her fiction for an imaginative exploration rather than a reductive attempt at theological totalizing. *Gilead*, then, is Robinson's means to imagine the ramifications of the incarnation for the human self and its outward relation to the other. Ames, struck by the power of the human face, only vaguely suggests that it has 'something to do with incarnation', yet his letter, when read with this suggestion in mind, can be seen to be an extended meditation on the outworking of the doctrine of incarnation, results which have a profound impact on conceptions of self and other. In exploring the incarnation's central role in selfhood, Ames evokes the language of Levinas and, as will be developed, invites interpretation from beyond Levinas' work, developing a notion of transcendence that profoundly alters the way *Gilead* is to be read.

'Any human face is a claim on you, because you can't help but understand the singularity of it, the courage and loneliness of it' (Robinson 2004: 75). As a preacher Ames feels the truth of his own claim often: notably in baptism (he says that the earlier noted astonishment caused by human face is 'truest of the face of an infant', specifically recalling the memory of his own child (Robinson 2004: 75)) and also in his visits with members of his congregation. Jack, it becomes clear throughout Ames' letter, is entirely other to the minster; his behaviour totally beyond Ames' understanding, and the preacher simply cannot comprehend how Jack emerged from the pious Boughton family, especially with his best friend and devout ministerial colleague as his father. Jack's otherness is compounded by proximity, and as a godfather, Ames feels responsible for and to an individual who simply exceeds his capacity to understand. The frustration of much of Ames' letter is born out of the claim Jack has on his attention and his simultaneous failure to fulfil his responsibility to him. In structuring Ames' consciousness in this way, Robinson evokes Levinas' analysis of the other and his notion of infinite responsibility. Reading Robinson's writing of the relation between Ames and Jack through a Levinasian lens allows for the alterity of the two men to one another while also leaving room for the radical draw their difference has. Bringing Robinson into dialogue with Levinas opens the possibility to examine the notion of transcendence in *Gilead*, beginning with Levinas' writing of the transcendence that emerges out of and is discovered in the relation between self and other. Shifting focus from Levinas' model of self–other relations to Rivera's notion of interrelational transcendence highlights how Robinson ultimately imagines a transcendence that operates in the physical touch between two irreducibly different individuals, a transcendence that explodes horizontal/vertical axes and refuses spatial imagery in a turn to the physically rooted nature of transcendence.

Levinas: Language and the other

Levinas and Ames share the conviction that from the other, from the face of the other, a demand is issued. In a 1986 interview Levinas surmises, 'I have said that in my analysis of the face it is a demand; a demand not a question. The face is a hand in search of recompense, an open hand. That is, it needs something. It is going to ask you for something' (Bernasconi 169). For Levinas, the face exists as a source of an unspoken claim, a demand that requires something of the self. This call-and-response pattern contains, although prior to speech, the very structure of language and operates, for Levinas, as language itself. 'I think the beginning of language is in the face', he states, claiming, 'your reaction to the face is a response' (Bernasconi 1988: 169, 170). In the absence, or in the 'before', of language exists a prior language between self and other that structures the speech that inevitably follows, and, as Levinas puts it: 'Meaning is the face of the other, and all recourse to words takes place already within the primordial face to face of language' (Levinas 1961: 206). In Robinson's text, however, Jack laments the lack of common language between himself and his godfather, and, as such, Robinson's character's relation to one another is a failing attempt to address this unspoken call in speech. The unvoiced language of the self–other relationship creates in Ames the obligation he feels perpetually that he is absolutely unable to meet: 'I do feel a burden of guilt toward that child, that man, my namesake', he writes, admitting, 'I have never been able to warm to him, never' (Robinson 2004: 215). With this in mind then, Ames' struggle with Jack takes place in the arena of failed language, but the demand and obligation emerging from Jack to Ames is sourced in the antecedent call and response that predates speech, 'because the essence of language is the relation with the other' (Levinas 1961: 207). The specific words used by both Robinson and Levinas in their discussions of the human other reveal a shared conviction that the relation with the other structures the consciousness of the self. Ames uses 'claim' and Levinas uses 'demand', and certainly the other in both Robinson and Levinas sources an ultimate obligation; in *Gilead*, Jack controls the narrative to the extent by which he eludes Ames' conceptual mastery. This is a fundamental part of Levinas' thinking too: the other must always exceed the self's grasp. Indeed an other can only be worthy of the name through an exceeding of the self's categories and ability to label. 'The Stranger is also the free one. Over him I have *no power*. He escapes my grasp by an essential dimension, even if I have him at my disposal. He is never wholly in my site', argues Levinas in a perfect commentary on Ames' experience of Jack (Levinas 1961: 39). The other resists the self's totalizing impulse and, from this simple foundation, Levinas develops his conception of transcendence. Otherness is experienced, here in *Gilead*, and in Levinas, as a call, and it calls simply because it refuses conceptualization or control and it is the stranger's face that fronts this ultimate alterity. Ineluctable strangeness, a foundational premise in Levinas' philosophy, central also to Robinson's theology, is an idea she roots in the image of God, a theological notion absent from Levinas' writing. Crucially, Ames is writing his letter in 1956, five years before Levinas published his first analysis of the face in *Totality and Infinity* (1961) and therefore, within the world of the novel, Levinas' philosophy is unaccessible to Ames. In lieu of Levinas' work then, Ames turns to Calvin in order to understand his intuition about the human face and, Calvin, in more overtly theological language, provides the transcendent foundation for a theology of the other. 'I fell to thinking about the passage in the *Institutes* where it says the image of the Lord in anyone is much more than reason enough to love him', writes Ames, consciously connecting Calvin's *imago dei* to his own thinking on the treatment of the other (Robinson 2004: 215). 'It seems to me', he continues, 'people tend to forget that we are to love our enemies, not to satisfy some standard of righteousness, but because God their Father loves them' (Robinson 2004: 215). For Ames, loving treatment of the other is an imperative emerging from both the image of God *in* and the love of God *for* the other person. The demand that he and Levinas detect is, for Ames, a call that must be interpreted theologically, for it emerges from the image of God within that person. Calvin, in an extended passage, sets out emphatically and clearly how the image of God should act as a corrective to the self's base and selfish response to the stranger:

> Therefore, whatever man you meet who needs your aid, you have no reason to refuse him. Say, 'He is a stranger,' but the Lord has given him a mark that ought to be familiar to you . . . . Say, 'He is contemptible and worthless,' but the Lord shows him to be one to whom he has deigned to give the beauty of his image. Say you owe nothing for any service of his but God, as it were, has put him in his own place in order that you may recognize toward him the many and great benefits with which God has bound you to himself. Say that he does not deserve even the least effort for his sake but the image of God, which recommends him to you, is worthy of your giving yourself and all your possessions. (Institutes, III.vii.6)

Ames' thinking is clearly directed by Calvin, particularly with passages like the one above in mind, and in his insistence on the primacy of the human face in human interaction, Ames reveals himself to be a proto-Levinasian. 'When you encounter another person, when you have dealings with anyone at all, it is as if a question is being put to you', Ames muses, in an almost direct echo of Levinas (Robinson 2004: 141). Robinson situates Ames between the two thinkers and in so doing provides her readers with the means to read the blessing that concludes the novel. In this creative space, between Calvin and Levinas, with the strangeness of the other held together with the image of God,[3] Robinson creates a startling ending to her novel, a conclusion that profoundly deepens her exploration of self, other and God in *Gilead*.

---

[3] Where Robinson's *Housekeeping* exhibits a classically Freudian uncanny, *Gilead* presents a theological reimagining of Freud's theory, one in which the unknowability of the other is bound together with a profound feeling of kinship and of a deep sense of familiarity, all anchored in a belief in God. As the author notes elsewhere, 'the alterity of the other is ultimately, as a Calvinist, the mark of a God who remains elusive', and 'this is the essence of the theological uncanny. Where Freud's concept involved an embroilment of familiarity and strangeness that *repels*, Robinson [. . .] envision[s] an uncanniness in the stranger that *calls*' (Kearney 2017: 275).

From face to flesh

The relation between I and the other is, for Levinas, an ethical one, for the demand arising from the other 'faces me and puts me into question' (Levinas 1961: 69). The other, put simply, demands a response and, for Levinas, any response to the other is necessarily ethical. As Eagleton puts it, in Levinas' work, 'the traditional ethical question "What am I to do?" becomes "What does the Other want of me?"' (Eagleton 2009: 224). Rivera makes the point in *The Touch of Transcendence* (2007) that 'in the ethical relation, it is the Other who presents himself; I can never take his place, assume his perspective, or challenge myself in the way the Other does. I must *face* the Other' (Rivera 2007: 64). The other is altogether not-I and presents an alterity that is absolute to my own apprehensible reality. For Ames, this is Jack; for Levinas, the infinite distance between self and other (Ames and Jack in this case) is what constitutes transcendence. The otherness of the other is limitless and 'for Levinas, the transcendence of the other is that separation, a distance between the self and the Other' (Rivera 2007: 63). Transcendence, a space in which concern for the other has displaced self-interest: it is this ethical *ekstasis* that merits the term 'transcendence' and certainly Robinson's text ends with Ames' own disgust at himself, his town and the manner in which he has allowed the other to be systemically excluded from Gilead; the judgement he levels at himself and his town is a product of his intercourse with otherness, a communion that inevitably renders returning to his same-old patterns of thought utterly untenable. In Robinson's novel, an open-handed blessing of otherness does not dispel strangeness, but instead reveals the strangeness of the self.

The separation between self and other is imagined in Levinas as spatial. 'Transcendence designates a relation with a reality *infinitely distant* from my own reality', he notes, and, later in his *Totality and Infinity*, concludes that I and other must face one another across an 'abyss of separation' (Levinas 1961: 41, 295, emphasis added). Alterity is figured spatially, as distance, infinite distance and these metaphors of separation have been critiqued for their relational implications. Eagleton observes, '[a]t the centre of Levinas' moral thought lies a relation with the Other, which – since the Other is *wholly* other, enigmatic and inaccessible – is also a non-relation' (Eagleton 2009: 225). Levinas' imagining of the ethical relation is fundamentally fatalistic to Eagleton, for the possibility of genuine encounter dissolves in the infinite nature of the distance separating I and the other. Metaphors of distance limit the opportunity for contact and, as Keller concludes, 'in Levinas exteriority trumps relationality' (Kearney 2016: 66). Levinas' conception of the other has the face at the centre, yet it places the other at such a remove as to make an embodied response wholly impossible, for, as Kearney notes, 'in Levinasian ethics we have a voice from a distance rather than a hand across a distance' (Kearney 2016: 65).

Rivera, in a concentrated effort to move away from Levinas' spatialized imagery, seeks a concept of transcendence that is fully embodied, arising out of the material reality of the interaction of two bodies. Levinas' notion is too 'lofty', too abstracted, ultimately too immaterial for Rivera, and his vision of transcendence all too readily eschews the body (Rivera 2007: 85–6). She writes, 'the spatio-temporality of transcendence in Levinas' imaginary – its heights, exteriority, and straightforwardness – presupposes the exclusion of eroticism' (Rivera 2007: 88). While it is sexual encounter to which Rivera devotes her attention, what she theorizes can be extended to touch in general. 'The caress', she argues, 'retraces the borders of the Other. Neither totemic verticality nor one-dimensional separation describes the space between lovers. That space is traced by the contours of bodies' (Rivera 2007: 89). Levinas' imaginary falls short in the case of physical touch between self and other. Indeed where language obscures and confuses meaning when passed from one person to another, as has been discussed earlier with regard to Ames' speech, touch offers a simple, undiluted site of encounter. 'When we touch someone, it is not just a physical event of flesh meeting flesh, but a language for our very beings', argues Naylor; this is a conclusion springing from a theological foundation, for, as she observes, 'as Christians, we can [. . .] speak in terms of body as sacrament: the outward and physical sign of inward and spiritual truth and grace' (Naylor 1996: 73). Naylor's encouragement to speak of the body as a sacrament comes indeed from the incarnation, a doctrine felt to be prescriptive in its honouring of the flesh and blood of the human body and a doctrine of central importance to Robinson's novel. 'Incarnation, as Christianity has taught us, needs its stable', Rivera notes and touch is the point at which bodies meet in a specific time and place, a physical rooting for the transcendent nature of encounter (Rivera 2007: 92). In *Gilead* Ames and Jack share a touch that seems to communicate more in a moment than they ever shared in a lifetime. If indeed this is to be called an instance of transcendence, then Levinas' model will not provide a helpful guide, for it has little to say about the transcendence of touch. Robinson's novel culminates with an embrace and, when read with the incarnation in mind, as Ames invites his readers to do, it becomes a scene of *incarnational transcendence*, a theological reimagining of an encounter that acts as a nexus of meaning for the novel. For all the ink Ames has spilt in the course of his letter, the hundreds of sermons both written and preached, it is this moment that speaks most of all and its meaning is, while accompanied with words, communicated in silence. The Levinasian silence prior to language of the self–other relationship is presented here and Robinson ultimately expands on Levinas' conception of transcendence by drawing attention to the physical nature of the encounter, a laying on of hands that roots its transcendence in the material reality of bodies.

Physical embrace and blessing

The discussion between Ames and his godson, near the close of the novel, in which Jack reveals his family situation, his marriage to Della and his son, Robert, ends with an embrace. Both men offend the other unintentionally during the conversation, Jack by suggesting Ames' marriage to Lila is scandalous and Ames by mentioning Jack's first child. 'We can't let the conversation end here', laments Ames and decides the only course of action is physical (Robinson 2004: 263). 'He stopped by the door and I went over to him and put my arms around him' (Robinson 2004: 263). This embrace prevents yet another breakdown in communication, but it does not fix the fundamental problem of language between the two men. Ames writes: 'here I was supposed to be a second father to him. I wanted to say something to him to that effect but it seemed complicated, and I was too tired to think through the implications' (Robinson 2004: 263). The relationship between Jack and Ames is indeed complicated: both men in marriages that have caused consternation, and both have lost a child and wife; these similarities only make their differences all the more striking. Ames is a minister and a respected figure of authority in Gilead; Jack is known to be of questionable character and has been a source of real regret to his father. That they now share a situational empathy makes Ames profoundly uncomfortable for a number of reasons, most crucial of which will conclude this chapter. Language is not the adequate vessel for communication between the two precisely because any reference to one man's situation necessarily invites comparison and evokes the memory of the other man's troubles. Ames' decision to embrace Jack reveals a strategy of communication that eschews the necessity of language and takes the task of language into the physical realm of embodiment.

'There are those who feel that the spiritual is diminished or denied when it is associated with the physical. I am not among them' claims Robinson, a statement which marries well with Ames' approach to blessing at the close of novel (Robinson 2012: 8). For all his praying and writing and speaking, it is ultimately the placing of a hand on Jack's forehead at the close of the novel that finally gives both men the moment of communion they had been seeking and it is in this physical gesture that the spiritual significance of encounter is produced and acknowledged. The scene is pregnant with meaning and its significance moves in many directions at once:

> He took his hat off and set it on his knee and closed his eyes and lowered his head, almost rested it against my hand, and I did bless him to the limit of my powers, whatever they are, repeating the benediction from Numbers, of course – 'The Lord make his face to shine upon thee and be gracious unto thee: The Lord lift up his countenance upon thee, and give thee peace.' Nothing could be more beautiful than that, or more expressive of my feelings, certainly, or more sufficient, for that matter. Then, when he didn't open his eyes or lift up his head, I said, 'Lord bless John Ames Boughton, this beloved son and brother and husband and father.' Then he sat back and looked at me as if he were waking out of a dream. (Robinson 2004: 275–6)

The second half of Ames' blessing, the improvised speech beyond the scripture quotation, immediately stands out as a verbalized commentary on what Ames has internally recognized since his conversation with Jack about Della and Robert: Jack is a beloved son, brother, husband and father. Not only this, by using his proper name, 'John Ames', the minister extends the meaning of the words to himself also, for both men are John Ames, and both men are father, brother, son and husband. In an earlier passage, and one now burdened with significance, Ames wonders at the example of biblical fathers and their treatment of their children. 'At the very end, poor old Jacob rebukes his sons as he blesses them. A remarkable thing to consider' (Robinson 2004: 155). This is indeed remarkable and it is all the more remarkable when read alongside the scene between Ames and Jack, for the commingling of blessing and rebuke is present there too. Ames blesses Jack as he rebukes himself. The admission that Jack is all these things is a rebuke in itself for it challenges all the warnings Ames has put in his letter to his son against Jack and more importantly, the blessing of Jack follows Ames' learning that Jack is married to an African American woman. This revelation provokes Ames' realization, only implicit in the text of the novel, that Gilead has become a town in which Jack's wife may not be welcome. Jack's marriage to Della is in itself a rebuke of Ames' entire work in Gilead and the blessing Ames gives affirms Jack's marriage and, by necessity, puts into question Ames' ministry, his life's work.

Relational transcendence and otherness

Earlier it was noted that Rivera's critique of Levinas focuses on his emphasis on distance in his imagining of transcendence. Rivera instead works towards a concept of 'relational transcendence', an imagining of transcendence that prioritizes physical touch over abstracted notions of infinite separation. She roundly rejects Levinas' limitless conceptions of obligation, distance and demand in favour of an embodied transcendence and 'as irreducibly relational, the work of the flesh – incarnation, transcendence-as-incarnation – is never without limits. It is always transcendence within, becoming within the constraints and promises of embodied existence – never dislodged from it' (Rivera 2007: 93). At and within the limits of bodies is the work of transcendence produced and, for Rivera, the essential gap between self and other is much better imagined in terms of difference than distance. Where for Levinas alterity gives way to a philosophically topographic separation, in

Rivera it is translated as an irreducible difference: 'transcendence is a relation with a reality irreducibly different from my own reality' (Rivera 2007: 97).[4] A relational transcendence is one that makes room for touch while acknowledging difference. Levinas' emphasis on exteriority means that the otherness of the other functions as a block on the actual relation. The assertion of absolute alterity risks ensuring the notion of relation between self and other is nothing more than a category mistake, but a relational transcendence that opens the space for touch closes the gap on which Levinas insists. Not only does this conception of transcendence make room for touch, but it also prescribes for its necessity: built into Rivera's notion of transcendence is the essential failure of language. Unlike Levinas, Rivera posits proximity between self and other and, where language fails, touch provides the site of communion.

This relational transcendence is imaginatively sketched in *Gilead* between Jack and Ames, and Rivera's notion of irreducibly different individuals is perfectly exemplified in their relationship. Where Rivera speaks of a transcendence that is *relational*, Robinson would be more inclined to speak of a transcendence that is *incarnational*, that is, rooted in the incarnation, a concept of self-other relation that finds its theological footing in the doctrine of Christ made human. Ames casually notes that the claim of the other's face has 'something to do with incarnation' and it makes sense that Ames' ultimate encounter with Jack is fully incarnational, that is, embodied. Indeed if incarnation produces the effect of the face, an incarnated response is the only one appropriate and ultimately satisfactory.

Taking Rivera's notion of relational transcendence seriously in a reading of *Gilead* means recognizing an important truth about the text's primary relationship: Ames and Jack are irreducibly different, not infinitely distant.

---

[4] To read Rivera alongside Robinson reveals Rivera's concept of the other to be 'Ordinary' in the Robinsonian sense, which is to say, excessively meaningful. As the introduction to the book makes clear, there is a distinctive theology of the Ordinary in Robinson, one that relies on the surplus of meaning and the endlessly interpretable nature of the seemingly mundane. Rivera writes along these lines with her conception of the other, noting: 'There is always more to the Other. We do encounter Others: we hear their voices, see their faces, and touch their bodies, and yet in the very encounter we also see, hear, and feel there is more. The gleam of transcendence in the flesh of the Other, an "elusive mystery" that envelops the other person, evokes that which cannot be made present' (Rivera 138).

This implies the real possibility of a genuine relationship and this is what Robinson writes in the conclusion of the novel. However, if it is granted that Jack is indeed 'other' to Ames, it must be recognized that the brief moments of understanding and communion between them do not signify a simple, uncomplicated 'happy ending' nor are they the *telos* of the text, for the truth of the matter, as Rivera notes, is that 'multiple Others are implicated in the face-to-face encounter' (Rivera 2007: 117). As Ames discovers with Jack, the other always springs from a prior network of other others. In the case of *Gilead*, Jack comes to Ames from Della, an African American woman and, on that basis alone, 'other' to Ames. Gilead, it appears, has become a white town, despite its history of radicalism and the 'negro church' that once stood earlier in Ames' ministry. Rivera rightly argues that '[a] broad interrelationality necessarily implies a depth in time. The past haunts the present – our past and the Other's past, pasts that might already link us to one another. We might already be complicit in the exclusion of the Other' (Rivera 2007: 104). This is the uncomfortable truth Ames recognizes as Jack reveals his family situation. Following the initial revelation, Ames records in his letter: 'I woke up this morning thinking this town might as well be standing on the absolute floor of hell for all the truth there is in it, and the fault is mine as much as anyone's' (Robinson 2004: 266). This is a direct reaction to his realization that Gilead has become, under his ministry, a place in which Jack's family might not be welcome. Jack convicts Ames of his total failure, stating, 'there was a fire at the Negro Church' to which Ames replies, 'that was a little nuisance fire, and it happened many years ago' (Robinson 2004: 264). 'And it has been many years since there was a Negro Church', says Jack and Ames recognizes 'there wasn't much I could say to that' (Robinson 2004: 264). Jack's otherness to Ames becomes, in this crucial conversation, a gateway to an otherness Ames has ignored in his ministry.

> The Other puts the self in question, says Levinas. I suggest that such questioning entails not only the claim of the priority of our responsibility to welcome the Other today, but also the implication of our subjectivity in the process of exclusion through which a person becomes a community's Other in the first place. (Rivera 2007: 107)

Where it was once Jack's mischievous childhood behaviour that put Ames in question, Jack's existence and the very facts of his life become for Ames a rebuke to his entire life's work and his unconscious acceptance of the 'othering' of black people in his community. Jack's presence in Gilead calls into question the process through which African Americans became ostracized from the town and, by extension, from Ames' own consciousness.

Jacob and the Angel: The wrestle in and beyond language

Early in the text Ames records a sermon he plans to give on the Genesis story of Jacob wrestling with the Angel: 'I wanted to talk about the gift of physical particularity and how blessing and sacrament are mediated through it' (Robinson 2004: 79). That Ames finally gets the opportunity to bless Jack physically engenders this passage with a renewed importance. As an image of encounter, Jacob's struggle with the Angel could well be the best way to understand Jack and Ames, their troubled relationship and the meaning of the blessing given. The Old Testament story tells the story of Jacob, preparing for an expected attack from his estranged brother, Esau, sending his family away to safety. While alone, Jacob encounters a stranger in his midst and the two figures begin to wrestle. Robinson's allusion to this story deserves attention and, when read side by side with Jack and Ames in mind, Robinson's novel begins to mirror and merge with the Old Testament tale.

Robinson is careful to ensure that both Ames and Jack do not become easily reducible to either Jacob or the Angel; rather, both characters can easily identify with either figure, and this blurring of the biblical archetypes is instructive. In their latter encounters at the close of *Gilead*, both men, like Jacob, are without their families, and both are engaged throughout the novel in an emotional and communicative struggle akin to the wrestling between Jacob and the stranger. The Angel, simply called, 'the man', in Genesis, wounds Jacob when he realizes he cannot overpower him and, likewise, the history of Jack's relationship with Ames is one of wounding, and within the events of the novel Ames too wounds Jack several times. However, the crucial moment of intersection between Robinson's text and the Old Testament story comes when

Jacob demands to be blessed by the Angel, asserting 'I will not let you go until you bless me' (Gen. 32. 26[b]).

With this in mind it would initially appear that Ames is the Angel as he is the one, finally, to administer the blessing. Indeed it was Ames' most clearly expressed desire to bless Jack, particularly because his initial baptism of Jack was so lacklustre. He writes, 'I do wish to christen him again, for my sake. I was so distracted by my own miserable thoughts I didn't feel that sacredness under my hand that I always do feel, that sense that the infant is blessing me' (Robinson 2004: 215). Here, though, Ames becomes more like Jacob, for it is also blessing that he seeks for himself. In the first baptism of Jack, neither person was blessed and the tortured relationship, the 'wrestle' between Ames and Jack that followed the baptism, should be read as both men's refusal to let the other go until they are blessed.

After his blessing Jacob receives a new name, 'Israel', 'because you have struggled with God and with men and have overcome' (Gen. 32.28). Jack, it is revealed, was to be called 'Theodore Dwight Weld', after the abolitionist organizer and preacher (1803–95). 'I thought that was an excellent name', writes Ames, continuing, 'my grandfather had heard Weld preach every night for three weeks until he had converted a whole doughface settlement to abolitionism, and the old man numbered it among the great experiences of his life' (Robinson 2004: 214). Of course, Reverend Boughton surprised everyone at Jack's baptism by having his son christened 'John Ames Boughton', and this change of name, making Jack Ames' namesake, places a huge burden on Ames' sense of self and his interpretation of his life's work.

Jack ultimately wounds Ames in a profound way, and the blessing that follows Ames' realization of his failure is the most he can do to make the situation right. Blessing is not necessarily a balm, as Ames' grandfather told him: 'being blessed meant being bloodied', and certainly it is a psychically bloodied Ames that blesses Jack (Robinson 2004: 41). Jack should have been called Theodore, a fact that compounds Ames' shame, for his namesake turned out a better man than he was, and Jack is, as Ames declares, 'another self, a more cherished self' (Robinson 2004: 215). Ironically, after all Jack had done to Ames as a child, this wound, the revelation of his wife and son, is the shock that shakes Ames most of all, and it has occurred altogether without malice. The injury Jack inflicts on Ames is one from which a reorientation to self and other springs and Kearney, reading the Jacob and the Angel story, writes, 'receiving a divine mark upon his hipbone and the new name of Israel, Jacob opts for peace, ultimately acknowledging "the face of God" in his mortal enemy' (Kearney 2010: 20). Ames, like Jacob, must acknowledge a newly uncovered reality: first that his status as minister and 'man of God' has not prevented his exclusion of the black community in Gilead; and second that Jack has avoided both Ames' and his own father's ethical shortcomings. Kearney continues, 'it is significant that, the day after he wrestled with the angel, he is able to finally embrace God in the guise of his estranged rival brother, Esau' (Kearney 2010: 20). Time and ailing health prevent Ames from making right his mistakes, so the blessing of Jack functions as his means to bless Jack's marriage, to rebuke his own role in its difficulty and to offer Jack the affirmation of being loved, forgiven and admired. Ames' wound is a wound of consciousness and, as death draws ever closer, it is a consciousness of an ultimate failing on his part but one that can, as is always the way in *Gilead*, be righted by a son.

Hope deferred

'Hope shapes intention. It leaves improbable possibilities open.' (Robinson 2018: 233)

This chapter began by discussing what Ames found cannot be said, that which exists beyond the grasp of the human language. While this is a central drama of the text, it becomes clear by the end of the novel that, running parallel to the frustration of what cannot be said, is the struggle Ames has with what he is *not prepared to say*. Ames' recognition of his failure in the town is only ever implicit in the text as is his standing by as the black population of Gilead is driven out. Where Ames finds God and ultimate reality inexpressible, he finds his own role in the othering of people of colour difficult to admit to plainly. What Ames cannot put right in this life, he must leave at the feet of Robbie, his only son. The letter that is *Gilead* is, of course, for Robbie to read, and its close discloses a hope for his life and a faith that Ames' own failings will not be final. 'This whole town does look like whatever hope becomes after it begins to weary a little, then weary a little more', writes Ames and, certainly, with his new consciousness of the whitewashed town he has ministered over, he cannot now see Gilead apart from its withdrawal from its once radical roots (Robinson 2004: 281). Town and self are inseparable for Ames, a man who has lived and worked in Gilead forever, and both have defected from their calling with regard to the marginalized black community in the American Midwest. 'The word "preacher" comes from an old French word, *prédicateur*, which means prophet. And what is the purpose of a prophet except to find meaning in trouble?' asks Ames, inviting his readers to judge his own ministry through the question (Robinson 2004: 266–7). Ames knows that he has failed to be a prophet a great deal of the time, and his tendency to reflect back on the one sermon he burned reveals his regret at his frequent lack of courage. Interpreting the Spanish influenza of 1918–20 as 'a sign and a warning to the rest of us that the desire for war would bring the consequences of war', the sermon was intended to be a reading of disaster as a divine sign, a mode of exposition consistent with the Old Testament prophets (Robinson 2004: 48). 'It was quite a sermon, I believe [. . .] But my courage failed', and this is all the more striking as, he admits, 'it might have been the only sermon I wouldn't mind answering for in the next world' (Robinson 2004: 49). The fire took his one truly great sermon, and soon '[he] too will solder away the time until the great and general incandescence', thus ending any reasonable hope he might have of compensating for his prophetic failings (Robinson 2004: 282).

Ames finishes his letter with a prayer: 'I pray that you grow up a brave man in a brave country. I pray you find a way to be useful' (Robinson 2004: 282). Ames, contrasting his own lack of courage, hopes Robbie will display open-hearted treatment of the stranger and will allow his father's failures to educate him. Ultimately, the wound inflicted on Ames' consciousness is the place from which Robbie's own sense of utility should spring. It is the mark left on the old minister after his wrestle with God, and, as father gives way to son, it is not a new name that Ames is given, but an heir that may fare better in being attentive to the humanity of the stranger. The sins of the father are not, then, to be visited upon this son, and in Robinson's *Gilead*, there is instead a *promise*; the literal promise a child brings, the promise of a future free from the limiting power of his father's errors. The future, then, is not under a curse borne of Ames' sin, but is open to the promise of grace provided by the son. In Robinson, readers are not so much presented with a doctrine of original sin as they are with a promise of future grace, and in her thinking the greatest sin individuals fall prey to is inattentiveness. Inattention to the Ordinary is given no room in *Housekeeping* and with her second novel in mind, inattentiveness to the stranger emerges as a particularly grave transgression. With a child, though, there is potential and promise of a renewed vision, and a more complete perception honed by attentiveness to the stranger. The letter of *Gilead* is a written request to Robbie to learn from his father's mistakes, an attempt to convict the son of paternal sin, and an imploring from a minister to his son to better understand difference, plurality and the incarnational truth that the divine is to be found ultimately in otherness.

3

Home

Robinson's radical grace

'What is grace, after all? What is the soul?'

(Robinson 2015: 35)

Introduction

Up to this point it has been demonstrated that 'the Ordinary' is the foundation of Robinson's thinking and, with this established, it remains to turn to the absolute heart of her world view. Grace is the unavoidable core of Robinson's theology, and no study of the significance of her work is complete without paying attention to her writing and construction of it in fiction. Post-*Housekeeping*, grace is the explicit concern of Robinson's writing and this can be seen very simply in the sheer number of times the word appears in both fiction and essays and, as will be highlighted, in the relationships she explores in her *Gilead* novels. *The Givenness of Things* devotes a full essay to grace and, certainly in the fictions, both Boughton and Ames are preoccupied with grace, its definition and its implications. There is a problem, though, in designating such an elusive concept as the centre of Robinson's work: writing about grace has always presented unique challenges for theologians. As Stephen Williams has noted 'we have no claim upon God's mercy – that grace must never be understood except as grace – is religiously and theologically fundamental' (SN Williams 139). It has been so thoroughly its own concept that no substitute or analogy is acceptable by way of making it easier to understand or write about, its essence distinct from justice, forgiveness or compassion, so comparison or equivalencies do not 'do justice' to the nature of grace. Interestingly, in the essay entitled 'Grace', Robinson turns to Shakespeare, 'my theologian', as she calls him, before she turns to Calvin (Robinson 2015: 49). In a discussion of Shakespeare's later plays which, she argues, are engaged in the 'intimation of a great reality of another order, which pervades human experience, even manifests itself in human actions and relations, yet is always purely itself', she seeks to piece together what she sees as the dramatist's deeply theological method of staging grace (Robinson 2015: 34). Speaking here to an interplay between narrative and grace in an echo of Williams' sentiment, she enquires 'grace is grace. How would this be staged?' (Robinson 2015: 37). Grace, for Robinson, resists description and translation and she turns to Shakespeare in order to find a way in which grace might be *expressed*, how it might be *enacted*. It is the staging of grace that has Robinson's attention here because, as an author of fiction, she has faith in the power of narrative to embody and express truths that resist philosophical statement. It is her implicit belief here that the essence of grace is best understood when it is seen and experienced, much more so than when it is described. Just as Robinson turns to Shakespeare, it is appropriate to read Robinson with the expectation that she will shed light on how grace may be staged.

In *Home*, grace is discussed openly and often by Rev. Boughton as the absolute foundation of his theology and faith. 'Nobody deserves anything, good or bad. It's all grace' he states, near the novel's end, and certainly it is his focus on the grace of God that abides in Glory's memory, '[standing] at the front of his own church year after year, hoping to be able to preach again about grace and the loving heart of Christ' (Robinson 2008: 283, 222). Beyond what is said in the text, by Rev. Boughton or Ames, about the theological centrality of forgiveness or the necessary justice of God, the real staging of grace is carried out in what is *not* said, what is implied, what is done and what is avoided by the principal characters. At the heart of the novel is the expression of a radical grace that dissolves any and all binaries, problematizing the kind of thinking that results in theological certainty at the expense of the other. Before delving into the deep and rich theology of grace offered in the text's exploration of familial relationship, it will be instructive to examine what can be referred to as 'intimations of grace'. These intimations function as economic, supralinguistic, *Ordinary* expressions of grace, 'grace-full' in their own right, yet also orbiting the ineffable core of grace that exists at the centre of the family and of Robinson's theology. Specifically, these intimations of grace in the novel are fragrance, music and house. These sustaining reminders are profoundly Ordinary, in the Robinsonian sense of the term, inherently valuable for what they are in themselves and also for what they point to, what they participate in beyond their physical or tangible existence, what they *open on to*. An examination of these intimations will draw the discussion towards the novel's struggle with reformed theological thinking and will shed light on the implications of Robinson's staging of grace for her own theology and her writing of transcendence. As will be developed in the chapter that follows, if Robinson's third novel is to be considered a study of grace, then its title, *Home*, is apt, for in Robinson's work grace is always connected to return, restoration and the often uncomfortable business of reorientation.

Intimations of grace

Fragrance

Robinson's third novel can be read as a contemporary midrash on the gospel's Prodigal Son parable. While the text allows the details of the gratuitous life of its errant son to enter in via memory and story, it is the period following his difficult return home that is evocatively conjured here. The novel explores the question, 'how did family life settle around the return of the prodigal?', an issue that exists beyond the point at which the biblical parable ends. When Jack does arrive he is visibly shamed, cautious about the welcome awaiting him and still clearly recovering from a hangover. 'Here he was', thinks Glory, 'in her kitchen, pale and ill at ease and in no state to receive the kindness prepared for him' (Robinson 2008: 33). Having seen his son and subtly noticed the state he was in, Boughton suggests coffee and leaves Jack alone. Glory, initiating a pattern of intercessory action between father and son, is the one to make the coffee, taking the first tentative step towards becoming the central familial conduit of grace in the text. Her first words to Jack, 'I was about to give up on you', are ironic when read in light of the extraordinary lengths Glory goes to make Jack feel comfortable, forgiven and at home (Robinson 2008: 31). Coffee is the first outward sign of what will become Glory's graceful, sustaining presence in the home, continually attempting to re-orientate Jack to himself, his family, his memories and his future.

Grace is, in Robinson's terms, a homecoming, a 'return'; or, in Ames' language, 'the Greek word *sozo*, which is usually translated "saved", can also mean healed, restored, that sort of thing' (Robinson 2004: 273). It is found in *Home*, too: 'he spilled coffee down his sleeve and winced with irritation, and she thought how kind her father was to give him time to *recover himself* (Robinson 2008: 35; emphasis added). In the 'Grace' essay she notes that the effect of grace in Shakespeare is 'the restoration of lost loved ones' (Robinson 2015: 48). Glory answers the call of this grace and in her words and actions seeks to make Jack feel welcome, to facilitate his homecoming in subtle and gentle ways. Later in the text it is revealed that much of her work is self-conscious in its attempt to restore Jack to his place as son and brother in the family: 'she went down to the kitchen and started a pot of coffee, and sat in the porch while it brought itself to the kind and degree of fragrance her family had always preferred. Then she poured a cup for Jack' (Robinson 2008: 205). Glory's embodiment of Ordinary grace has profound attention to detail, extending to the fragrance of coffee, all for the purpose of somehow reminding Jack that he is fully at home. After Jack's suicide attempt it is Glory who takes it upon herself to recover Jack, to restore him. Aside from the obvious washing of her brother and clothing him in fresh clothes, Glory once again turns to fragrance as a means to communicate grace. 'How to announce the return of comfort and well-being except by cooking something fragrant', thinks Glory, recalling, 'that is what her mother always did' (Robinson 2008: 263):

> After every calamity of any significance she would fill the atmosphere of the house with the smell of cinnamon rolls or brownies, or with chicken and dumplings, and it would mean, This house has a soul that loves us all, no matter what. It would mean peace if they had fought and amnesty if they had been in trouble [. . .] And her father would offer the grace, inevitable with minor variations, thanking the Lord for all the wonderful faces he saw around his table. (Robinson 2008: 263)

The fragrance of grace is reliant on the memories it conjures. Here, Glory is attempting to evoke recollections of wholeness, peace and a family that is held together by ties that exist beyond present difficulties. Of course the problem in stirring these memories is that Jack is so often absent in them. Jack himself confesses to Glory, 'when I was a kid I used to wish I lived here. I used to wish I could just walk in the door like the rest of you did and, you know, sit down at the table and do my homework or something' (Robinson 2008: 287). Glory hopes that the fact that Jack did not participate in much of the family's rituals of reconciliation does not preclude the power of the memory from reminding him of his status as brother. She is hoping that Ames is right in his assertion that 'memory can make a thing seem to have been much more than it was' and that the mere suggestion of an illusory familial peace might be enough to instil it once again (Robinson 2004: 75). Painter observes that 'Glory's example is a contemporary re-visioning of the biblical parable that places divine mercy and acceptance in human hands – often female hands at that, an example somewhat lacking in scripture' (Painter 2010: 336). Where Jack's difficulty with the theological doctrine of predestination becomes the novel's dramatic core, Glory's tending to her father and brother contrasts the abstract debates with an embodied grace, a grace made simple, quotidian and tangible. Coffee and fragrance are introduced in the text as a means to recover Jack from a hangover and persist as a symbol of grace extended to a disreputable brother from an alienated and equally ill-at-ease younger sister.

Music

If grace, through Glory, is performed in the Ordinary and self-conscious rituals of daily family life, then it is clear that Jack's initial awkwardness at being at home precludes him from reciprocating in this way. Glory's mediation of grace is just as often staged as spoken, taking place in careful, attentive acts as well as vocal assurances. Jack, however, as the last chapter has demonstrated, finds language difficult, particularly when talking to those with whom he should be most familiar. As a participant in the grace evident throughout the text, Jack finds his utility in non-linguistic methods, in actions that communicate without speech. In very plain language at the beginning of the novel it is stated 'Hope was serene, Luke was generous, Teddy was brilliant, Jack was Jack, Grace was musical' (Robinson 2008: 15). While this list of siblings and their defining characteristics serves as a brief introduction to figures who will remain at the periphery of the text, the phrase 'Grace was musical' stands out due to what follows. Music is indeed an intimation of grace in the text, existing as it does in contrast to Jack's 'twenty-year silence'. In many ways Glory and Jack, as part of their grace work, seek to 'fill' the house once more: Glory with the scents of family and Jack with piano music. Extending the 'Grace' as 'sister and theological concept' significance further, the following passage can be seen to connect silence with the absence of grace: 'then there were those other years, after even Grace was gone, those tense years only she and her mother and father had lived through together in that house, when they lost the habit of mentioning Jack by name' (Robinson 2008: 56). 'Never had it entered her mind', notes Glory, reflecting on this time, 'that their household could contain so desolate a silence' (Robinson 2008: 60). Grace, the sister closest to Glory's age, left the house and with her the music went too as she was the family's most gifted musician. The silence that envelops the house, caused by Jack's abandonment of his child and his family, is only truly alleviated once Jack returns home and to the piano.

Glory laments that the initial period following Jack's return was characterized by a lack of conversation and a real awkwardness between them. Glory voices this concern to Jack, framing it from their father's perspective, saying, 'he just worries that we don't talk. He hates a silent house' (Robinson 2008: 48). Jack's first song on the piano, 'Smoke Gets in Your Eyes,' while initially rebuked as a choice by Glory, reveals to him that he and his sister may have more shared experiences than he ever would have imagined. The lyrics of the song, 'I chaffed them and I gaily laughed / To think they could doubt my love / Yet today my love has flown away / I am without my love', alluding to a lost beloved, express a struggle central to Jack and Glory's present situation, the reason they have returned home ('Smoke Gets In Your Eyes', The Platters). It is the exchanging of their mutual mistakes with each other that forms the basis of their genuine relationship as it exists at the end of the text. Jack's inability to hold on to his would-be wife and Glory's failed engagement, while remaining painful for both, are facts about their history that humanize Jack in Glory's eyes, and vice versa. Hearing Glory's tale of deception at the hands of a married man, and the break-up of a marriage that never was, leads Jack to the revelation 'I have just been told that I am not the only sinner in this family' (Robinson 2008: 125). While Calvin's insistence on the absolute sinfulness of humankind has theological problems for Robinson, it is worth noting that the realization that he is not the only member of the family to have experienced disgrace permits Jack to relax. The Marxist critic, Roland Boer, calls this egalitarian streak in Calvin's theology the 'democracy of depravity', meaning that if humans do indeed share without exception in a tainted nature, then no one ought to feel especially separate on account of their sinful character, an idea that will be returned to later in a discussion of the radical nature of grace in Robinson's work (Boer 2009: 25). The initial phrases on the piano are, then, the foundations on which a deep bond is formed and past wrongs healed, literal grace notes in the development of their relationship.

If music makes possible a connection between Glory and Jack, it becomes one of the few ways Jack can please his father. Having played a couple of chastised bars of 'Smoke Gets in Your Eyes', Jack goes on to play his father's favourite hymn, 'Sweet Hour of Prayer', taking his lead from Boughton singing it from the other room. Jack meets his father's implicit request and 'played the hymn through, embellishing a little but respectfully enough' (Robinson 2008: 93). The visual metaphor of this scene is striking, Jack finding a means to communicate with his father, even as they inhabit different rooms on either side of a separating wall. Playing hymns for his father becomes for Jack a way to 'meet' him, an activity in which both men can be wholly engaged. It is clear that it is primarily in the playing of the piano that Jack returns to himself, or, in other words, it is in his playing that he ceases to be parodic, once removed from his own life, but present and inhabiting his body and its moment. At a dinner with Ames, Jack decides once more to play. Through Glory's eyes, this quiet event becomes a moment of grace from son to father, godson to godfather:

> He went to the piano and sat down and began to play 'Softly and Tenderly', a favourite hymn of his father's. He played it softly, and, she thought, very tenderly. She went into the hallway to listen, and he glanced up at her sidelong, as if there were an understanding between them, but he played on

pensively, without a hint of detachment or calculation. 'Come home, come home, ye who are weary, come home.' (Robinson 2008: 204–5)

The silence that follows the singalong is thick with meaning, a change in atmosphere consistent with the outside conditions as 'it had begun to thunder and rain, one of those storms that come after dark and change the weather' (Robinson 2008: 205). The old men sit and ponder the significance of the returned prodigal in a silence that is qualitatively altered due to the preceding communion in music. Jack playing this hymn, with its lyrics speaking of a need to return to one's father, is his way of revealing his all-too-apparent struggles and communicating his gratitude for the frail, yet open, arms that greeted him when he returned. It is uncommon in theology to associate grace with the efforts of the sinner, yet Robinson goes to considerable lengths to ensure that the omnidirectional reality of grace proceeds from a troubled son as much as it does from a preacherly father. Robinson's conception of grace is staged in *Home* and it consistently subverts expectation. Jack, as will be discussed, becomes the channel of a divine grace that explodes any distinction between Christian and non-Christian, saved and unsaved, chosen and not chosen.

House

The house in Robinson's third novel comes to signify a core duality in the experience of grace. Jack's cognitive dissonance in terms of his familial home, his desire to see it remain as it is and his simultaneous anxiety at actually being there, are contrasting feelings mirrored in his equally complex encounter with grace. Reflecting on the house, Glory notes,

> It seemed sometimes as if her father must have meant to preserve all this memory, this sheer power of sameness, so that when they came home, or when Jack came home, there would be no need to say anything. In terms of the place, they would always have known everything. (Robinson 2008: 91)

This thoughtful gesture, sustained through decades of prayerful separation, is ultimately recognized by Jack in his final moments in the house. Seeing her brother carefully taking in last glances of its particulars, she thinks 'Dear Lord, he is missing it all in anticipation' (Robinson 2008: 312). This comfort in sameness, however, stands in contrast to Jack's inability to relax in the benefits of his old home. The text is marked by references to Jack's awkwardness, his desire for privacy and his almost ironic politeness in treating his closest family like courteous strangers. Jack's means of making himself more comfortable in his house is to try to restore it to the one he holds in his memory, as Glory concludes 'against her advice and to her surprise, he had undertaken a furtive campaign to make the house look a little less forbidding' (Robinson 2008: 90). Jack's conflation of God and father, as will be discussed, ensures he cannot imagine a God that transcends his father's limitations. It is also true that Jack views his childhood home as an image of divine grace: at once a place of welcome, yet also a refuge he never truly felt was his. The forbidding nature of the house is a visual reminder of the forbidding nature of his father's theology and the double-edged nature of Jack's experience of grace. If grace is a 'homecoming', then Jack exists as a challenge to any simplistic notion of redemption. Gardening, tending to the old car, trimming back the obscuring hedges, are all attempts by Jack to engage in a restoration, a project of graceful rehabilitation for the ageing house of his childhood. This double-sided experience of homecoming is a central motif of the novel, a feeling shared by Glory and Jack: 'what kinder place could there be on earth, and why did it seem to them all like exile?' (Robinson 2008: 294). This sentiment is obviously applicable to both siblings and its significance deepened further when applied to Jack's theological enquiry into the nature of grace.

Her father used to say: 'He lets us wander so we will know what it means to come home' (Robinson 2008: 106). For Boughton, the return home of Jack is both an example of the grace of God and an opportunity to demonstrate this very same grace. Glory herself observes that 'grace seems to answer every question, as far as he's concerned' (Robinson 2008: 161). In his insistence on the absolute centrality of the mystery of grace, Boughton closes himself off from the possibility of understanding his son's struggle with the doctrine. In the crucial predestination discussion, Boughton once again affirms the primacy of grace, stating 'the grace of God can find out any soul, anywhere' (Robinson 2008: 230). Jack's response to his father, 'then isn't grace the same as predestination? The pleasanter side of it?' reveals either the logical or moral collapse in his father's thinking here (Robinson 2008: 230). Indeed, in an earlier conversation with his sister, Jack argues that if grace is indeed the answer to his father's every question, 'then he shouldn't have to worry about his reprobate son, should he [. . .] it does seem like a contradiction, doesn't it?' (Robinson 2008: 161). In logical terms, Jack cannot understand how his father cannot see that the limited nature of grace involved in predestination theology means that grace cannot be the last word for those unfortunate people for whom grace was never intended. However, logic aside, Jack's most serious concern is that his father thinks he is correct in his theology and is simply blind to the implications it has for his own son's destiny.

Grace as a synonym for predestination is Jack's primary theological struggle for much of the text. In his mind, grace is grace when experienced by the elect, and perdition when extended to the sinner, and, 'one way or the other, it seems like fate' (Robinson 2008: 230). Jack experiences this dual nature of grace all at once in his own life: leading a life of disrepute, abandoning a child, stealing, drinking, yet also knowing the assurances of a welcoming home and a place in a family. However, Jack largely garners his theology from a reading of his own experience and concludes 'perdition is the one thing that always made sense to me' (Robinson 2008: 124). Jack sees his history as evidence of the unpleasant side of the 'grace' his father preached from his pulpit. 'It is possible' he states simply, 'to know the great truths without feeling the truth of them', and it is important to note that in saying this Jack has in mind the 'Fatherhood of God' and the existence of a 'gracious intention behind it all' as examples of doctrines that have no emotional hold on him (Robinson 2008: 109). Jack finds himself existentially stranded between his father's theology of pervasive grace and a permanent experience of perdition. The problematic nature of grace as it is understood by Jack is mirrored in his return home: a reminder of his difficult relation to his pious family, his taunting of Ames, his thieving, yet also, a source of comfort, a reminder of place and welcome. If grace is a 'homecoming' for Robinson, then her third novel exists as a means to exemplify the problematic and complex nature of homecoming grace. While what has been discussed so far is little more than an introduction to Robinson's theology of grace, it should be noted that in her writing she is constantly working on a number of levels and at a multitude of interfaces, most notably between the Ordinary and the transcendent, the divine and the human, the symbolic and the actual. In what follows it should be made clear that Robinson is insistent on the centrality of grace and is extremely hesitant to limit the power of that grace in any way, her fiction existing as an *apologia* for the multifaceted, infinite capacity of grace to transform and restore people and relationships. Grace, as will be seen, does not so much break down binary theological thinking, that is, distinctions between saved and unsaved, elect and unelect, but instead operates above and beyond these categories, *in spite* of them, its power not reducible to simplistic and reductive accounts of 'us and them'.

Robinson and grace

Thus far the discussion of grace in *Home* has been largely confined to an exploration of human relationships. The messy, complex histories shared by Jack, Glory and their father mean that, as with all human ties in Robinson's fiction, their potential for grace is complicated by limitation. In Robinson's writing, despite the focus on human capacity and potential, it is always a transcendent Reality that permits human participation in the divine realities of love, grace and faith. As Ames puts it to Jack:

> There are certain attributes our faith assigns to God – omniscience, omnipotence, justice, and grace. We human beings have such a slight acquaintance with power and knowledge, so little conception of justice, and so slight a capacity for grace, that the workings of these great attributes together is a mystery we cannot hope to penetrate. (Robinson 2008: 229)

Robinson is fundamentally theological in all her thinking: that is, the arguments she forwards and the positions she takes are always grounded in theology. It is imperative, then, that an account be made of the transcendent, the 'divine' foundation of grace as it figures in her writing. Robinson is interested in humans in so far as they are carriers of the divine image, and she is interested in God simply because he 'is of a kind to love the world extravagantly, wondrously [. . .] This is the essence of the story that forever eludes telling' (Robinson 2012: 128). The grace that passes between individuals is, for Robinson, participating in however small a way in a grace that pervades from the 'rapturous love' of the Cross (Robinson 2012: 128).

In an interview with Rebecca Painter, Robinson speaks directly about the Prodigal Son parable, commenting: 'I really see this as a parable about grace, not forgiveness, since the father runs to meet his son and embraces him before the son can even ask to be forgiven. Or it is about love, which is probably a synonym for grace' (Painter 2009: 488). Here she voices a statement absolutely central to her theology, a sentiment repeated by Ames, 'love is holy because it is like grace – the worthiness of its object is never really what matters' (Robinson 2004: 238). Robinson affirms the synonymity of love and grace, an assertion that runs contrary to Jack's conflation of grace and perdition. However, to say that love and grace are the same thing is not, on the face of it, to have said anything that does not require further explanation. Taking Robinson at her word here means that anything she writes about love can equally inform an exploration of her theology of grace and, love, she argues, 'however elusive, however protean, however fragmentary, seems to have something like an objective existence' (Robinson 2015: 78). Again Robinson emphasizes the *reality* of love, the connection between the lofty metaphysical nature of love and the everyday experience of love, and in a statement characteristic of her thinking, writes, 'God so loved the world. God is Love. Love one another as I have loved you. These sentences are intelligible to us because we do, in however misdirected or dilute a form, participate in this attribute' (Robinson 2015: 80). It is crucial to note the explicit assertion that it is the experience of love that renders scripture meaningful, and this is the kind of thinking Ames embodies, who argues, 'it is religious experience above all that authenticates religion' (Robinson 2004: 165). Human love, for Robinson, allows the lover to extrapolate from his or her experience upwards, to gain some insight into what it might mean for God to love, to *be* love. Grace and love are known in their grandest sense through the Ordinary practice of them. Equally, for Robinson, Ordinary acts of love and grace garner their power and character because they participate in the transcendent reality of love and grace. With this in mind, the relationship between experience and belief can be seen to be reciprocal, the Ordinary daily revelation of grace is recognized as such because of the metaphysical, theological grace of God, and the transcendent grace of God is known, if only partially, through these quotidian experiences of grace. Robinson is careful in her essays to keep all talk of metaphysics and transcendence anchored to the Ordinary. At times, her predisposition to the Ordinary demands she address issues of injustice, racism and inequality. *Gilead* and *Home*, however, have been criticized for their supposed muteness or lack of historical grounding, a charge of quietness levelled at Robinson for a perceived lack of attention to the reality of America in the 1950s. This is worth discussing, first to correct such a misreading of Robinson's work, and, second, to demonstrate how her theology of grace is, as noted above, garnered from and applied to the reality of human life and struggle.

Robinson, Cone and the charge of quietness

Two very different perspectives on theology are presented in *Home*: the approach of its ministers, Ames and Boughton, and the route taken by its errant prodigal, Jack. This difference of approach and assumption is brought into sharp focus in the text's dealing with the historical reality of America in 1956. Where the ministers enjoy debating the finer points of doctrine, or Barth, or Calvin, Jack cannot see past Christian inaction in the context of a segregated United States.[1] Robinson sets up a striking contrast in *Home* between abstract, contextless theological debate and a concern for the material reality of injustice. As a thinker instinctually attuned to the Ordinary and to the physical world, Robinson's third novel asks the question, 'What good is theology when it looks past reality?' Brueggemann's *The Prophetic Imagination* (1978) asks similarly charged questions, and approaches the Hebrew Bible with the expectation that the prophets may have some answers. Speaking of the Exodus narrative, Brueggemann writes, 'it is only a poem and we might say rightly that singing a song does not change reality. However, we must not say that with too much conviction. The evocation of an alternative reality consists at least in part in the battle for language and the legitimisation of a new rhetoric'

---

[1] It could be argued that Jack's perspective is not an approach to theology at all, but a *rejection* of it. However, as will be demonstrated, Jack rejects theology on theological grounds, out of a clear-sighted analysis of the utility of theology, and from a view of the chasm separating his own sense of justice from his father's theology.

(Brueggemann 1978: 18). The drama of *Home* does takes place in discourse and in the breakdown of dialogue. Jack brings to his family home a new way of speaking about the world and, by extension, a new way of being in the world. The reality of racism is not diluted by Jack, and, as Robinson's theological mouthpiece, he disrupts a settled, inactive, white theological consensus. For Robinson, theology should always be restless with itself; indeed, a theology that bypasses injustice necessarily delegitimizes itself, and Jack's voice in the novel is her device for rupturing sedate theological debate once removed from the world in which it takes place.

Jack's narrative arc and presence in the novel invite close reading because Jack himself is the key to unlocking Robinson's theology of grace. Moreover, it is difficult to read *Home* without hearing distinct echoes of James Cone's widely influential *A Black Theology of Liberation* (1970).[2] A central theme of Cone's theology – that it always must be done with full, self-conscious awareness of particularity – finds a home in Robinson's *Gilead* novels. She avoids the error Cone diagnoses in so much of what he calls 'white theology' – the mistake of making universal, prescriptive claims about God – by building in the security of uncertainty to her statements on ultimate reality. 'I don't like to say prescriptive things about God because I know I would be wrong', states Robinson in a recent interview (Chapter 5). There is a profound difference in Cone's writing between prescriptive descriptions of God and prescriptive ethical judgement. For this reason, for Cone, it is possible to say 'racism is inherently evil', but impossible to claim 'the providence of God always brings good out of evil'. Experience is Cone's guide here, validating his ethics while particularizing his theology. 'To suggest that black suffering is consistent with the knowledge and will of God and that in the end everything will happen for the good of those who love God is unacceptable to blacks', argues Cone; and as he rejects universalizing a theological statement, he also rejects the 'tendency of classic Christianity to appeal to divine providence' (Cone 1970: 16). As

---

[2] Robinson has never referenced Cone in her written work, or mentioned his work in interviews. However, such is the extent of *Home*'s crossover with Cone's thinking that it seems highly unlikely Robinson has not read and wrestled with Cone's theology. Whether the crossover is conscious engagement in Robinson's part or serendipitously similar thinking, there is a fruitful interface between the two thinkers.

Cummings argues, 'the universalising tendencies of white theology lead to the rejection of black theology's particular claims and, more troubling, rejection of black theologians' particular voices' (2009: 399).³ Divine providence, the doctrine Jack struggles with throughout the text of *Home*, does not situate well in a theology sourced from the experience of the ostracized and oppressed.

For Cone, black theology is not to be a direct replacement or competition for white theology, for such an aim would risk compromising the essence of what makes black theology distinctive and identifiably itself. No: for Cone it is essential that black theology not become like its oppressor and cede to the temptation to control theological discourse with totalizing claims. The white ministers in *Home* do not often make sweeping, universal statements about the God they worship, or the theology they read. Instead, a more subtle and insidious pattern of discourse unfolds within the novel, one in which Ames and Boughton, when pushed on the logical and ethical end points of their theology, find it all too easy to use the word 'mystery' to justify their inaction. As Ames says of God's character in *Home*, '[it is] a mystery we cannot hope to penetrate' (Robinson 2008: 229). As will be seen in what follows, mystery has a privileged place in Robinson's theology, but it is never used as an escape from sustained analysis of material injustice. Mystery should never be a conceptual retreat from a theological scrutiny of oppression, not only because this is immoral but also because the genuine mysteries of the Christian faith – the incarnation, the creation of humans in the image of God, for example – effectively rule out this use of mystery. Ames and Boughton find mystery as the terminus of their theological thinking, where Jack begins with the reality of oppression. Black liberation theology has no room for talk of objective divine truth, and never seeks to explicate the Christian faith in these terms. As Hopkins notes, 'theological language is not objective, or neutral, a transparent

---

[3] John D. Caputo, although coming at theology from a different perspective to Cone, nonetheless shares Cone's passion for 'weakening' the claims made by traditional, orthodox theology. He argues: 'theology in the strong sense is characterised by a classical Greco-philosophical discursive mode, by a system of propositional claims [. . .] By weak theology I do not mean something debilitated, ineffective, and anaemic, but a theology that abandons the mode of claiming and gives itself over to a prior being-claimed', he posits (Kearney 2017: 45). What Cone rejects as 'white theology', Caputo rebukes as 'strong theology', and both are united on the need for a return to existential experience as the primary guide for theological thinking.

transmission of God's will to the human domain', continuing, 'a black theology of liberation [. . .] must submit any language of God-talk to the question: how does this language aid in the conditions of possibility for poor and working class emancipation' (Batstone et al., 1997: 217). Theology, here, begins not with an attempt to divine the theological facts of God or reality, but with an analysis of the pervasive cases of injustice and alienation in the physical world. Nothing useful can be said of God, then, if it cannot be said in full sincerity in the face of racist oppression; and, even more importantly, if it cannot be affirmed by people who are powerless.

Cone's work is well known for its assertive, undiluted tone; characteristic of his style, he argues: 'the Jesus-event in twentieth-century America is a black-event – that is, an event of liberation taking place in the black community' (Cone 1970: 5). What Cone declares emphatically only ever enters Robinson's novel at the margins, in hushed tones. Jack very gently asks agitating questions, troubling the settled mindsets of his father and godfather. He does not shout, exclaim or preach. Indeed, hushed is an apt adjective for a novel that, as Sykes argues, 'embodies an aesthetic that is calm, private, and peaceful before it is loud, public, and obtrusive' (Sykes 2017: 109). Sykes notes the 'quiet' nature of Robinson's *Gilead* novels, situating it against 'the work of novelists such as Franzen, DeLillo, Pynchon, and Wallace, who are often seen as the century's key chroniclers because, within a culture declared to be loud, quiet is viewed as reticence, at best, and conservativism, at worst' (Sykes 2017: 109). This has certainly been the case, as reviewers and critics have often picked up on a perceived lack of 'background noise' and atemporality in the *Gilead* trilogy.[4] However, an emphasis on the trilogy's lack of historical grounding must make a clear distinction between the novels themselves and the consciousness of their characters. It is certainly the case that the ministers of Robinson's prose are indeed ignorant of their particular moment, but this should not to be taken to

---

[4] Schmidt argues *Gilead* is 'anachronistic' (Schmidt 559); Petite says that the characters of Robinson's trilogy suffer from an 'historical amnesia' (Petite 119); and Tessa Hadley refers to *Gilead* as 'old fashioned' (Hadley 19). Sykes, surveying these critical opinions, comments, 'Schmidt, Hadley, and Petite all acknowledge that the Gilead novels are set in the past but are not immediately identifiable with a particular moment, and it is this aspect of Robinson's prose that reviewers often describe as "quiet"' (Sykes 115).

mean that the novels exhibit this same lack of awareness. Sykes rightly argues that 'the struggle for civil rights is a driving force of the second Gilead novel, which picks up the discussion of segregation introduced in *Gilead*'s final pages' (Sykes 2017: 113). Quietness need not imply political quietism, and where Robinson's ministers can and should be critiqued for inactivity, the novels simply cannot be read as texts blind to history or deaf to injustice. Indeed an interpretation of *Home* that fails to appreciate the quiet, theologically grounded critique of American Christianity is one that has not taken Robinson's non-fiction – or Robinson as a theologian – seriously enough. *Home*, read alongside essays in, for example, *The Givenness of Things*, is simply not open to the charge of ahistoricism or of ignorant complacency. If, as Cone argues, the Jesus-event of the twentieth century is the narrative of black liberation in the United States, it is hardly presumptuous to expect a theological novel set in 1956 America to have something to say about this unfolding historical story. Where Cone's rhetorical style is loud, Robinson's prose is quiet, an aesthetic choice that in no way dilutes the ethical and theological significance of her third novel. 'Theology can never be neutral or fail to take sides on issues related to the plight of the oppressed', writes Cone, continuing, 'there can be no theology of the gospel which does not arise from an oppressed community (Cone 1970: 4). This is so because God is revealed in Jesus as a God whose righteousness is inseparable from the weak and helpless in human society' (Cone 1970: 5). The connection Cone makes here – between justice and the revelation of God in Jesus in the incarnation – is absolutely key to his theology and, as will be developed, to Robinson's world view, her theology of grace and, indeed, her third novel. Cone shouts his theology in *A Black Theology of Liberation*, convicting American Christians of hypocrisy, where Robinson whispers, letting her readers piece together her fundamentally theological critique of white conservative theology and the immoral silence such theology incubates.

Cosmic Christ and God as Father

'My Christology is high, in that I take Christ to be with God, and to be God. And I take it to be true that without him nothing was made that was made'

(Robinson 2015: 188). Robinson places herself firmly in Barth's legacy with her emphasis on the divinity of Christ, his primal role in Creation and the centrality these Christological doctrines have in her theology. For Robinson, the place of Christ in the Trinity is fundamental and means that reality is inscribed with divinity: 'reality is sacred, and, as expressed in the being of Christ, is also profoundly human-centred'; for Robinson, this has profound implications for both the reading of scripture and for action in the world (Robinson 2015: 192). She writes,

> In light of the unvarying solicitude of the Old Testament toward the poor, it might be metaphysically respectable to infer that Christ was in some sense present even in the least of them from the primordial moment when human circumstance began to call for justice and generosity. (Robinson 2015: 195)

This is logical for Robinson, a passionate Trinitarian, as without this notion of the cosmic Christ, 'this cleavage leaves the being of Christ unexpressed from the beginning until the Incarnation' (Robinson 2015: 196). Christ's pre-existence and place in the Godhead, far from being abstract theological notions, are, for Robinson, the reasons why the call of social justice has infinite importance and universal resonance.

For Robinson,

> To embrace the thought that the presence of Christ in the moment of Creation would have meant that the nature of Christ is intrinsic to Creation, and an aspect of the relation of God to the world from the very outset. The Trinity would be conceptually unsustainable if this were not true. (Robinson 2015: 196–7)

The knitting of Christ into the fabric of reality means that it is 'reasonable to suppose that he was to be found, so to speak, among the nameless and vulnerable, whether of Galilee or Babylon, whether of Egypt, God's people, or of Assyria' (Robinson 2015: 200). Christ's incarnation, then, is to be understood as a revelation, a making known of truths that were always true, 'that there was a love that could only be made known to us through a gesture of such unthinkable grandeur and generosity – over and above the grandeur and generosity of Creation itself' (Robinson 2015: 197). This revelation means that the vulnerable and the poor have God's attention and, 'when society seems to have an intrinsic order, it is an unjust order. And the justice of God disrupts it' (Robinson 2015: 199). This divine disruption of injustice finds its paradoxical power in the weakness of Christ, as Robinson states: 'Jesus of Nazareth is the great and culminating instance of the exaltation of the humble. He takes his place among them as one who is despised and betrayed' and this is where the call of the cosmic Christ lies (Robinson 2015: 200). This is a call to engage in the work of upending societal systems, deconstructing hierarchical structures and freeing the captives. As Robinson puts it, 'in history as God sees it, they [the poor, the humble, the nameless] are the great potential who make his power in human affairs actual, and through whom his justice is vindicated' (Robinson 2015: 200). It is this vision of God, as Trinity, with the revelation of the incarnated Christ as much a part of the Godhead as Father and Spirit, that generates an essential, necessary, desire for social justice. 'Christ humbled himself and took the form of a slave. He humbled himself not in the fact of being human, but to show us the meaning of making slaves of human beings' (Robinson 2015: 200). The subversive nature of the gospel, as Robinson sees it, entails a laying low of the powerful and a radical vindication of the poor and marginalized.

It is with Robinson's ethical imperative in mind that Jack's theological struggle, its causes and implications, come into view. The relationship between Jack and his father is at once tense and loving, gracious and difficult. Boughton makes it clear to Jack that forgiveness and love are his and that he will never be a stranger in his home. However, this spirit of grace is undercut in the novel when scenes of police brutality against black people in Montgomery are shown on the Boughtons' new television set. The minister's reaction, 'there's no reason to let that sort of trouble upset you. In six months nobody will remember one thing about it', invites a gentle response from Jack, commenting, 'some people will probably remember it' (Robinson 2008: 101). As the police turn dogs and fire hoses on the crowd, Jack exclaims 'Jesus Christ!', which in turn invites a strong rebuke from his father: 'that kind of language has never been acceptable in this house' (Robinson 2008: 102). This brief exchange is possibly the single most illuminating passage in the text for understanding Jack's perpetual wrestle with Christian belief and the theology of grace. As the reader later finds out, Jack has married a black woman called Della. His exile from his familial home involved coexisting with people of colour and led to his conclusion, which he voices to Ames and his father, 'they are very fine Christians, many of them' (Robinson 2008: 227). Later in the conversation Boughton '[falls] back on his experience of Minneapolis, his closest equivalent to foreign travel' (Robinson 2008: 229). Robinson makes clear here that Jack is speaking out of a rich experience and Boughton out of a naive ignorance and surprising absence of empathy. When Jack uses the name 'Jesus Christ' as an exclamation, it is the sin of blasphemy to which his father objects. However, the irony in this moment is clear, the minister of grace being far more concerned with the supposed misuse of the Lord's name in a moment of deep shock than with the more obvious blasphemy involved in the mistreatment of human beings, as seen on the TV news. The implicit issue at stake here is indeed one of blasphemy, and the unvoiced conflict between father and son is where they each, as individuals, see it taking place.

Jack raises this issue with Ames and Boughton, directly challenging his father's blind eye. Commenting on an article he has both men read, he says, 'the seriousness of American Christianity was called into question by our treatment of the Negro. It seems to me there is something to be said for that idea' (Robinson 2008: 227). Jack's gentle insistence here on the ethical task of genuine faith is Robinson's own, and it is impossible to read Boughton's response to his son without hearing Robinson's voice, channelled through Jack, critiquing a theology that does not result in Christlike action. The old man says, 'I don't believe in calling anyone's religion into question because he has certain failings. A blind spot or two. [...] My point is that it's very easy to judge' (Robinson 2008: 227). Jack replies, 'true. Remarkably easy in this case, it seems to me' (Robinson 2008: 227). This can be read in two ways, both hammering home the point that, for Jack, the treatment of African Americans is the most important theological issue of his time. Either judgement is remarkably easy because it is prima facie obvious for Jack that a Christian response to the issue is to side with the marginalized black folks, or, it is remarkably easy for his father to judge simply because he does not wish to think about it. This is the crux of the divide that separates father and son. Boughton retreats from the call of social justice, into theology, whereas Jack begins with this call and sees an inactive Christianity, morally vacuous. Boughton says, 'if there is one thing the faith teaches us clearly it is that we are all sinners and we owe each other pardon and grace. "Honor everyone", the Apostle says' (Robinson 2008: 227–8). 'Yes, sir', Jack replies, 'I know the text. It's the application that confuses me a little' (Robinson 2008: 228).

Jack's struggle with predestination, with the nature of a providential God, is inseparable from his experience of his own father. Frequently, throughout the novel, prayers offered to God the Father are typological, consciously blurring the lines between earthly and divine fathers, between Boughton and God. In Boughton's welcome prayer at Jack's first dinner back at home, he offers, 'dearest Father [. . .] whose love, and whose strength, are unchanging, in whose eyes we too are unchanging, still your beloved children, however our fleshly garment may soil and wear' (Robinson 2008: 42). Clearly this prayer is about Jack's status as son and the reference to 'earthly garments' causes Jack to touch the scar under his eye in recognition of his ageing appearance. By implication, then, the father being both prayed about *and* to here is also Boughton, the prayer functioning as a reminder to Jack that his father (both paternal and supernatural) has an unchanging, gracious view of him. However, while this linking of father and God may have the intention of comfort, it is the foundational cause of Jack's problem with grace. Jack conflates God with his father and, in so doing, cannot imagine a God that transcends his father's 'blind spots'. Boughton embodies the contradiction at the heart of Jack's struggle. On the one hand, he is a preacher of the absolute centrality of divine grace and, on the other hand, a Christian who resists the conclusion that divine grace implies its extension, through believers, to those who need it most, those with whom Christ identified, the persecuted. If this is the God that Jack imagines, it is little wonder he cannot 'feel' the truth of grace, absent as it is where it is most needed. Boughton, from this perspective, stands at the antithesis of Robinson's insistence that Christianity is not simply a metaphysical thesis, but a partnering, on the behalf of believers, with Christ in the exaltation of the weak, the forgotten, the defenceless. Christianity, as a way of seeing, cannot overlook reality.

Christ: God through particularity

As noted, Robinson is staunch in her advocacy of the Trinity as a model for thinking about God. She asks 'is there any great Christian theology that does not have the Trinity at its center? Does the highest sense of the sacred abide where the Trinity as a concept is disallowed? Well, I think not, for what that is worth' (Robinson 2015: 210). Fundamental to this, then, is the equality of Christ, Father and Spirit in the Godhead. A Trinitarian conception of the divine does not permit one of the three images of God to dictate the overall theology of God: it is a wholly democratic, non-hierarchical theological principle. What Robinson wishes to recover, then, in line with her Trinitarianism, is the fact that Christ was and is God and is not therefore divorceable from the Godhead, or somehow less Godlike than the Father. Interestingly, Robinson plants this truth in moral grounds as much as she does in scriptural authority. Commenting on a pervasive and persistent Marcionist impulse that 'wrenched the Testaments apart', separating the supposedly judgemental God of the Old Testament and the compassionate Christ of the New Testament:

> The obvious solution to the problem is to make Jesus of Nazareth simply a man who appears at a particular historical moment as the rest of us do. But this is not interesting. Metaphysics collapses around it. And it abandons that widow who must not be deprived of her garment, the laborer whose heart is set on his pay, all those wandering orphans and strangers, all those pagans who do not know their right hand from their left – to Sheol, I suppose, or its conceptual equivalent. (Robinson 2015: 196)

Of course, Jesus did indeed appear at a particular point in history, but this is not what Robinson is disputing. Rather, the fact that Christ was and is indeed God means that the particularity of Jesus' brief life might indeed be opened up to deeply meaningful interpretations, readings that do not respect the limits of a typical inquiry into a figure from ancient history. Indeed, Robinson's insistence on the eternal nature of Christ ensures that the grace made evident in his incarnation is not limited by particularity, but mediated through it. The idea that Jesus was a good man, an excellent moral example, a genius of ethical teaching, may well inspire his admirers to act accordingly. However, for Robinson this is not enough: 'metaphysics collapses around it'. Removing the divinity of Christ alters the very core of Robinson's conception of Christianity, and it profoundly dilutes the force of the call at the heart of the faith. Jesus, the man, has not the means to make absolute claims about the treatment of the other, but, when these statements are made by Christ, the incarnate God, the social and ethical imperative of Christianity is not merely one voice among many; rather, it is a command stitched into the very fabric of reality. Indeed, if Creation was made through this Word, this Christ, his life and words are fundamental to Reality itself. To reach out to the alienated, the forgotten, the humbled is to enact the work of Christ, to 'participate in the grace that saved me' as Ames puts it (Robinson 2004: 141).

The notion of God working through particularity, discussed in the last chapter in relation to blessing and physicality, is important to Robinson's Christology and is also central to her soteriology. Robinson only entertains the notion of predestination when it is in line with her reading of the ethical call at the heart of Christianity. For Robinson, the Old Testament and the work of Jesus, in the New Testament, reveal that, if predestination is to be taken seriously, it must be rescued from any rendering that leaves the already advantaged certain of their election. Commenting on the words 'elect' and 'elite', she notes that they 'come from the same root and mean the same thing. Their [Calvinists'] elect were unknowable, chosen by God in a manner assumed to be consistent with his tendency to scorn the hierarchies and overturn the judgements of this world. Our elites are simply, one way or another, advantaged' (Robinson 1998: 169).[5] This latter kind of thinking ignores the scriptural solicitude for the stranger, for the ignored. Predestination should not result in self-righteousness, and if it does, the doctrine is in conflict with the gospel and needs to be reimagined. To be clear, Robinson is not positing a pragmatic approach to doctrine, the sort of thinking that says 'as soon as the idea stops producing desirable results, it should be rethought'; what she *is* saying here is much more interesting. Robinson is insisting that predestination is fundamental to the ethics of Christianity, not simply an additional idea that, if it helps believers act well, can be layered onto more important theology. Predestination is the secret heart of grace, just as grace

---

[5] This should not by any means be read as an endorsement of Calvin's election theology. What Robinson is doing here is a comparison between the idea of 'the elect' in Calvin and 'elites' as they exist now, making the point that in shifting away from theology, society has not moved away from Calvin's elect, but merely secularized it. More insidiously, the elites of contemporary society find certainty of their status in their already privileged status.

is the heart of Robinson's theology. This idea of being 'chosen', then, does not apply to those who already have power, for it was Jesus who chose to subvert the religious elites and who chose to spend his time with the forgotten and the despised. Seen in this light, the doctrine of predestination begins to look more like an embodiment of Christ's inclusivity rather than a hidden cosmic thesis that is indifferent to the weak. Careful attention to Robinson's subtle dealings with this doctrine in *Home* reveals a profound and radical core to her theology of grace.

Predestination versus universalism

Home is not a novel about good and evil, but about frail loyalty between imperfect individuals. It is a text uninterested in simplified binary thinking regarding heroes and villains and is, instead, involved in exploring the complexities of family life, limited perspectives and the difficulties in balancing loyalty to loved ones with commitment to one's own moral sense. If the text has anything to say about the doctrine of predestination, then, it will not be reduced to the elect/unelect, saved/unsaved language that has so often characterized its discussion. 'Granting all complexities', Robinson writes, 'is it conceivable that the God of the Bible would shackle himself to the worst consequences of our worst behaviour?' (Robinson 2015: 216). In her writing of human individuals and in her evocation of the complex interior lives of characters, Robinson displays a keen awareness of the intricacy and ambiguity of human experience. For her, as will be explored in Chapter 4, all definitions of the Self are partial at best, and in her creation of characters she aims to faithfully reproduce the ineffable experience of being human. On this theme she writes,

> There is a tendency to fit a tight and awkward carapace of definition over humankind, and to try to trim the living creature to fit the dead shell. The advice I give my students is the same advice I give myself – forget definition, forget assumption, watch. We inhabit, we are part of, a reality for which explanation is much too poor or small. (Robinson 2012: 7)

If interior human experience is as complex as Robinson allows for, with moral seriousness perpetually competing with a bias towards errors of all kinds, it follows that no single idea or distinction will ever have the potency to binarily separate humankind into saved and unsaved. The soul of the individual is the site of such rich and contradictory experience that any totalizing and final statement of its fate seems paltry. This objection to the doctrine is bound up with the seeming arbitrariness of the divine choice to save or not to save. Indeed, predestination, when understood as the hidden will of God, as an unknowable theological secret, begins to look like a crude reactionary doctrine that ensures the contemporary Pharisaical groups are certain of their salvation. It cannot be overstated how contrary this idea of predestination is to Robinson's own writing in *Home*.

Predestination is available in *Home* in radically different terms than what has been discussed above. In questioning the state of his soul, Jack reveals his inherited belief that predestination is a metaphysical secret, off limits to, and unaffected by, human action. 'I've wondered from time to time if I might not be an instance of predestination in my own person', Jack comments in the second half of the novel (Robinson 2008: 235). What he is referring to is his impulse to interpret the misery of his own life as the direct result of a divine fatalism that has chosen not to choose him for the salvation his family seems to enjoy. Tellingly, while discussing his fate at the end of the text, Jack is playing with cards in a subtle nod towards the apparent randomness and chance predestination theology seems to imply. In Jack's pondering if he is an example of predestination, Robinson is implicitly asking for her readers to take up this question, God's question: is Jack beyond saving, beyond restoration, that is, beyond *grace*? In the interview with Painter, she brings this up directly: 'very few readers seem to find Jack beyond their compassion. On what grounds do so many of them assume he would be beyond God's compassion, or his love? I think I let him be available to understanding in other terms' (Painter 2009: 489). Predestination, then, in the manner in which Jack conceives of it, is alien to what Robinson achieves in the novel. Glory comes to the conclusion that 'if I or my father or any Boughton has ever stirred the Lord's compassion, then Jack will be alright. Because perdition for him would be perdition for every one of us' (Robinson 2008: 329). Not only does Glory conclude on the nonsense of arbitrary perdition, but she also finds she cannot reconcile this doctrine with the character of a compassionate God. Looking closely at Robinson's subtle characterization of Jack will illuminate the radical, grace-full heart of Robinson's theological position here.

Jack is deployed in various ways throughout the novel as a Christ figure. He is the man of sorrows who can find no place to lay his head. He, like Christ, experiences estrangement from the Father: Jesus on the cross with his cry 'Why have you forsaken me?' and Jack when his father 'turned onto his right side, away from Jack, toward the wall' (Robinson 2008: 121). Jack builds a den out of wood and nails, and even undergoes a kind of death and resurrection, with a faithful woman discovering and tending to his body. The importance of Robinson's evocation of Christlike imagery in her descriptions of Jack is obvious, particularly when read in light of the text's dealings with predestination. Jack paradoxically experiences himself as an arch-sinner and yet is figured in the text as Jesus, the source and means of salvation. This is taken a stage further when he returns from a conversation with Ames who has been telling Jack about his grandfather and his religious visions. Jack tells his father:

> He told me the story about his grandfather leaving Maine for Kansas because he had a dream that Jesus came to him as a slave and showed him how the chains rankled his flesh. I'd heard the story before, of course. I always thought it sounded enviable. I mean, to have that kind of certainty. It's hard to imagine. Hard for me to imagine. (Robinson 2008: 213)

Boughton replies that 'certainty can be dangerous', to which Jack responds, tellingly, 'yes sir, I know. But if Jesus is – Jesus, it seems as though he might have shown someone his chains, I mean, in that situation' (Robinson 2008: 213). Jack here voices, albeit in faltering terms, the conviction of Robinson's that Jesus did indeed take on the role of a slave in order that an unjust order may be disrupted. In gentle terms, spoken to a father that does not share his ethical conclusion, Jack reveals his own belief that Jesus is and, by extension, Christianity ought to be, centrally concerned with the vulnerable and oppressed. Jack is deployed in Christlike fashions precisely because he shares

Christ's passion for the forgotten and powerless. The irony of Jack's character, then, is that, while he wrestles with the idea that he is on the receiving end of the graceless will of a metaphysical demagogue, Robinson simultaneously paints him as the mediator of divine grace. The conclusion to be drawn here is that Jack is not the *victim* of predestination, but the *vessel of it*.

Roland Boer, as quoted earlier, sees Calvin's doctrine of predestination as fundamentally conservative. He contrasts, as noted, Calvin's 'democracy of depravity' with his 'aristocracy of salvation' (Boer 2009: 32). What Boer is getting at here is Calvin's reactionary impulse to control that which should remain unlimited, namely, divine grace. Indeed, as he argues, if sin is such a levelling force in its democratic flattening of all human claims to righteousness, grace, if it is to save this depraved species, must be at the very least equal to sin in its potency. What Boer anticipates from Calvin is a radical grace, in line with his radical conception of depravity for, as Boer argues, 'the greater the extent of our depraved and corrupt state, the greater becomes the task for grace' (Boer 2009: 22). However, Calvin intervenes at this point with his doctrine of predestination, introducing a 'careful itinerary for grace, designating what it cannot do and what it can do, and when it can do so' (Boer 2009: 32). As Boer observes, 'Calvin has not quite abolished ranking in terms of privilege or inheritance. He may have removed any privilege or status when it comes to the merit of works, but he has replaced it with the distinction between the elect and damned' (Boer 2009: 38). For Boer this is frustrating as it subverts the natural conclusion Calvin was heading towards, the realization of a grace that is pervasive, democratic and universal. He comments, 'grace may be a life-changing, indeed a world-changing experience, but it runs all too quickly into a controlling and repressive regime' (Boer 2009: 40).

Predestination, in its classic formation, is, for Robinson as well as for Boer, simply too undemocratic. She, like Boer, requires a radical conception of grace that answers and heals the profound faults at the heart of the human self. Commenting on the nature of democracy, she writes, 'democracy in its essence and genius, is imaginative love for and identification with a community with which, much of the time and in many ways, one may be in profound disagreement' (Robinson 2012: 27). Democracy is the political expression of the theological imperative for imaginative empathy and for

Robinson classical predestination effectively rules out the necessity of this engagement with its arbitrary and hidden choices. Democracy preserves the inherent worth in each human individual by assuming each self is worth the same as any other. In this rendering, democracy becomes a theological ideal, as it was for Whitman, who, as Robinson writes, '[believed] a great presiding spirit of Democracy would check, or correct for, the worst deficiencies of the civilization' (Robinson 2012: x). For Robinson, democracy, like grace, is a natural product of the recognition of the value of the individual human self and 'to identify sacred mystery with every individual experience, every life, giving the word its largest sense, is to arrive at democracy as an ideal, and to accept the difficult obligation to honour others and oneself with something approaching due reverence' (Robinson 2012: xiv). Robinson equates grace with love and, in rereading her above comment on democracy with this in mind, it becomes clear that democracy as an ideal is imaginative grace, extended to the realm of the political. Her theological project in *Home* is fundamentally subversive, aiming as it does to uncage grace from ideas that seek to limit it. In his empathy for the oppressed black groups in Montgomery and in the connection he makes between Jesus and the necessity of social justice, Jack embodies Robinson's real notion of predestination. Just as Christ came to raise the lowly, Jack is present in the text as the graceful site of agape. Christ, for Robinson, makes known the will of God, which springs from an undeviating love for the poor and a desire to see power overturned. The weak and despised are the subjects of predestination because it is their plight that has God's ear, according to Robinson and, in *Home*, she reveals her belief in the power of an imperfect man to in some way embody this perfect will of God. Robinson is not writing about some white saviour, but rather is gesturing towards the power Jack has in his utter vulnerability to demonstrate grace.

There are times Robinson seems to defend predestination, or at the very least, refuses to critique it explicitly. The reading of *Home* presented in this chapter has demonstrated that Robinson's refusal to give up the doctrine is not explicable simply by recourse to some traditionalist impulse on her behalf, but rather is due to her radical reinterpretation of the doctrine that shifts the emphasis away from the hidden will of God, to the revealed will of God in Christ. Indeed Robinson's commitment to Calvin is made clear in reinterpretation, not mere appropriation, as Shy argues: 'in seeking to reclaim tradition, she frames an early modern theology in very modern terms. What she wants perhaps is the wine of older zeal poured into new wineskins' (Shy 2007: 254). In the absence of any clear critique of Calvin's doctrine, Robinson subtly hints towards her acceptance of a theological position that appears fundamentally at odds with Calvin's formation of predestination. She ventures, 'maybe his [God's] constant blessing falls on those great multitudes who lived and died without any name for him, for those multitudes who know his name and believe they only have contempt for him' (Robinson 2015: 216). Despite its somewhat hesitant phrasing, this statement betrays, in plain writing, what *Home* gestures towards, namely that universalism is the logical end point of Robinson's theological thinking.

Shy is absolutely right to note that 'what Robinson admires in Calvin, first of all, is the grandeur of his vision of what God intends for humanity', and Robinson's own writing of theology, while certainly influenced by Calvin's, is more often centred on human experience, its partiality and the conditioning effect it has on knowledge (Shy 2007: 253). 'I take the Jamesian view', she writes, 'that what we know about anything is determined by the way we encounter it, and therefore we should never assume that our knowledge of anything is more than partial' (Robinson 2015: 229). Robinson emphasizes the importance of the limited nature of the human self in theology because theology itself is a report on the transcendent from the finite; it is talk of God in the necessarily restricted arena of human language. Religious experience is central to Robinson's theology precisely because the discipline itself is unintelligible outside of religious experience and, therefore, her writing will always emphasize the human, and focus on the self in theological discourse. This is not to say that the differences between Robinson and Calvin's theology are explainable simply by a differing placement of emphasis – one on God, the other on the human. Indeed, there are real discrepancies between Calvin and the Calvinist Robinson and, as this chapter has developed, one of the major examples of such a contradiction is Robinson's exploration of predestination and embrace of universalism.

A theology of grace

Robinson's theology, while self-consciously emanating from the human and offering language approaching appropriateness for the experience of God, is concerned always with grace. *Home* is preoccupied with grace, both in the everyday struggle to be graceful to others and in the metaphysical questions of God's providence and divine will. Robinson's fiction post-*Housekeeping* is infused with images of human grace; whether it be Lila's appearance in Ames's church, Boughton's prayerful wait for Jack to return or Glory's sustaining presence in the family home, each instance of grace is always a movement towards restoration. With such an imagining of Ordinary grace, it is of no surprise that Robinson finds herself yearning for an ultimate, metaphysical Grace, a final and total restoration that completes the human graces her characters enact for one another. She writes, 'I feel a distinctly Christian dread at the thought that any good thing ultimate reality holds for the patient, the kind, the humble, the lovers of truth, the hopeful and enduring who are Christian will be denied to those excellent souls who are anything else' (Robinson 2015: 207). This is not a ventriloquizing of the Calvin who spoke of the 'sad spectacle of our ignominy and corruption', of the human race 'descending from an impure seed [. . .] tainted with the contagion of sin' (Calvin 2008: 213–14). In Robinson's thinking, humans can be 'excellent souls' and it is impossible for her to imagine a God that insists on assent to specific doctrinal statements as the means to salvation. The character Jack is an imaginative critique of any theology that posits a God that is anything less than infinitely graceful. Robinson writes, with full sincerity, 'by the grace of God, we have God as our judge', because in her theology God is love, or, to use her synonym, God is grace (Robinson 2015: 208).

Jack, as a Christlike figure in Robinson's fiction, is the figurative product of Robinson's own assertion that 'only a radical Christocentricity can address the problem of Christian exclusivism' (Robinson 2015: 216). Jack does not acknowledge the distinctions his father makes between whites and blacks, believers and unbelievers, and, in a similar vein, Robinson asks, 'is it conceivable that the reach of Christ's mercy would honor the narrow limits of human differences?' (Robinson 2015: 216). Robinson's Christ, as intrinsic to the Godhead and Creation itself, is more expansive and elusive than narrow denominational claims allow for and certainly Robinson's high Christology in turn produces a grace that is equally ineffable. Robinson entertains a universalist position with regard to salvation because her vision of grace rules out the possibility of a populous hell. In an important essay she writes,

> It might be that the Christ I place at the origin and source of Being would be called another name and would show another face to all those hundreds of billions who are or were not Scots Presbyterians or American Congregationalists or anything remotely like them. This is my devoutest hope, not least because it promises our salvation, too. (Robinson 2015: 216)

This is not a surprising admission from the author of *Home*, a novel that places divine grace in the hands of its unbeliever. Shy writes, with *Gilead* in mind, although the sentiment applies equally to *Home*, 'it is the melancholy triumph of this book that religious grace glints at certain angles only, and does not swallow other light with superior incandescence' (Shy 2007: 261). Shy is right that Robinson's theological novels do not privilege religious grace, but he introduces a distinction Robinson would not wish to make. 'Grace is grace', she writes, and with her universalism in mind, there is no such thing as an unreligious grace, for a cup of coffee for a hungover brother is participating in the same divine grace as the Eucharist in a church (Robinson 2015: 230). Grace may or may not be religious in context, but it is always divine in nature and is ultimately the final word in Robinson's theology, a concept so central to her world view that it is the check put on all other theological questions. Noting the common objection to universalism – what about murderers and tyrants, is their salvation also assured? – she simply replies, 'I am not willing to open an abyss, conceptually speaking, just to accommodate Hitler or Stalin [. . .] My thoughts on the ultimate disposition of the great villains and monsters of history might incline me to curtail my conception of grace. The cost would be too high' (Robinson 2015: 217). Paradoxically, grace is known through human experience and is recognized as grace because of its inherent divinity. Beginning from the quotidian experience of grace and extrapolating upwards to what the grace of God might be leads Robinson logically to a universalist conception of grace.

Conclusion: On the anti-economy of grace

Robinson does not doubt the gravity of human error, but she does question how useful the religious obsession with 'sin' is: 'ultimately a compassionate Lord must find our errors and insights to be of extremely limited interest in themselves [. . .] however fascinated we may be by the project of attempting to distinguish one from another, one mode of belief from another' (Robinson 2015: 190). Sin, for Robinson, while very real, is ultimately eclipsed, corrected and covered over by grace. However, despite her conviction on the centrality of grace, Robinson admits she has difficulty in accepting what has been the dominating interpretation of Jesus' death: penal substitutionary atonement. She writes 'I confess that I struggle to understand the phenomenon of ritual sacrifice, and the Crucifixion when explicated in its terms' (Robinson 2015: 194). Noting that this interpretation risks a means of forgiveness that is itself scarcely different from the acts it is meant to atone for, Robinson cannot accept a view of the cross that posits Christ's death as sacrificial. She argues that this kind of theological thinking posits Jesus as 'in the ancient or the modern sense, the victim in an act that seems to epitomise the sinfulness of the world and nevertheless to be what God requires' (Robinson 2015: 194).

An interpretation that proceeds on substitutionary grounds receives no assent from Robinson, as she simply finds no meaning in the model, though she defers to those who do: 'the concept is so central to the tradition that I have no desire to take issue with it, and so difficult for me that I leave it for others to interpret' (Robinson 2015: 194).[6] Negatively implied here is Robinson's notion of grace that stands at odds to economic or legalistic language. Penal substitution relies on the assumption that Jesus' death paid a debt, a satisfaction that made forgiveness possible. However, as Derrida has noted, forgiveness cannot exist within the contours of conditionality:

> And does one have to deserve forgiveness? One may deserve an excuse, but ought not forgiveness be accorded without regard to worthiness? Ought not a true forgiveness (a forgiveness in authentic money) absolve the fault or

---

[6] Although one might reasonably object that even in this hesitant phrasing, Robinson has already 'taken issue' with penal substitutionary atonement.

the crime even as the fault and the crime remain where they are? (Derrida 1992: 163)

Robinson finds herself much closer to the Derridean position here than dominant orthodox theological interpretation. Robinson's writing of grace avoids legalism, for, taking *Home* and its historical context as an example, miscegenation laws sought to prevent Jack and Della's marriage – a relationship that is crucial to the concept of grace inscribed in Robinson's third novel. A theology of grace must remain unlimited by law simply because law is always a limit placed on the possible. The objection may be made that a law prevents danger or loss of life, for example, but this surely reveals grace, as a lawless phenomenon, to be a genuinely risky business. Indeed, if Christ's death is a symbol of grace, it is also possible to interpret his death as the inevitable repercussion of a life lived obediently exhibiting grace. Jack and Della pay little heed to a law that would have restricted and made their marriage impossible, and in the same way Robinson cannot understand the Cross in a fashion that cedes authority to a *theological* legalism. The language that often characterizes penal substitution, phrases like 'God required', or, 'God was satisfied', evoke a picture of a God intent on the upkeep of a system. In Robinson's writing, however, grace is the disruptive force that upends systems, so it makes little sense to confine grace to a legal framework and, it should be noted that, for Robinson, as soon as grace is confined it ceases to be grace.

Caputo's *The Weakness of God* (2007) presents a Derridean reading of Christian grace and, like the quotation from Derrida earlier, Caputo argues that grace must flow free from conditionality. Caputo's discussion sets grace against economic language in order to highlight its radically different essence: 'in the great religious traditions, in both Jewish and Christian theology, forgiveness always functions as an economy, where it is regulated by a certain calculus' (Caputo 2006: 211). Now, this is clearly an overstatement, as Robinson herself, a prominent Christian thinker, stands as an example outside of this economic interpretation of grace; however, Caputo is right to note the economic character of much theological thinking in this area. He continues: 'reconciliation is not a bad economy and certainly not a bad thing, and it is to be preferred to vindictiveness and endless cycles of retribution. But it is not the gift of the event or the event of the gift, which is not an economy but an excess'

(Caputo 2006: 211). For Caputo, grace resides beyond the language of debt and repayment: true forgiveness has its own logic that is really no logic at all and it pays no heed to the inevitable limitations put on it by human language. He argues: 'the gift of forgiveness would go beyond the law, in the direction of a certain saintly excess that forgoes power and the returns that bring promises' (Caputo 2006: 211). The 'excessive' nature of grace, an idea central to Robinson's thinking too, implies its elusiveness to definition and sense. For Robinson, this excess bears the imprint of a divine reality, a reality that permits grace its Ordinary status. Robinson's writing privileges the illimitability of grace, and specifically emphasizes the capacity of grace to lift humans out of repetitive cycles of self-interest, out of patterns built on economic notions of 'owing', 'merit' and 'debt'. Asked about her conception of grace, Robinson replies:

> I know this is a crude simplification, but if you imagine a sort of double vision where there is the world as you see it, and the world as God sees it. Everything tells you that they are not the same thing at all no matter what you bring to bear on it. Trying to imagine the second perspective is interesting to me and the only way I can even begin to address that is the concept of grace, which is truly transformative. It makes the rules; and the fact that we never understand the rules does not alter that fact. (Chapter 5)

The absolute lack of a theological system in Robinson's thinking is striking here. Grace is Ordinary in the Robinsonian sense in its necessary wildness. It can be spoken of, written about, but never adequately captured in language. As the introduction to the chapter initially stated, grace, if it is to be adequately *felt* in writing, must be staged. Yet, grace's Ordinary status also ensures its excessiveness and its elusiveness. Grace is not tamed in Robinson's work, and Jack's presence in *Home* ensures that abstract and comfortable musings on the nature of grace and God are continually anchored to the historical reality of 1950s America. *Home* does not present a simple, stable conception of grace, and this is illustrative of Robinson's theology more widely. The Ordinary never cedes to a system, and the radical nature of grace refuses to be controlled by prior theological principles.

Dietrich Bonhoeffer (1906–45) is a thinker held up in Robinson's essays as worthy of sustained attention on these issues. Robinson celebrates his theology of grace as laid out in *The Cost of Discipleship* (1937) for its 'appealing over the head of conventional theology, to shared experience', and her essay devoted to Bonhoeffer is littered with praise for both the man and his thinking (Robinson 1998: 119). He writes of a 'costly grace', imagined as 'the call of Jesus Christ at which the disciple leaves his nets and follows him' (Bonhoeffer 1948: 4). Where economic metaphors of grace ought to be rejected for their reduction of soteriology to a game of debts and payments, Bonhoeffer shifts his discussion of grace from the economy of salvation to the costliness of grace:

> Such grace is *costly* because it calls us to follow, and it is *grace* because it calls us to follow *Jesus Christ*. It is costly because it costs a man his life, and it is grace because it gives a man the only true life. It is costly because it condemns sin, and grace because it justifies the sinner [. . .] Costly grace is the Incarnation of God. (Bonhoeffer 1948: 5)

Robinson cites Bonhoeffer on grace, and his well-known notion of 'cheap grace'. Bonhoeffer's language could be initially interpreted as yet another economic model of grace but, in reality, he highlights the poverty of these metaphors by moving the discussion from how salvation was 'won' to how grace operates in practice. Grace, genuine grace, is 'costly', for Bonhoeffer, not because of a debt that is owed, but because of a call at its heart that demands ethical action. Notably, grace is inextricably bound up in his theology with the incarnation of God. The grace presented in Christ's life, offered to all, cannot but be passed on through the conduit of his followers. Grace is restless with itself, by definition, for as soon as grace resists replication and transmission, it has stopped being grace. Jack's perpetual unease at being at home is, in part, because he cannot settle into the rhythms of a home that is out of step with his own internal sense of justice. Robinson's staging of grace is a radical theology of democracy, and a reclaiming of the apophatic nature of what is ultimate. For Robinson, there could be nothing more plain than what is most important to theology – God, grace, truth, love – is also ultimately ineffable. 'Modern religious thought', she ventures, 'has shied away from the unfathomable, as if grace could have other origins and truth another character'; for Robinson, there could be no better form for staging inexpressible grace than the novel, and no better example of the disruptive, contrarian spirit of grace than Jack Boughton (Robinson 2015: 210).

4

Lila

The myth of the self

Introduction: Time and the self

As a fiction writer, Robinson is inevitably implicated in the portrayal of what it means to be subject to time, both in the more mundane aspects of temporality – noting 'I do have to deal with the nuts and bolts of temporal reality – from time to time a character has to walk through a door and close it behind him' – and in the deeper philosophical and theological questions that time and its movement raise (Robinson 2012: 20). This is not to say that authors are necessarily constrained to produce a perfect likeness of time boundedness in their writing. Rather, by writing a character who does, in some way or other, move through time, is to enter into the question of what it means to do precisely that: move through time. This inevitably invites questions of memory, subjectivity and self, and how these notions operate in a reality in which time is a given. One's passage through time is perceptible to the individual, at least in part, through the function of memory, an activity that takes place in the present and permits access, in however full a form, to the past. Equally, memory helps retain a sense of self and a feeling of coherency through time, allowing the individual to stretch a conception of self across moments past, present and future. As Manning et al. argue, 'time past and time future are experienced with a sense of a unitary self since past and future only exist in the human mind' (Manning et al. 2013: 236). Robinson's fourth novel, *Lila*, raises intriguing questions with regard to the function of memory and the seeming absurdity of a sense of self that persists in spite of the contingency of time. As her most theologically illiterate character, Lila's mind and voice are the means

Robinson has to disrupt the often abstracted theological jargon of Ames and Boughton. The text itself frequently focuses on the nature of memory and on notions of self, soul and causality through the eyes of the itinerant Lila. As Williams states in his review of the novel, 'the Lilas of the world are those who challenge the ways in which the good refuse to know what they do not know' (Williams Review). It is both the text and character of Lila that ultimately succeed in forwarding what is perhaps Robinson's most important theological formulation: that in a reality in which time is a given, the possibility of change is inevitably redemptive.

In Robinson's writing, the present is never simply the present. While attention to the immediate moment is, of course, one of her most clearly stated theological commitments, the notion that the present opens up the extent to which attention is paid to it is, itself, reliant on the past as a phenomenon that resides in and haunts the present. Certainly, with Robinson's novels in mind, the experiential depth of the present is a product of the lingering nature of the past on the mind. For Ruth, every glass of water is the lake that took her mother; for Ames, every communion is cause to reflect on the ashy biscuit his father shared with him; and for Lila, the river is a constant reminder of the life out of which she has been baptized. Equally important as the lingering nature of the past, for Robinson, is the quality of that lingering. In her work she is clear that the present exists as a gateway to both the remembered past and the awaited future; with this in mind, the past is therefore knowable only through interpretation and, by extension, is known only through the fallible and limited lens of human subjectivity. 'As we perceive, we interpret', she writes, 'and we make hypotheses. Something is happening, it has a certain character or meaning which we usually feel we understand at least tentatively, though experience is almost always available to reinterpretations based on subsequent experience or reflection' (Robinson 2012: 9). The past is available to us by way of memory which itself bears the marks of human limitation and a desire for meaning, in all its limits, biases and defensiveness. Taking the predestination conversation common to both *Gilead* and *Home* as an example, the fragmented, prejudiced nature of memory becomes clear to see. The conversation takes up just over five pages of *Gilead* (170–5) and thirteen pages in *Home* (226–38), a considerable difference in terms of length; when read side by side, it reveals just how much

Ames left out, or forgot, in his telling of it in his letter. One particular moment stands out: in *Home* – a narrative written largely from Glory's perspective, in the third person – the conversation is initiated by Jack within the more general context of race relations in America and the role of Christianity in the contemporary political situation. In Ames' narrative, however, the theological debate ruptures an otherwise sedate conversation about Boughton's one-time trip to Minneapolis: 'Jack broke in and said to me, "So, Reverend, I would like to hear your views on the doctrine of predestination"' (Robinson 2004: 170). That Ames leaves out the uncomfortable discussion about the 'Christian' treatment of African American people is no accident, and stands as a startling reminder, from Robinson to her readers, that memory is not only partial due to cognitive limitation but fragmented, too, by moral failure. *Gilead* can be read as a highly selective account of Ames' life and, indeed, much of the drama of the text is buried in throwaway comments and suppressed narrative. This amnesiac quality of *Gilead* has been explored in a number of articles[1] that draw attention to both the unconscious and conscious suppression of certain important subtexts in the novel. It is important to recognize that Robinson is indeed engaged in a demonstration of the faulty nature of memory, but, in addition, she is also keen, more widely, to demonstrate the theological potential of memory and its role in meaning making for the human self. It is crucial, then, to make a distinction between Robinson's writing of particular cases of suppressed memory and her more general exploration of the ways in which memory demonstrates the manner in which meaning is sought. It is with this latter strand of Robinson's thought that this exploration of her writing of time begins. What follows commences with an exploration of Robinson's thinking on myth as a biblical genre, and how individual memory functions similarly to the communal remembering that occurs in myth. Arguing that meaning making is central to both activities, and that subjectivity is the inescapable realm of all human thinking, it is demonstrated that Robinson engages the

---

[1] See, for example: Lisa Bailey, 'Fraught with Fire: Race and Theology in Marilynne Robinson's *Gilead*', *Christianity and Literature*, Vol. 59, No. 2 (Winter 2010) and Susan Petit, 'Field of Deferred Dreams: Baseball and Historical Amnesia in Marilynne Robinson's *Gilead* and *Home*', *MELUS*, Vol. 37, No. 4, Media(s) and the Mediation of Ethnicity (WINTER 2012), pp. 119–37.

question of the existence of the self in order to shift the territory on which the issue is debated. She charts an important move from positivist philosophy and neuroscience to literary and theological modes. Finally, the chapter will demonstrate how Robinson views the 'self' as an unfolding story, a fiction (akin to Wallace Stevens' 'Supreme Fiction') one that gives form to the stories and memories that report to it and, ultimately, how the narrative self relies on a divine 'reader' and a grace that sustains its coherence in and through time.

Robinson on myth

As a thinker engaged in the reading of biblical narratives and as a teacher of the Old Testament,[2] Robinson is understandably concerned with the notion of memory not only in the case of an individual's remembering but also as a cultural phenomenon, as a means to conjure and secure a community's identity. The recording of memory, in this cultural setting, in the time and place of the Hebrews in the ancient Near East, was achieved through myth, and 'myth – never to be confused with fable – is ontology, since its terms attempt to describe the origins and nature of reality' (Robinson 2015: 145). Myth, for Robinson, is a narrative that attempts to house grand truths about the human experience of the world, and indeed of the very existence of the world itself. The Hebrew Bible is full of these narratives: the Creation stories, the Fall, the Flood, the Exodus, all of which are, to Robinson's mind, cultural rememberings of a truly meaningful nature. In using 'myth' as her descriptor, Robinson is not opening up a debate about the historical veracity of these accounts, for myth is a genre term and not a statement about the historicity of their claims. As Hoffman rightly states, 'to call something a myth is to say nothing about its truth value [. . .] They are, however, certainly out of tune with modernity's melodies' (Hoffman 2010: 235). Robinson, in line with Hoffman, calls these narratives myths not to denigrate them, but to allow them to be read properly,

---

[2] Robinson has noted several times publicly that during her tenure at the Iowa Writer's Workshop she frequently taught the Old Testament to her students.

also noting the discordance of myth with contemporary, post-Enlightenment thought: 'I was taught that the demythologising of Christianity was a step forward, or at least such a deft strategic defeat that it came to the same thing' (Robinson 2015: 145). Rejecting this approach in favour of interpreting myth with expectations shaped by the intentions of the genre, Robinson reinstates its role as a means to understand perception of reality and situate our conceptions of self, free from the narrow concerns of positivistic truth.

Myth is, above all, a mode of remembering. As Bosman notes, 'in the end we must probably resolve ourselves to the realisation that we cannot go back to the exodus itself, but that it is entirely meaningful to engage with the different ways in which the exodus has been remembered' (Bosman 2014: 5). Taking myth seriously does not entail believing its details are an accurate account of a historical event, but instead are read with an eye for the importance of memorialized detail. Consequently, myth should be interrogated as follows: 'why was this event remembered in this way?'; 'what does the myth contain that is revealing about the worldview of its writers?'; 'how does this myth construct reality and in what ways does it speak of the self, the community, of reality?' As Assmann argues,

> The theme of the myth was not the essence of deities, but rather [. . .] the essence of reality [. . .] Myths establish and enclose the area in which human actions and experiences can be orientated. The stories they tell about deities are supposed to bring to light the meaningful structure of reality. Myths are always set in the past, and they always refer to the present. (Assmann 2001: 112)

In orientating its reader in and to the present, by way of an imaginative remembering of the past, myths raise interesting and crucial questions about the nature of truth and meaning, and their relation to human memory. Robinson, interestingly, defines myth as ontology and, in so doing, elevates the genre as a valid 'way in' to the ultimate questions of existence. Applying her thinking to the Hebrew Bible, she notes:

> That strange old verse in the first chapter of Genesis, 'in the image of God he created him, male and female he created them,' is meaningless by the standards of positivism or the higher criticism. It is unfalsifiable, undemonstrable, and dependent on terms for which we have no stable

definitions. It is dependent as well on a conception of God that compels reverence and will make us reverent of one another. It tells us every essential thing about who we are and what we are, and what we are a part of. It is ontology. It is metaphysics. (Robinson 2015: 171)

The Genesis account of Creation is ontology in so far as it seeks to make inroads on a grand statement of what it means to be human, folding the conception of human nature into a wider, metaphysical vision of reality. In the same way, the gospel stories of Jesus's incarnation, crucifixion and resurrection function as myth for Robinson, in that they, 'are all highly charged statements about the nature of Being and human being. They are profound, and, so far as I know, unique assertions of the transcendent value of human life' (Robinson 2015: 168).

What is myth?

Robinson does not engage much in the wider debates surrounding the definition of myth, preferring instead to discuss the theological value and potential of the narratives themselves. It is worth noting, though, just how contested and complex the study of the genre is, if only to properly contextualize Robinson's embrace of the term. When she dismisses the demythologizing of the Bible, Robinson implicitly rejects the approach of Rudolf Bultmann (1884–1976), the foremost theologian in the demythologizing movement. For Bultmann, myths are to be stripped of their surface content, of what they appear to refer to, and should no longer mean simply what they are about. As he writes, with ancient Israel's approach to historiography in mind, 'it is interested not in knowledge of the immanent powers working in history but in the intention and plan of God who as creator is also the ruler of history, and leads it to a goal' (Bultmann 1955: 18). Instead, myths are read as tales more revealing of inner human states, a psychology of experience rather than anything approaching cultural history. Scarborough notes how Bultmann subverts readers' expectations of myth narratives by having them disregard their literal content:

> Problems of credibility, consequently, arise for us in the modern world as a result of our mistakenly assuming that myths are about objective realities.

The remedy is not to abandon myths but to demythologise them – that is, to interpret them in terms of existential self-understanding. (Scarborough 1994: 23)

For Robinson, this approach arbitrarily rules out the metaphysical. In Bultmann's hands, myth becomes less potent and ambitious, referring merely to human psychology, untethered from the potential that these myths may indeed mean – in some sense – what they say. Bultmann reads the Hebrew Bible's myths as an exercise in existential storytelling, a narrative to generate self-knowledge for a people living before Enlightenment inspired historiography. He writes,

> If there is an interest in knowledge [in ancient Israel's myths] it is in self-knowledge, and the historian calls his people to self-knowledge in reminding them of the deeds of God in the past and of the conduct of the people [. . .] Therefore historiography is not a means of education for politicians but a sermon to the people. Looking back into the past means critically examining the past in order to warn the present. (Bultmann 1955: 18–19)

Critics have noted that Bultmann's approach ignores, or 'brackets off', the metaphysics of myth. Macquarrie, for example, has noted that in Butlmann's theology 'the question of fact is no longer being raised. We are no longer asking about what happened but about what the story says to us in our situation now' (Macquarrie 1960: 19). Robinson sees no reason to bind together the non-literal nature of myth with a rejection of the metaphysical reality inscribed within them. For her, the former does not imply the latter; and reading myth as an imaginative representation of reality does not rule out the transcendent reality embedded within the narratives themselves. That myth is a genre found across antiquity, embedded in a wide range of disparate religious cultures is not something Robinson spends a great deal of time discussing. Accepting this fact, Robinson focuses on the Hebrew Bible and the myths of its books, preferring to excavate the particular collection of narratives for their significance than engage in a meta-discussion of myth as a genre in itself.

In her reading of myth as a cultural memory, Robinson does find herself among a broad sweep of scholars who agree on the societal and communal authorship of myth. Doty, in his survey of myth scholarship, records, 'what does seem to remain valid from earlier definitions is the suggestion that important myths appear on the scene not as authored by individuals, but derived from collaborative social experience over a period of time' (Doty 2004: 19). This is crucial to Robinson's understanding and use of the term. Myths garner their meaning in communal construction, by the marks left on them by the many hands that have shaped them and passed them on. The result is a narrative that combines a very particular construction of reality with the theology of its community, a story that aims to evoke the deep meaning of societal memories. 'What myths struggle with is not so much "how" something began in terms of the natural sciences but rather what it signifies, its meaning, and of course, how the human race is to be related to it', notes Doty, and certainly this conception of myth is closely allied to Robinson's (2004: 23).

Barthes' *Mythologies* (1957) defines myth as 'a type of speech chosen by history', and 'speech justified in excess' (Barthes 1972: 132). The preservation of myth is, in itself, illustrative of its importance to the community that fostered it, and, with this in mind, what remains of a myth has been filtered by the passing of time: 'chosen by history'. Barthes' use of excess here connects his study to Robinson's own theology of surplus. Myth is a genre-specific response to the irreducibility of the relation between power and language, for Barthes, and, as such, is always inscribed with an implicit ideology. Robinson does not devote space to a Barthesian analysis of power relations in the Hebrew Bible narratives, but she does share his conviction that myth proceeds under the logic of an implicit ideology, or – to use Robinson's preferred term – an 'implied' theology. Where Barthes' inquiry is inspired by semiology, Robinson's is led by theological concerns. Despite the marked difference in approach, both thinkers agree that myth is best read with an appreciation for the specific intentions of the genre. As Barthes puts it, 'the third type of focusing is dynamic, it consumes the myth according to the very ends built into its structure: the reader lives the myth as a stay at once true and unreal' (Barthes 1972: 153). The fluidity of a myth's interpreted signification ensures both its survival and relevance through time and history, and Robinson, too, apprehends myth with no expectation that its meaning will be static and its implications unchanged.

Myth, like memory, is open constantly to the possibility of reassembly and reinterpretation.

Myth and memory

If myth is indeed to be considered a theological remembering, it must be engaged within the present in order to retain its meaningfulness, and this is what Rogerson, in his important work on the defining features of myth, makes clear. A central quality of myth, he notes, is its communal remembrance by way of ritual celebration (Rogerson 1974: 174–8). The Passover cedar, for example, functions as an entry point for Jewish people into the Exodus myth. For Robinson, as a Christian, 'Baptism, Communion, and worship are all participations in this metaphysical, ontological vision [of the gospels]' and become imaginative gateways into the drama of the original narrative (Robinson 2015: 168). Where fable is reducible to a moral lesson, myth is constructed to allow its reader into the narrative, through ritual or sacrament, in order to 'join the remembering' – to, in effect, allow the story to enter the present. The narratives of myth were written to be continually remembered, their images and stories reassembled each time they are told and, with each telling, they are edited and emphasized in ways that allow myth's meaningful application to the present.

With all this in mind, an individual's memories are functionally similar to myth. Where myth conveys the world view of its community and constantly allows itself to be reinterpreted in accordance with the shifting consciousness of its readers, memory, on a smaller scale, writes itself on an individual mind and, like myth, is shaped by the conditions of remembering. Indeed, what myth achieves in conjuring the effect of an event for a community, memory does the same for the individual self. For Robinson, memory's meaning is not fixed and its purpose is not to conjure the literal truth of a past occurrence, but instead to capture the meaning operating beyond a reductive collection of facts. Memory evokes the 'sense' of an event or a person in a manner that speaks to the current set of circumstances; myth, too, is a malleable cultural memory that is changed, even if only subtly, by each remembering. Memories, then, can take on a sacramental[3] significance in the way that baptism and communion allow believers to enter into the theological significance of the narratives they symbolize. For Lila, the knife, the river and the sound of crickets are all sacramental in quality, allowing access to memories of her old life that are never static, but build and layer one another, influenced always by the concerns of the present. Robinson's writing of memory in her novels, and particularly in *Lila*, will be discussed below with reference to the mythic qualities to which she draws her reader's attention.

Robinson is emphatic that the way in which myth and memory operate should not disqualify them from their status as meaningful routes to truth. In fact she argues that their eschewal of objective truth paradoxically enables them to be more truthful. Writing of the inconsistencies of the gospel account of Jesus' resurrection, she states: 'if let us say, memories were transposed to prove eloquent detail, or even if some details were invented, it would be in the service of creating a likeness, not a history, and discrepancies would matter not at all' (Robinson 1998: 242). Memory and myth both privilege truthfulness over truth, or, in other words, both forms of remembering seek to evoke the essence of an event that communicates what it might *mean* rather than simply what happened; they are necessary responses to the inadequacy of facts. As Ruth puts it, 'all this is fact. Fact explains nothing. On the contrary, it is fact that requires explanation' (Robinson 1980: 217). Robinson herself asks 'what is myth, after all? It is a narrative that conveys a kind of truth by nonliteral

---

[3] Sacrament and sacramentality are interesting recurrent themes in Robinson's work. Potts reads *Housekeeping* with an eye for the significance of its use of sacrament and sign. Incorporating a Rowan Williams' 1989 article on Augustine into his reading, he argues, 'what matters about sacramental signs is not really the matter of the signs themselves – the bread, the wine, the water, the oil – because, again, "all that is present to us" is "potentially a sign of God"' (Potts 492). In the same way, memories 'give way' in Robinson's fiction to that which transcends and forms them. Potts goes on to argue: 'What is real about the sacraments, then, is not just the material stuff that makes them but the love that stirs them; a love that, if we're to follow even loosely any typical Christian ontology, is as deep and certain a reality as matter anyway' (Potts 493). For Robinson, memories are functionally similar to bread and wine – ordinary material – in how their significance is constantly open to reconfigured, reinvigorated interpretation. And in this endless interpretability, memories act as a sign of the inexhaustibility of the divine, for, 'were signs simply stable and fixed, they would fail to indicate or embody God's own eternity, God's endless infinity' (Potts 491). They are also reminders, as this chapter develops, of the unfolding nature of the self in Robinson's fiction.

means. This is a definition meant to exclude the influence of a common sense of the word, that a myth is unreal, untrue' (Robinson 2018: 72). The distinction between the meaning of an event and the facts of what actually happened is what Robinson rigorously maintains in her writing on memory. Using an example from the gospels, she argues,

> To say that a literal representation is different from portraiture is to make a distinction like this: Jesus, even in the interval before his ascent into heaven, did in fact address a woman with courtesy and deference. Or, it would have been *like* Jesus, even in the interval before his ascent into heaven, to address a woman with courtesy and deference. A statement of the second kind could easily be truer, and is certainly more meaningful, than a statement of the first kind. (Robinson 1998: 242)

Hans Frei, a theologian intimately engaged in excavating the importance of narrative to theology, shares Robinson's conviction that what has commonly been referred to as 'history' in Christian theology is, in actual fact, nothing of the sort. He writes,

> Even if I say that history is first of all the facts – and I do have a healthy respect for evidence – I come across something else. Is Jesus Christ [. . .] a 'fact' like other historical facts? Should I really say that the eternal Word made flesh, that is, made fact indeed, is a fact like any other? (Frei 1993: 211)

Theological thinking arises not out of verifiable facts, but out of the meaning operating in and between these facts. Robinson treats myth not as simply the incidental mode the biblical writers happened to use but, rather, as an instructive genre in itself. Myth is written to allow for imaginative reinterpretation because it is itself an embodiment of the manner in which memory works. As noted, myth isn't history in the post-enlightenment sense of an inquiry into 'what really happened'; rather, it is a collection of narratives that commit to tradition a community's memory of a past occurrence, filtered and constructed always by the world view of the remembering community. It is, like all forms of human remembering, an account both of an event and the beliefs and underlying connection of self or identity of those whose memory it is. Writing of the various Flood narratives that pre-existed the account in Genesis, Robinson comments,

> The Gilgamesh epic was found in various forms throughout the ancient Near East. It is absurd to imagine that the most dramatic part of it could be patched into the Hebrew Genesis and no one would notice the plagiarism. To retell the story with changes would be to defend it against its pagan theological implications, and also to address what are, after all, questions of very great interest. (Robinson 2010: 25–6)

Clearly demonstrated here is Robinson's willingness to read the Old Testament story in line with the genre in which it is written. Myth invites its readers not into a debate about what really occurred, but instead to ponder the conception of reality that has been inscribed in the story. Speaking about another Genesis narrative, Robinson argues, definitively,

> One of the things that's amazing to me is the positivist notion of what the Creation narrative is about. When did that start? The eighteenth century I suppose. You can't find anything but myth in antiquity, that's how they expressed important ideas. It is absolutely naive to imply that standards that did not exist on earth at the time should be applied to these narratives. (Chapter 5)

Myth, more akin to poetry than to contemporary history, bridges the gulf between history and theology by making no acknowledgement of this truly modern distinction. As Lloyd puts it, 'where history merely tells us what did happen, the poet describes "a kind of thing that might be". The difference makes poetry something more philosophical and of graver import than history' (Lloyd 1993: 165). Where moderns inevitably seek an objective account of the past, the writers of biblical myth sought no such thing, a fact that makes these accounts of great interest to Robinson, bearing self-consciously as they do, the marks of human subjectivity.

In *Lila*, Robinson's narrative darts between the past and present and, in doing so, raises concerns about the nature of memory and history that are also interrogated in her non-fiction. In *The Death of Adam* she writes:

> The true past is veiled in mystery, to the extent that it can be said to exist at all. Insofar as we receive it, it is liable to record itself in us culturally as assumption too fundamental to be reached by inquiry, or as memory so painful it must be rationalised, falsified, or suppressed. It is liable to being

reconstructed to bear the blame for present vice of failure. (Robinson 1998: 126–7)

The inaccessibility of the 'true' past is a feature of Robinson's fourth novel which opens with Lila's memory of Doll's night-time rescue of her. Finding her alone and abandoned on the stoop she 'took her up in her arms and wrapped her in a shawl' (Robinson 2014: 4). This act of grace becomes a foundational memory for Lila, an event she returns to in her mind; indeed, with each remembrance, the event is slightly altered and reshaped. The early sections of the text acknowledge the mythical nature of memory: following Doll's stealing of Lila, 'the door *might* have opened, and a woman *might* have called after them, Where are you going with that child?' (Robinson 2014: 5; emphasis added). The novel is consistent with Robinson's earlier writing on the subjective content of memory and how this subjectivity is to be embraced as a route to meaning. Lila knows that her memories are being continually shaped by her situation and current patterns of thought but, as will developed, she also demonstrates how memory itself reveals the human impulse towards meaning.

'Lila knew it couldn't have been the way she remembered it, as if she were carried off along the wind': yet, importantly for Lila, knowing that a memory is an exaggerated, edited or even false record of how an event happened does not lead her to disregard or suppress her memories (Robinson 2014: 5). Instead, she accepts the manner in which memory operates and allows herself to remember, giving herself permission to accept the fictional additions memory makes to the past, primarily because the past exists only as interpretation anyway and, secondarily, because these interpretations and additions are revealing in and of themselves. In doing this she can become consciously aware of the inevitable narrativization of memory, of how the self cannot help but read the past through the present and, equally, view the present through the lens of memory. A few pages later, Lila, now married to Ames and pregnant, eats a carrot straight out of the ground and remembers having the thought of stealing away her own son, 'carrying him away to the woods off down the road so she could have him to herself' (Robinson 2014: 17). The memory of this thought in turn gives way to an imagined scenario in which Ames calls after them, 'Where are you going with that child?' (Robinson 2014: 17). Here, Lila visualizes a scene in which her husband has taken the role of the woman who might have called after her and Doll, and 'the sadness in his voice would be terrible' (Robinson 2014: 17). Moreover Lila 'remembered that sadness from somewhere, and it was as if she would understand something if she could hear it again' (Robinson 2014: 17). The initial memory, already in dubious relation to actuality, provides Lila with an image and a voice by which her own thoughts in the present are read through. Robinson is here consciously weaving memory and imaginative anticipation; in this brief paragraph, past, present and future are all evoked: the past of the woman calling in the doorway, the present self remembering and the future scenario of stealing away the child, freely imagined by Lila. The only time that has any degree of tangible existence is the present and out of the current moment emerges an interpretation of the past and a projection of this past onto the future. This is not to say that the past's and the future's lack of existence discredits what can be said about what has happened and what might happen. Rather, Robinson's point is that any memory or imagined future reveals more about the individual than it does about the truth of past- and future-tense statements. Robinson is not so radical as to doubt the occurrence of events in history, but, as is seen through Lila's recurring memories, she is keen to note the meaning-making nature of memory and is a staunch advocate of reading memory like a myth, taking into account the conditions surrounding its remembrance and the world view of the individual doing the remembering. Ames, too, has an appreciation of the contingent and malleable nature of memory, which, he notes, 'can make a thing seem to have been much more than it was' (Robinson 2004: 75). Folding memory into an overarching conception of blessing in *Gilead*, Aronociwz writes, 'it is impossible in the end to reduce blessing, as *Gilead* presents it, to just one meaning' (Aronociwz 2017: 48). Blessing is 'tied to so much that eludes our understanding – time in all its unpredictability and nonlinearity, the vitality within everything that we both see and do not see' (Aronociwz 2017: 48–9). Memory, in both *Gilead* and *Lila*, reveals not the static facts of a perfectly recollected past, but the ever-shifting meaning of events, given their significance through time and subsequent experience and reflection.

The implication of Robinson's writing on myth and memory is a positive reappraisal of subjectivity and its role in truth, meaning and faith. For Robinson, the operation of myth and the conditions that allow memory its function are only understandable as products of human subjectivity. Moreover, it is only through an embrace of this subjectivity that the stories that myth and memory contain can be rightly read and assimilated. Niebuhr writes, 'we are in history as the fish is in water and what we mean by the revelation of God can be indicated only as we point through the medium in which we live' (Hauerwas and Burrell 1997: 24). The point Niebuhr makes here – that all genuine theological knowledge is gleaned only through a reading of history, when taken alongside Robinson's own reservations about the supposed objective truth of historical narratives – implies that history is to be treated as inescapable and, in actual fact, the conditions through which we know anything. Granting Robinson's assertion that history is accessible only through the interpretative lens of human subjectivity, Niebuhr's argument should be extended from the inescapability of history to the inescapability of subjectivity. The subjective nature of history and memory are not conditions to be transcended for Robinson, not only because this is a doomed project but also, and more positively, because embracing the human context in which revelation emerges is the only way to embrace revelation itself. Robinson writes, 'the elusiveness of the mind is a consequence of its centrality, which is its potency and its limitation. The difficulty with which objectivity can be achieved, to the extent that it is ever achieved, only demonstrates the pervasive importance of subjectivity' (Robinson 2010: 36). When Niebuhr writes, 'faith cannot get to God save through historic experience', Robinson would want to add, 'the mind, whatever else it is, is a constant of everyone's experience, and, in more and other ways than we know, the creator of the reality that we live within' (Hauerwas and Burrell 1997: 42; Robinson 2010: 1). Robinson's take on the centrality of subjectivity to all theological thinking mirrors the writing of James Cone, who similarly argues that 'there is no "abstract" revelation, independent of human experiences, to which theologians can appeal for evidence of what they say about the gospel' (Cone 1970: xix). Memory and myth, then, in their profoundly human ways, offer a route into history and its meaning through present interpretation and experience, and, as Robinson is eager to make clear, invite a total embrace of the human subjectivity they emerge from and about which they report.

(Para)Science and the self

Memory is a story told by the self, to the self and about the self, for the purpose of preserving the meaning of the past and to maintain a sense of coherency through time. It is also a means of safeguarding one's identity. Where written myth is a record of an oral tradition, memory remains largely unspoken as a silent dialogue between the remembering self and the self being presented with the memory; it is, as Robinson has said, a 'companion' (Chapter 5). It is impossible to speak meaningfully about memory, then, without considering its stabilizing role in a conception of self. Being profoundly concerned with the ways in which the self is talked about in contemporary writing, Robinson pays particular attention to what she perceives to be a dismissive rhetorical tone present in much popular scientific discussion. *Absence of Mind*, originally given as the Terry Lectures in 2009, was written as a response to the unchallenged and, to Robinson's mind, groundless conclusions certain contemporary writers had forwarded with regard to religion and the self. She states:

> What I wish to question are not the methods of science, but the methods of a kind of argument that claims the authority of science [. . .] that assumes a protective coloration that allows it to pass for science yet does not practice the self-discipline or self-criticism for which science is distinguished. (Robinson 2010: 2)

Dennett, Pinker, Vattimo and Rorty[4] are all critiqued for various kinds of 'threshold thinking', for their assertions that at a certain point in human

---

[4] Dennett is critiqued in *Absence of Mind* for his impulse to treat religion as solely a social phenomenon. In so doing, Robinson counters, '[he] sheers off the contemplative side of faith, its subjectivity, as if the collective expressions of religion and the inward experience of it were nonoverlapping magisteria' (Robinson 2010: 9). By approaching religion with just the tools of the sociologist or anthropologist, Robinson argues, everything that makes religion meaningful to an individual person is missed or overlooked.
  Similarly, Robinson challenges Pinker on his dismissive talk of religion and his mission to 'debunk [. . .] belief in the soul' (Robinson 2010: 16). Pinker is frequently held up as an example of a thinker

intellectual history a threshold was crossed, an event which made ever returning to old ways of thinking simply impossible for the well informed. The death of God, the rise of evolutionary biology and psychology, the collapse of metaphysics are, in modern thought, Robinson argues, assumed to be threshold moments of a kind that falsified what came before and opened a novel way of thinking for the future of whichever disciplines they influenced. Robinson's critique varies in its subject matter but returns most often to the human self, to the insidious denigration of the basic experience of being, and having, a self. 'Neuroscientists seem predisposed to the conclusion that there is no "self"', Robinson writes in *The Givenness of Things*, and it is this predisposition, born out of the modern trend of deep-rooted suspicion of 'that old romantic notion of the self still encouraged by religion" that invites her sustained attention in her non-fiction writing (Robinson 2015: 7; Robinson 2010: 2). It is as if the self's inevitable and historical theological connotations have, prima facie, led to the assumed conclusion that it must be an illusion, and now that we have crossed over the demythologizing Nietzschean–Freudian threshold, there can be no home for the self in the contemporary imagination. For Robinson, the conclusion that the self is an illusion is akin to the statement 'God is dead', in that both have been absorbed by intellectual culture to the extent that they are treated as self-evident truths upon which entire theories can be constructed. The problem with this kind of thinking, or at least one that is most striking, is that at the same time as these statements are taken as given by the individuals who would think of such things, they have absolutely nothing to say to the

engaged in what Robinson calls 'parasceince'. Principally, she rejects the implicit assumption found in his work that the highest thoughts of humans across millennia – namely religious and theological ideas and expressions – could be wiped out or 'debunked' with the stroke of an enlightened person's pen. He writes, notes Robinson, 'with the certitude typical of his genre', a certitude based not in scientific evidence but, to Robinson's mind, unverifiable assertion (Robinson 2010: 114).

Robinson singles out Rorty and Vattimo's *The Future of Religion* (2005) as an example of the kind of threshold thinking she rejects. Despite being a 'good-hearted, even rather joyful book', Robinson is suspicious of its tendency to chart tightly and prescriptively the state and history of Western Christianity (Robinson 2010: 6). The text, she notes, 'announces the passage of Western Christianity from a law of power through its Nietzschean moment to an embrace of the law of love' (Robinson 2010: 6). Robinson concludes, 'I am eager to welcome the first sign of the reality of this transformation' (Robinson 2010: 6). Her objection is that Rorty and Vattimo write about Christianity as if it were not made up of millions of individual subjectivities completely devout and unaware of Nietzsche's 'deconstruction of metaphysics', implicitly raising the question: what could this apparent threshold mean to the initiated?

experience of a person in the grip of a religious experience or to the Ordinary awareness many people have of the holy, of the sacred or of the *self*. Discussing Nietzsche's supposed 'deconstruction of metaphysics' as an example of an apparent threshold, Robinson asks how ideas such as these are to be lived out by the millions of individuals who are and will remain unaware of them:

> These questions are not meant to invoke any sort of populist standard, as if I were to say 'The man in the street may be wholly unaware that metaphysics has been deconstructed, and might not approve the project if he were aware of it'. No, quite the opposite. They are meant to call to mind the voice of the Psalmist, the voice of any ancient poet, saint, or visionary on the far side of the threshold who has attested to his or her own sense of the holy, and all those who are moved by these voices and attest to the truth of them. (Robinson 2010: 7)

Robinson is questioning neither the value of philosophy nor intellectual progress on questions of ultimate importance and profundity; rather, she is rejecting the kind of thinking that is allowed to progress despite a total blindness to the usual experience of human beings. She is staunchly opposed to any mode of intellectual discourse that ignores the strangely consistent religiosity of humans across time and space and that ends in the patronizing conclusion that advances in science necessarily invalidate an individual's experience of themselves. 'The thing that is lost in this kind of thinking', Robinson argues, 'is the self, the solitary, perceiving, and interpreting locus of anything that can be called experience' (Robinson 2010: 7).

There is a worrying overreach in statements like 'there is no self' for Robinson. 'We shed error, and we have to be willing to', she comments, in an implicit critique of this over-confident scientific assertion (Chapter 5). 'Identity is one of those intractable mysteries and I expect it to remain so. It has led people to say things like "There is no self", because there is no way of accounting for the fact that I have a self that is not highly mistakable for other selves, and I think the same is true for everyone else', she explains, noting the disconnect between human experience and unfounded parascientific statement (Chapter 5). Neuroscience has not yet the means to explain the uncanny sense of a unified, coherent self that persists for individuals and, as Robinson argues, this should not be taken to necessarily imply its non-existence. She engages in the scientific question of the self, first, only to highlight the logical errors in certain pronouncements based on scant current evidence and, second, and more crucially, to show that the question of the self is not merely a scientific or psychological issue, but one that exceeds the scientific method and invites philosophical, theological and literary discussion. Implicit in Robinson's writing on the self is the compelling argument that, as a writer of fiction, she has a way into the issue that is more appropriate to the humanness of the question. In addition, even if the reach of currently available scientific knowledge could make a positive statement like 'there is no self', this would not rid the human of the *experience* of having a self, and one that, in its remarkable consistency through time and contingency, would stand as a rebuke to such an assertion. The self is felt to be both a constituent and a creator of experience, so being told it does not exist would do nothing to exorcise the haunting presence of the 'I' in each passing moment. In other words, the self persists independent of what current scientific or philosophical opinion on its status is. This invites the conclusion that, where science necessarily has nothing to say to the felt experience of having a self, fiction, poetry and art are the means by which the subjective nature of experience cannot only be tolerated, but explored, examined and expressed. In Robinson's words, 'rationalistic accounts of mind and self do not suit their subject any better than a mechanistic physics suits a quantum universe': it is with Robinson's own approach to the question of the time-bound self that the rest of the chapter is devoted (Robinson 2015, 219).

Theology as narrative

While Robinson devotes a considerable amount of space in her essays to dealing with the apparent 'suspicion of the self' in contemporary thought, she also demonstrates the richness of her alternate vision in and through her fiction. At no point in her work is the notion of the self resolved to something simple or straightforward, yet it emerges as a mystery so fundamental to the human experience that it cannot go unexplored. In *Lila* particularly, a way of conceiving of the time-bound self is presented that demands careful attention so that its profound theological implications are laid bare. Lila's initial encounter with John Ames is one of the most illuminating passages in Robinson's fiction with regard to her own thinking on the relation between self, memory and narrative. It is here that a discussion of Robinson's distinctive contribution to theological reflection on the self may begin.

Showing up on Rev. Ames doorstep, unannounced and uninvited,[5] Lila introduces herself as the surprising, disruptive presence she will continue to be in the town of Gilead. When Ames asks her to tell him a little about herself, Lila replies, 'I don't talk about that. I just been wondering lately why things happen the way they do'; and with that, she initiates the central theological question of the text (Robinson 2014: 29). The silence that follows the question, the making of coffee, and the exchange of pleasantries about the weather, is finally broken by Ames with a story. He recollects for Lila the history of his family, how most of his brothers and sisters died before he was born, and how many of the scars his old house exhibits were marks left by the siblings he never knew: 'so when he found a scratch or a mark or something, he still thought, One of the children' (Robinson 2014: 29). 'There's been a good deal of sorrow in this house', Ames reflects, 'some of it mine. Some of it I used to wish were mine. So I sort of live with this question. Why things happen. I guess this isn't much help' (Robinson 2014: 30). Lila's reply – 'I liked that story' – causes Ames to realize that that is exactly what it was: 'It *is* a story, isn't it? I've never really thought of it that way. And I suppose the next time I tell it, it will be a better story. Maybe a little less true' (Robinson 2014: 30; emphasis in original). Not only does this admission connect to the earlier discussion about Robinson's writing on the subjective nature of memory, but it also makes explicit the surprising fact that Ames' response to Lila's question was to tell a story and not to immediately explain the doctrinal basis of his faith. The initial question could well have been interpreted scientifically, as one of causation, but to Ames' mind, it is inevitably a theological question and one that invites him to account for his faith and his vocation. That he does this, not with formal theology, nor by quoting Calvin, nor with an exegesis of scripture, but through

---

[5] In typical Robinson style, the Parable of the Lost Sheep is turned on its head here. Lila seeking out the minister rather than waiting to be found: an act of female agency so often absent from biblical narrative.

the telling of a story is revealing of his own reading of the question and indeed the context in which it was raised. Theological questions require theological answers, and Ames' eschewal of what would be most readily recognized as theology should not imply that his response is itself not 'theological'; rather, this encounter invites reflection on the status of the story within theological thinking. Ames does eventually, after being asked about his sermons, proceed to mention the grace of God and the mysterious nature of its outworking, but that his initial response is a story is crucial and requires unpacking.

Niebuhr makes some key assertions about the role of narrative in historic theology that connect to Ames' own discursive approach in his initial encounter with Lila:

> What prompted Christians in the past to confess their faith by telling their story was more than a need for vivid illustration or for analogical reasoning. Their story was not a parable which could be replaced by another; it was irreplaceable and untranslatable. An internal compulsion rather than free choice led them to speak of what they knew. (Hauerwas and Burrell 1997: 23)

Ames is an example of this impulse to convey the 'truth' of religious belief through personal narrative; he is, despite his profound interest in Christian doctrine, an illustration of the necessity of a story in the demonstration of the validity of a religious life. Apologetics, for Ames, is not an activity of formal reasoning or rigorous logical argumentation, but a relaying of one's own subjective experience. The grace of God and its role in causation, temporality and God's providential care for Creation are theological discussions that are secondary to the foundational nature of story because story itself is an orientating activity that provides the experiential context through which these more abstracted notions may be believed. As Kearney observes, 'what works at the level of communal history works also at the level of individual history. When someone asks you who you are, you tell your story [...] And in so doing you give a sense of yourself as a *narrative* identity that perdures and coheres over a lifetime' (Kearney 2002: 4; emphasis in original).[6] Story is crucial to

---

[6] Kearney and Robinson are of one mind here, and the discussion here constructs Robinson's own thinking on the narrative self.

Robinson's world view, for theological belief does not arise in a vacuum, and it is therefore a mistake to divorce someone's stated beliefs from the experiences that give rise to and ground these ideas. One's own story is not incidental to one's theology: it is both the casual and underpinning structure that gives these beliefs human depth and context. This is not to set up a dichotomy between story and theology, as if the two are necessarily distinct; for the rise of postliberal theology in 1970s America, for example, saw the two not only as compatible, but inextricably bound together. Niebuhr makes the point that narrative has been the sustaining force behind the cohesion of Christian theology and the community of the church:

> We may remind ourselves also of the fact that despite many efforts to set forth Christian faith in metaphysical and ethical terms of great generality the only creed which has been able to maintain itself in the church with any approach to universality consists for the most part of statements about events. (Hauerwas and Burrell 1997: 22)

That Robinson would agree that 'metaphysical statements have not been able to maintain the intellectual life of our community' is very unlikely (Hauerwas and Burrell 1997: 23). Robinson is very clear that she wishes to see a return to Christian metaphysics and she nowhere makes any real distinction between biblical narrative, on the one hand, and the metaphysics they may be thought to imply, on the other hand.[7] However, Robinson does share Niebuhr's stress on the centrality of story in theological reflection. At the beginning of this chapter, the identity securing nature of myth and memory was introduced, and it should be noted that Ames, too, has an implicit faith in the power of story to orientate its teller and its listener to both the subjective quality of the question being asked and, more widely, to the conception of self that is operating beneath any account of one's faith. Lila's first words to Ames are 'I got nowhere to be', and the discussion that follows can well be read as a response to this initial admission (Robinson 2014: 28). With Lila's words in mind, it becomes clear why Ames

---

[7] Robinson's comment on the metaphysics of the Creation narrative, quoted earlier, is a clear example of her refusal to acknowledge any distinction between scriptural narrative and the metaphysics they can be said to assume, or imply.

does not immediately launch into pure theology, for this kind of response is not appropriate for someone who clearly already feels out of place and is not asking her question as a challenge to the legitimacy of belief. Ames recognizes the hidden story behind her question, observing that 'I think you are asking me these questions because of some hard things that have happened, the things you won't talk about' (Robinson 2014: 31). In responding to someone who has no place to be, Ames tells his story and the purpose of the telling is to both contextualize his own struggle with Lila's question and to invite her into a dialogue, to encourage her to reciprocate in sharing something of her own story. Posed in the context of shared story, potentially abstract questions like Lila's are planted firmly in the ground of human experience and any answers ventured are implicitly subjective in nature: they are responses arising from a purely personal perspective and individual history, and any theology contained in the subsequent answers is not forwarded as objectively accurate or universally true. Ames continues: 'if you did tell me about them, I could probably not say more than that life is a very deep mystery, and that finally the grace of God is all that can resolve it. And the grace of God is also a very deep mystery' (Robinson 2014: 31). Ames believes this and has 'said these words too many times' in his counselling of his congregation (Robinson 2014: 31). Walter Benjamin's essay *The Storyteller* (1936) usefully theorizes what Ames actually does here. He writes, 'in every case the storyteller is a man who has counsel for his readers [. . .] After all, counsel is less an answer to a question than a proposal concerning the continuation of a story which is just unfolding' (Benjamin: 5). For Benjamin, counselling and storytelling are one and the same, and certainly for Ames, metaphysics is secondary to achieving empathy through the telling of a story. After saying these words to Lila, '[he] watched his finger trace the scar on the table' (Robinson 2014: 31). The conversation with Lila is bookended with this tracing of a scar and, as an image of what it encloses, is revelatory of Ames' prioritization of memory, personal story and the sharing of difficulty over theological doctrine. It is, in micro, an image of what Niebuhr argues is fundamental to Christian theology: the tracing of scars and the recollection of events for the purpose of creating a community and a context from which belief in the metaphysical can rightly arise.

The narrative self

Asked specifically about the curious sense of self that persists across time, Robinson comments: 'for my purposes identity means there is an arc of self-consistency and this is the self' (Chapter 5). This self-consistency does not necessarily rely on a predictable life or an unsurprising set of experiences, but that whatever actually occurs in the course of a life, the recognizable presence of the 'I' is continually present to register its responses. The self may be surprised, threatened, bereaved or elated at any one moment, but it is felt through time as a consistent presence and this consistency relies on memory and anticipation for its existence; as Crites notes, 'without memory, in fact, experience would have no coherence at all' (Hauerwas and Burrell 1997: 73). For example: Oliver Sacks, in *The Man Who Mistook His Wife for a Hat* (1985), records the case of Mr Thomson who 'remembered nothing for more than a few seconds' and was therefore forced to 'literally make himself (and his world) up every moment' (Sacks 1990: 109). Sacks concludes from this case that 'each of us constructs and lives a "narrative," and that narrative *is* us, our identities' (Sacks 1990: 110). The synonymity between narrative and identity Sacks proposes is striking, but arises out of his observation that, without the narrative of memory, identity has no grounding and must be created ex nihilo. Commenting on Sacks' conclusion, Eakin argues 'what is arresting about this radical equation between narrative and identity is the notion that narrative here is not merely *about* the self but rather in some profound way a constituent part *of* self' (Eakin 2016: 101). Robinson's phrase 'self-consistency' hints towards a conception of self similar to Sacks; in *Lila*, the narrative quality of the self is demonstrated through her protagonist's mythic memory and her projection of past onto the future. In the novel, a conception of a 'timeless' or static self untethered from memory and anticipation is implicitly shown to be absurd and, while the self is experienced in the present, it is a phenomenon granted its form by time.

Lila herself is drawn to narrative. She saves money to go to the movies twice a week, 'and when she was sitting there in the dark, sometimes, when it was crowded, with somebody's arm or knee brushing against hers, she was dreaming some stranger's dream, everybody in there dreaming one dream together' (Robinson 2014: 208). In extension of this, Robinson imagines a secular version of the church's attraction at Easter and Christmas: 'I have a theory that the churches fill on Christmas and Easter because it is on these days that the two most startling moments in the Christian narrative can be heard again' (Robinson 2012: 126–7). No doubt Robinson would attribute the magnetism of these particular stories to their content and the inexpressible meaning residing beyond their content; for her they 'become so beautiful as to acquire a unique authority, a weight of meaning history cannot approach' (Robinson 2012: 127). These are narratives that imply a larger story, one that always resists expression. As Crites suggests, 'even the myths and epics, even the scriptures, are mundane stories. But in these [. . .] the sacred stories resonate. People are able to feel this resonance, because the unutterable stories are those they know best of all' (Hauerwas and Burrell 1997: 71). This is a crucial distinction, and one that connects well to Robinson's thinking on the self, as will be discussed later. It is worth noting that these narratives (Easter and Christmas) are, like all myths, stories about the past, read in the present and intended to shape engagement with the future. In their temporality and the coherence with which they stretch across these modalities, they are akin to memory in their strange and malleable endurance through time. When Lila goes to the movies she is not a passive receiver of story, but an active and creative participant who carries the narrative in her mind and cannot help but recreate it. The movie 'was all there was in her mind for an hour or two, a week or two. She might look like some woman going about her work, sitting by the window, but she'd be remaking the story in her mind' (Robinson 2014: 209). That she is drawn to narrative, and that she cannot help but recreate, edit and reshape it is demonstrative of an innate recognition of the narrative form within the self, which is, in turn, a suggestion of what the self may well *be*.

Lila is capable of memory and anticipation in the present and is able to combine all three 'tenses' in a unified sense of self while also maintaining their distinct qualities. For example, she often recalls Doll from the past and allows this memory to alter both her present behaviour and her imagining of the future: 'she lived for Doll to see. Lila made the old man smile for the pleasure in his eyes, because Doll would have been so happy to see it.' A little later, she imagines how a resurrection would surprise Doll: 'Doll [was] just the way she used to be but with death behind her, and with all the peace that comes with that [...] Doll would laugh at the surprise of it all, because she'd probably never heard of such a thing' (Robinson 2014: 97, 100). Robinson presents a character that, without effort, accesses the past, present and future with a consistent sense of self, and with the ability to differentiate between these divisions of time. This is a strangely human capability, as Crites argues, which implies that consciousness itself has a narrative structure: 'the whole [of] experience, as it is concentrated in a conscious present, has a narrative form. Narrative alone can contain the full temporality of experience in a unity of form' (Hauerwas and Burrell 1997: 78). Indeed, the self's ability to cohere through temporal contingency in a conscious awareness of the threefold structure of time is unthinkable unless it itself is considered to have a narrative form. The ability of Lila to hold the modalities of the past, present and future both in coherence and in separation strongly mirrors the temporal possibilities of narrative. For Crites, and for Lila, the present holds together the remembered past and the hoped-for future because experience itself is structured as a story; that is, consciousness of being in time is formed like a narrative which in turn allows for the coexistence of the past and the future in the decisive present, the moment in which the narrative self pivots. Crites argues: 'there seems to be a powerful inner drive of thought and imagination to overcome the relentless temporality of experience'; Lila embodies this imaginative response to the flux and propulsion of time and the self's vulnerability to its irresistible movement (Hauerwas and Burrell 1997: 84). She, as a participant in storytelling, as both listener and speaker, 'humanizes time', as Kearney puts it: 'transforming it from an impersonal passing of fragmented moments into a pattern, a plot, a *mythos*' (Kearney 2002: 4). Viewing the self as a narrative explains how its coherency manages to persist in spite of time, no doubt, but this begs the questions: what does this *mean*, and what *kind* of narrative can the self be said to be?

As a writer concerned explicitly with the question of 'self' and with its rejection in much contemporary thought, Robinson's fiction stands as a profound rebuttal to any dismissive rhetoric against it. *Housekeeping*, *Gilead*, *Home* and *Lila* are each, in their own ways and from varying narrative perspectives, engaged in helpfully complicating the notion of the self. In each text, the self is not reducible to a written narrative, for there is never the suggestion that the consciousness of a character is exhausted by the text of any of the novels. The clearest and most obvious example of this is Ames' letter, the text of *Gilead*. A careful reading of that novel reveals the complexity of consciousness, the simultaneous linear and non-linear nature of a self's conversation with itself and the ultimately unspeakable, unsayable nature of what it means to be and have a self. It would be absurd to think that Ames has made a final and total account of himself in *Gilead*, and it would be equally absurd to conclude that the self's exceeding of narrative necessarily means that *it* cannot ultimately be understood as narrative.[8] As the beginning of this chapter established, myth is a narrative that, through the recording of memorialized detail, seeks to evoke the *meaning* of an event. Implicit within this, then, is that a myth's failure to record exhaustively and plainly an event's meaning should not lead to a rejection of myth or should it be thought to suggest that the ultimately unsayable meaning of the event has not been faithfully served by narrative. In a paradoxical sense, the failure of myth is actually its means to achieve its purpose. Indeed, as Chapter 2 developed, words constantly and necessarily meet their own limits, and because of this inevitability, are forever burdened with trying to speak what they cannot say. It is the granting of this ineffable reality that frees narrative from the expectation of total explanation. To say that the self is a narrative is then not to suggest that the self is accounted for, without remainder, in what a person can say about themselves; for, as Robinson comments, 'I think that one of the primary mistakes people make is to take people's spoken language to be equivalent to the level of their thinking' (Schaub 237). Like Ames and the text of *Gilead*, the self always eclipses the narratives that speak of it. Narratives always 'fail' in this sense but, for Robinson, the failure of narrative in total description is just as instructive about the mysterious nature of the self as it is about the limits of language. To her mind, ultimate otherness necessitates partiality of description. To return to Crites's distinction between mundane stories and sacred stories, it becomes clear that if the self is to be thought of as narrative, it must belong to the 'sacred' category; that is, as a narrative to which all other narratives

---

[8] The sheer number of sermons Ames has written further evidence the linguistic inexhaustibility of both God and self. The existence of such a huge collection underscores the absurdity of ever finally housing the self in language.

report, and which they imply in the course of their own telling. Memories are, like myths, in the service of a 'sacred story', a narrative that resides in the background of these 'mundane' stories and one that is continually suggested by them. The narrative of the 'self', then, is given form by stories about the self and also, in turn, gives form to these stories in a give-and-take process. As Sacks argues, the self is known and grasped through the stories (memories) that are retained by an individual and, as such, cannot be accessed except through them. Robinson's Lila exemplifies this and her self-understanding is bound up with the narratives she tells herself about her past. Lila is not reducible to what she remembers, just as Ames is not reducible to his letter; 'Lila' is, rather, what these memories report to: the narrative self that generates narrative and judges the authenticity of them.

Wallace Stevens and Nietzsche: Fictions, supreme fictions and the self

Robinson, in a discussion of the strange, mysterious name God reveals for God's self – the 'I am what I will be' passage of Exodus 3 – notes how individuals use this same 'I am' phrase:

> Though always with a modifier of some kind. I am hungry, I am comfortable, I am a singer, I am a cook. The abrupt descent into particularity in every statement of this kind, Being itself made an auxiliary to some momentary accident of being, may only startle in the dark of night, when the intuition comes that there is no proportion between the great given of existence and the narrow vessel of circumstance into which it is inevitably forced. (Robinson 1998: 110–11)

Being, the mysterious reality shared by God, humans, animals and objects, is rendered conceivable by the human self through qualifying the 'I am' with a particular activity or quality. The self and existence are two constants and constituents of experience and, as Robinson notes earlier, it is in the nature of humans to particularize their self-experience from moment to moment in order to make more intelligible the greater mystery of 'I am'. Any 'I am' statement feeds the larger narrative of simply 'I am', and the modifiers provide the content for the overarching story of the self. Identity, then, for Robinson is not rooted in the Emersonian transparency of *Nature*, but in the mundane myths, stories and statements that proceed from and give shape to the unsayable nature of the 'I am' operating behind them all. This way of viewing the self finds a literary corollary in Wallace Stevens' idea of the supreme fiction. As Franke puts it, 'the supreme fiction is the one that cannot be said or represented at all. Like a negative theologian, Stevens starts from a position of critical reflection that can no longer naively believe in the myths of the gods' (Franke 23). The supreme fiction, for Stevens, cannot be finally represented but finds its partial representation in the fictions that seek to evoke it. Stevens' supreme fiction is equivalent to Crites's notion of a 'sacred story', that is, one that inhabits the background of other fictions and is, while being always ineffable in itself, constructed and implied by these mundane stories. Writing of these sacred stories, Crites notes, 'every serious attempt to express them creates poetry. The expressions admit of great variation in detail, but no variation fully grasps the story within these diverse stories' (Hauerwas and Burrell 1997: 69). The self, then, as a supreme fiction, must, like Stevens' sun, 'bear no name, gold flourisher, but be / In the difficulty of what it is to be' (Stevens 402).[9] For Stevens, 'There was a myth before the myth began. / Venerable, articulate and complete': for Robinson there is a self that, while no doubt present in the memories and stories about the self, ultimately exceeds their explanatory reach (Stevens 405). For Stevens, the supreme fiction animates other fictions, giving them form and content, and equally for Robinson – particularly with the importance she places on the role of memory – the self is an animator of story, recollection and projection. The sun is, for Stevens, an image of his supreme fiction because, while it would blind anyone who looks at it directly, it is also the means by which anything else is seen. Robinson's writing of the self in her fiction and essays outlines a closely allied view, with the self being equally 'unseeable' but also the only means by which the world is encountered.

---

[9] Robinson also makes use of similar light imagery in her writing of Jesus' death on the cross: a historical moment that 'lives in the world not as myth or history but as a saturating light, a light so brilliant that it hides its source' (Robinson 2012: 128).

This discussion of the self and fiction invites a brief exploration of the writing of Nietzsche, a thinker engaged deeply in investigating the depths of the self and its potential fictionality. Nietzsche's views on the actual nature of the self are notoriously hard to get at, shifting and contradicting as they appear to do, but Nehemas' *Life as Literature* (1985) presents a striking reading of Nietzsche's view of the self, one that argues Nietzsche was, essentially, an essentialist. Using the eternal recurrence passage in *The Gay Science* (1882) as a foundational text, Nehemas argues that Nietzsche's doctrine of the eternal recurrence of the same is inextricably bound up with a doctrine of essentialism, for, hearing the demon's famous speech, Nietzsche only allows his readers two reactions: despair or affirmation. Nehemas does not interpret the eternal recurrence idea as a cosmological doctrine, but instead as one that implies a denial of the substantial self: 'of the view that a person is something more than the totality of its experiences and actions' (Nehemas 154). The two reactions Nietzsche permits his readers, then, imply that to affirm the eternal recurrence of one's life, it is necessarily the case that each moment of that life is essential to the self itself. As Nehemas puts is, 'no person remains beyond the totality of its experiences and actions. If any of these were different, then their subject, which is simply their sum total, would also have to be different' (Nehemas 155). Nietzsche's well-known comment, 'there is no "being" behind doing, acting, becoming; "the doer" is merely a fiction imposed on the doing – the doing is everything', appears to be a staunch denial of the objective reality of the subject (Nietzsche 1887: 29). For Nietzsche, and this is particularly emphasized in Nehemas' reading of him, a thing is the sum of its effects and activities, and this includes the human person. The self, then, in Nehemas' reading of Nietzsche, is more of a literary flourish than a thing in itself, an artistic creation rather than an immutable blunt fact. For Nietzsche, a self emerges out of an enacted unity, through a process more akin to authorial intention than a settled metaphysical state of affairs.

Robinson does not take a strictly Nietzschean line on the existence of the self. Where for the philosopher, the self is nothing more than the sum of its activities, emotions and decisions, Robinson holds a belief in something called the self that transcends its effects. She continually, in both fiction and essay, underscores the unknowability of the self which implies – despite the necessary inaccessibility – its existence. While she entertains the notion of the self as fiction, she implicitly rejects Nietzsche's notion that selfhood is something that must be attained through conscious intention. Rather, the self comes into being in Robinson's writing not through artistic shaping and choice, but as a natural fact of existence. What is enacted artistically is, for Robinson, one's interpretation of oneself. For Nietzsche, the human is more an author of his or her self, where Robinson's characters find themselves as interpreters of themselves, readers of their own text: 'we choose an utterance, a gesture. By these means we identify ourselves and, in the same moment, discover and create ourselves', a statement that reveals Robinson's belief that the self, like a text, is to be read; for in the reading of a text, meaning is discovered and it is created in an impossible-to-untangle process of exegesis and eisegesis (Robinson 2018: 103).

Eakin argues that the self is only unified by the activity of storytelling, that without the narrativization of memory and story the self would be a fragmented set of disparate happenings and facts. For Robinson this 'solution' relies on a false dichotomy between fiction and truth. Lloyd argues that 'the unified self, lying behind language as the originator of meanings, is perhaps itself just such a fiction, taking different forms throughout the history of western philosophy' (Lloyd 13). Implicit here is an equivalency between fiction and falsity, and an assumption that designating the unified self as a fiction means that it does not exist. With Robinson's assertions of the pervasive nature of subjectivity with all human experience in mind, this invites the question 'What, after all, *isn't* a fiction?' This is not to ascribe relativism to Robinson, but rather to rescue fiction from an understanding that positions it as 'the opposite of facts' and instead view it as the natural and inescapable mode in which truth emerges; for, if truth is to be grasped at all, it must emerge within the arena of subjectivity. The denigration of the notion of a unified self seems, to Robinson, to have been paralleled by the rise of literary theory, and both are developments that, to her mind, seek to delegitimize an individual's subjective encounter both with oneself and with a text:

> As a professor of literature, more or less, I have seen scholarly criticism given over to quasi-sociology, or -psychology, or -economic theory, or anthropology, taking some sort of authority from the imposition of jargon

> that is either dubious in itself, wholly inappropriate to its subject, or both. This looks to me like the abandonment of literature as such, its reduction to data to be fed into theories. It is only logical in the circumstances that the individual student's encounter with a book should be marginalised in favour of a more knowing construction of its meaning. Nothing is lost except everything that makes literature the preeminent art. (Robinson 2015: 111)

The 'meaning' of a text is not, for Robinson, to be excavated in the imposition of a theoretical perspective on it, but emerges instead in the unmediated, unqualified encounter between a human self and the text: 'reading above the level of the simplest information, is an act of great inwardness and subjectivity [...] the soul encountered itself in its response to a text, first Genesis or Matthew and then *Paradise Lost* or *Leaves of Grass*' (Robinson 1998: 9). Literary theory that makes no allowance for the subjective experience one has with a novel or a poem makes the same mistake that the positivists make with regard to the self. As Robinson argues: 'neuroscience does not know what the mind or the self is, and has made a project of talking them out of existence for the sake of its theories which exclude them' (Robinson 2015: 77). 'Theory' has, for Robinson, a tendency to impose arbitrary limitations on encounter: 'experience demands a richer vocabulary than theory can give it, for all its neologisms' (Robinson 2018: 112). In fact, Robinson's objection to both literary theory and dismissive talk of the non-existence of the self reveals just how closely allied these phenomena – the self and the text – are. Both the self and a novel, for example, demand a willing entry into subjectivity in order to be understood, for both are products of human experience and activity. In other words, claiming an objective interpretation of a novel is, for Robinson, just as absurd as claiming the self can be approached with any kind of objectivity. The self is a story and, as such, must be approached with methods more familiar to the reader of fiction than the neuroscientist or positivist philosopher. In order to 'get at' Wallace Stevens' supreme fiction, a reader must rely on the poems, symbols and stories that point to it. Despite their partiality, this is the only gateway to that which Stevens means when he writes of the supreme fiction. In precisely the same way Robinson views the self as fiction that resides behind and beyond memory. 'Narrative is not merely a literary form but a mode of phenomenological and cognitive self experience, while self – the self of autobiographical discourse –

does not necessarily precede its constitution in narrative' (Eakin 100). Eakin here makes the startling claim that the self written in an autobiography is not a report of some prior thing that exists, but may well be the creation of a self in the actual process of writing. Indeed, in Robinson's fiction and essays, the self is conceived of more as an unfolding story than it is as a static fact that is carried from one moment to the next. 'At seventy years of age, I know myself as I eventuate, as I happen', comments Robinson, noting the emergent nature of the self (Robinson 2015: 219). The narrative self may well be a 'fiction', but only insofar as the human individual experience of anything is a fiction, which is to say, a subjective encounter with another, an object, a text, an event. There is nothing true 'beyond' subjectivity, for Robinson, which is another way of saying that subjectivity is inescapable and forms the conditions in which any 'knowing' must take place. Williams makes a very useful point in this regard, one that marries well to Robinson's thinking here:

> There is no way of abstracting from the passage of time some necessary, nonrevisable and exhaustive correlation between an inside and an outside, a set of determinate, entirely 'objective' stimuli and a 'correct' reception of and relation between them. This is in no way to say that there is no truthful relation between speech and reality, or however you want to put it. The process is one of generation, not creation from nothing, and what can be said is not decided by an inner 'free' subject involved in endless self-reflection. What you can meaningfully say is contained by the given. But truthfulness unfolds – it doesn't happen all at once – and makes possible different levels of appropriating or sharing in the activity that is the world. (Williams 2005: 137)

The unfolding nature of truth Williams describes here must, for Robinson, emerge within the limitations of human subjectivity, for a notion of, as Williams puts it, a 'truthful' relation between speech and reality is unthinkable unless it proceeds from subjective human experience and the necessarily partial human speech *of* that experience. The self exists in the manner in which a text or a story may be said to exist: it requires *reading* and, by extension, *interpretation*. Memory, then, is a gateway to self in the fashion that myth is a path to the sacred story of the Bible. Memory both constitutes the self and provides access to it, in a similar way that the biblical myths coalesce to form the narrative of the Bible while also testifying to the sacred story of the Christian or Jewish *mythos* that forever eludes telling. The narrative structure of the self does not ensure its intelligibility for, as Robinson comments, 'I will never know myself, nor will anyone else know me', but it does 'fence off' the area in which the question of the self is to be rightly raised (Robinson 2015: 219). The parascience Robinson scorns in her non-fiction treats the experience of having a self to be reducible to the observable features of the brain, a mistake by her lights, as the self is 'incommensurate with the nature and potentialities of the mind' (Robinson 2015: 219). A literary quest is called for, then, precisely because the persistence of what is called the self demands a study in line with the nature of its existence. This is, in part, what Robinson executes in her novels. They are demonstrations of the pervasive nature of subjectivity and explorations of the narrative or storied self that emerges from a literary appreciation of what it means to exist in time.

'I suppose it is inevitable that I should think of a fiction as a small model of the simulacrum of reality that is given to us by sense and perception, and as a way to probe anomalies that emerge in the assumed world when it is under scrutiny' (Robinson 2015: 218). Here Robinson once again acknowledges her conviction that subjectivity goes 'all the way down', as it were, and her use of 'fiction' here blurs any clear boundaries between literature and life. Indeed, there are no simple distinctions to be made between the two on the grounds that one is 'real' and the other is 'false'. We only know what we know and for Robinson it is too simplistic to suppose what we see and touch is the world as it really is. Like an apophatic theologian, Robinson is keenly aware of both the limits of language and of our empirical experience and is, by extension, doubly attentive to the unknowable reality that exceeds our perception and expression. It is in this sense, then, that the reading of fiction is an activity that mirrors the Ordinary human experience of the world much more closely than the objectivity-seeking activities of the scientists Robinson critiques. A text is encountered, like the world and the self, through subjective lenses, and with a limited capacity for any kind of objectivity; and, in lieu of being able to transcend our brains and think outside of thought itself, reading and interpretation become inevitable. 'I take the Jamesian view, that what we know about anything is determined by the way we encounter it, and therefore we should never assume that our knowledge is more than partial', she notes: taking her at her word here implies a total embrace of the pervasive nature of subjectivity (Robinson 2015: 229).

Conclusion: On time and change

At the close of *Lila*, Ames writes his wife a letter, finally expressing in full his response to her initial theological question of 'why things happen the way they do'. The model of time given voice to here is one that in no way simplifies the notion of causation. 'Things happen for reasons that are hidden from us, utterly hidden for as long as we think they must proceed from what has come before, our guilt or our deserving, rather than going to us from a future that God in his freedom offers us', he writes (Robinson 2014: 222). For Ames, it is both too simple and too untrue of experience to say that what has happened in the past is the necessary cause of what is happening in the present. Of course, there is a causal relationship between past and present, present and future, but the human understanding of any past event is partial to such an extent that the reach of its explanatory power is severely limited. 'You really can't account for what happens by what has happened in the past, as you understand it anyway, which may be very different from the past itself. If there is such a thing', he notes, voicing a concern about the interpretation of the past close to Robinson's own expressions in her essays (Robinson 2014: 222–3). Ames, like Robinson, does not believe an objective account of history is possible, and in the absence of an exhaustive factual knowledge of the past, the present exists, not as a product of the remembered past, but as a fundamental mystery. For Ames, the extra ingredient in causation that a purely rationalist world view would rule out is, of course, the will and character of God. As Chapter 2 noted, Ames has a real sense and appreciation of the apophatic nature of the divine, so he invokes 'God' in the question of 'why things happen the way they do', not to provide an answer but to explain why the question is there in the first place. Indeed, Lila's question holds already implicit within it the suggestion that the unfolding of a life and of history is not explainable simply by pointing to a long chain of cause and effect. Lila, Ames and Robinson are of one mind when it comes to the mysterious nature of the present and to the ineffable providence that seems to guide the movement of time. Robinson writes,

> The absolute and momentary present in which we all live might seem to be set apart by the slightest, most porous membrane from the moment that precedes or follows it. But this way of thinking excludes the fact that moments can differ in every property, and as they differ they change our experience of time. Only when we are threatened with an astonishment of some sort, a threat or an insight, are we inclined to realise that a moment is potentially capacious and transformative, and that we are subject to time far otherwise than in the most predictable of events, our mortality. (Robinson 2015: 90)

Ames' invocation of God in his letter gives him the freedom to expect more from the passage of time than what the past could reasonably be thought to generate. For Ames, Lila herself is an example of the ultimately mysterious but unmistakeable grace of God operating from beyond time, within time; and for Robinson, the surprising capaciousness of a single moment is an experiential truth she roots in the grace of God.

With this in mind, then, Lila's most important contribution to Robinson's written theology is her simple statement that brings to a close the heated predestination conversation in *Gilead* and *Home*: 'A person can change, everything can change' (Robinson 2004: 174; 2008: 238). In a world in which time is a given, change becomes the vehicle of grace. As Robinson describes, 'the great given, the medium of all gain and loss, the medium with which change is possible and inevitable and constantly persists through endless transformations, the medium of act, accident, and thought, disruption and coherency, is time' (Robinson 2015: 89). Where contingency and flux present real philosophical challenges for our conceptions of stable, unified selves, the inevitability of change also opens up the possibility of substantive disruptions ushered in by a grace that eludes sense and definition. It is a truth of existence that change can bring disaster but, as Robinson notes, it also implies that time itself can reconfigure the fragments of a life in new, more satisfying and surprising ways. In an interview, asked about the 'resurrection of the Ordinary', Robinson notes:

> When the ordinary is resurrected what that means is that the world is putting itself together in what she (Sylvia) finds a comprehensible experience, even

though she doesn't comprehend it. That's a *given*, that happens. The world of most mental experience heals itself after amazing things; it restores the ordinary. The mark of the divine presence in the world, which is pervasive although I don't understand its pervasiveness, is that things that are in themselves absolutely arbitrary, like the fact that we can live in the world as if we understand it. (Chapter 5)

Here Robinson is clear that, while time necessarily brings destruction and tragedy, it also implies the possibilities of reconstitution and reassembly, or, in gospel terms, where death is experienced, there is always the promise of resurrection.

The God revealed in and through myth is ultimately the God who ensures the story of the self is held together through time. As Ames says at the close of *Lila*, 'when I say that much the greater part of our existence is unknowable by us because it rests with God, who is unknowable, I acknowledge His grace in allowing us to feel that we know any slightest part of it' (Robinson 2015: 223). For the minister, the very notion of selfhood is itself a grace thrown over the flux of time, and the singularity implied by 'you' or 'I' is a source of amazement for him. That the self is formed and sustained by the passing of time underscores the notion that, like a narrative, the self relies on the possibility and inevitability of change for its existence. Change is indeed necessary in a storied world, and this is a truth Lila holds close:

Somehow there was always the notion that one day would lead to the next, mild today meant mild tomorrow, a sunny morning meant a decent afternoon. And then winter would take over everything before you knew what was happening. It would be like the world after sleep, a surprise and no surprise. (Robinson 2015: 156)

Lila has, above all, a faith in time to disrupt the given, and change is the redemptive force in Lila's life. The great storms that rise up in existence, as Lila often records, totally alter the landscape of the natural world, and as an image of trauma, delight or surprise, these storms have the power to drastically change the life of an individual. For Lila, Doll's rescue of her felt like being carried off by the wind, and her capacity to think of change in this poetic mode makes clear why she finds a thinking partner in the book of Ezekiel. As Ames notes, Ezekiel, 'is full of poetry. Even more than the rest of the Bible. Poetry and parables and visions' (Robinson 2015: 128). Lila is attracted to the text because, as a natural theologian[10] she sees bizarre imagery that is adequate to her unsheltered experience of the world: 'strange as it was, there was something to it. Well, there was the strangeness of it' (Robinson 2015: 74).

At the close of the novel, Lila reflects on the absurdity of her initial question of 'why things happen the way they do' and, voicing a thought with Nietzschean resonances, she thinks, 'things happen the way they do. What a foolish question. In a song a note follows the one before because it is that song and not another one' (Robinson 2015: 259). Here Lila equates time, self and causality with the melodic structure of a song. While on the surface this appears to embrace a kind of meticulous providence – the music score of a life being written by a divine composer – this would run contrary to Robinson's emphasis elsewhere on human freedom. The invocation of a song does not necessarily imply a strict, prewritten melody. A classical pianist may well be limited to the notes on a page, but for a jazz musician, Lila's statement could be read as an embrace of improvisation and a creative engagement in flux and change. In a jazz tune, for example, a great deal of unplanned improvisation is integral to the beauty of the song itself and Lila's notion of the inevitability of one note following the next could well be affirmed by both a classical musician and a jazz player, if for very different reasons. In truth, Lila's statement does not shed much light on her conception of time and causality, but instead suggests a Robinsonian conviction of the sort that posits aesthetics over morality as the only lens by which a life can viewed rightly. Nehemas' interpretation of Nietzsche emphasizes the literary nature of Nietzsche's conception of self and the 'styling' of self one must engage with in order to become an authentic individual. Lila's image of a song implies an aesthetic appreciation for the time-bound self, too: an interpretation that emphasizes the grace by which an individual moves through the world. This is a view that leaves the unanswerable questions of providence and causality behind as important issues, but

---

[10] Natural as in a theologian who begins with nature, and also a natural in that she cannot help but raise theological questions.

ultimately secondary to the pragmatic endeavours of living a life well. As noted in Chapter 3, Robinson firmly believes that if God is the judge of humanity, it would be peculiar for God to be fixated on the weakness and sinfulness of his creation rather than the beauty of what has been made. Ames says as much in *Gilead*, noting that 'Calvin says somewhere that each of us is an actor on a stage and God is the audience', a metaphor that interests him, 'because it makes us artists of our behaviour, and the reaction of God to us might be thought of as aesthetic rather than morally judgmental in the ordinary sense' (Robinson 2004: 141–2). God, for both Robinson and Ames, is more interested in beauty than in sin, more concerned with the aesthetic quality of a life well lived than in its inevitable moments of frailty.

This is a theological conviction Robinson feels the truth of in her writing of fiction. She notes in *What Are We Doing Here?* that as an author of novels she has an aesthetic sense of her characters, that they possess a certain 'musicality' against which her own inventions for them can be sounded out as authentic:

> Practically speaking, when I am writing I tend to think of a character as having a palette or a music. An aesthetic, in other words. While this is in some ways constraining, it establishes the limits within which substantive invention is possible and, more to the point, within which variation is meaningful. (Robinson 2018: 104)

This gives the life of a character a sense of inevitability that is not reducible to predictability. In the same way a composer establishes a key centre for a piece of music, Robinson has a foundational sense of a character's 'self'. In music, the key of the song provides the logic for what happens in the course of the piece. Indeed variations are only intelligible to listeners if the song already has a foundational logic or structure, as it is impossible to differentiate meaningfully between separate instances of chaos within a formless set of noises. The whole idea of a key change, too, is only really intelligible if a key has been previously established. In this way, then, a song proceeds under its own logic, varying and changing under the limitations of that logic. Robinson reveals her own sense of inevitability as she writes a character or reads a well-written one. For example, she states: '[a] great part of the pleasure of reading Dickens comes from the strange compound of utter originality and perfect inevitability invested in his best characters. After one or two brilliant details, every subsequent choice is disciplined by them' (Robinson 2018: 106). So it is from within the paradox of freedom in constraint that Robinson writes her characters; by listening to the musicality of a character, Robinson suggests she writes under the discipline of an aesthetic constraint, one in which a wrong authorial choice 'is an inaudible equivalent of a clang or a clunk' (Robinson 2018: 104).

Furthermore, Robinson's characterization, as with every aspect of her written work, emerges from a theological foundation. Asked about the relation between her fiction writing and her own theology, she comments:

> I think I start from a theological premise, or a complex of theological premises, and I'm glad I do. If you decide that people are very mysterious and you can watch them and respond to them and make aesthetic judgements on the basis of what they say and what they do, then you are very free in not over-determining them in any way. I do think that is the theological basis of my strategies of characterisation. (Chapter 5)

That character freedom emerges as a central concern of Robinson's writing is indicative of her theology as a whole, and the mystery she encounters as inherent to the process of writing a character is similar to her conviction of the utter unknowability of the self. Indeed, the self is presented in Robinson's writing as Ordinary, as an excessively meaningful phenomenon that can never be exhausted by any means of knowing. The greater part of the human self, for Robinson, will always remain hidden and utterly ineffable, and can only really be glimpsed through the Ordinary acts of particularity she details in her fiction. It is because the self is so shrouded in utter mystery that Robinson creates characters so entranced by the strangeness of their own existence. 'We remain unknown to ourselves', Nietzsche writes famously, and, despite her staunch opposition to Nietzsche's thought, Robinson can fully endorse this, his most haunting statement (Nietzsche 1996: 3). Ruth struggles throughout *Housekeeping* with her own transparency, with not understanding who or what she is, and Ames discovers just how much of his history, his motives and, by extension, his *self* he has repressed, finishing *Gilead* as a man conscious of his own lack of self-knowledge, convicted of his own moral blindness, and resigned to his imminent death.

By emphasizing the unknowability of the self, Robinson does not embrace a pessimistic denial of human freedom, but an open-hearted appraisal of the complexity of existence. Granting incomprehensibility its rightful place in theological thinking, she is freed up, as it were, to offer mystery a place at the table. Never reducing the self to character, emotion, memory or narrative, Robinson nonetheless demonstrates how the self can be seen, if only in partial glimpses, in and through these Ordinary phenomena. Just as divine grace is traced in quotidian acts of simple hospitality, the self is only truly suggested by the narratives of memory and the poetry and images these conjure. Contemporary science is a dwelling not roomy enough for Robinson's conception of self and, until the modern conversation catches up with her writing of the self and its myths, she is perfectly content to explore the implications of her own theology in both essay and novel.

Reflections on the Ordinary

An interview with Marilynne Robinson

The following interview took place on 4 November 2017 in Dey House, at the Iowa Writer's Workshop in Iowa City.

Andrew Cunning: The word 'Ordinary' seems so important to your work, and the more I read your fiction, the more it stands out as a significant term. Your novels focus on profoundly Ordinary things: family, ageing, light, water, loss, language, time and the natural world. I think this would be a good place to start our conversation. Where does your mind go when you hear the word 'Ordinary', and what is behind your conscious decision to write novels so attentive to the Ordinary?

Marilynne Robinson: I think the Ordinary is very mysterious. I think the Ordinary, given a reasonable span of time, might also be called the ephemeral. It presents itself as if it were not, as something that allows itself to be taken for granted, when nothing is finally granted. There's a sort of metaphysical mystery, I think, because the Ordinary can be so overlooked, even though it's basically the fabric of life. It is so important that it has to be very meaningful and at the same time so sort of self-effacing in a way that it is so seldom put into the model of reality from which people extrapolate statements about reality.

Cunning: It seems that it is overlooked, yet the more attention that is paid to it the more it seems to open up. In your fiction there is the sense that the Ordinary is inexhaustible.

Robinson: I feel that way, certainly.

Cunning: You've said before that our attention will never go unrewarded and that reality is available to us to the extent to which we are present to it. Ames seems so capable of presentness and I can't help read *Gilead* without Emerson in mind. Is he in the background in your attention to the Ordinary?

Robinson: Yes. Emerson had a huge impact on me when I first seriously read him, in high school and in college. He's just a very beautiful articulator of very essential things.

Cunning: There seems to be in your work, an exceeding quality to the Ordinary. Ames finds the Ordinary so beautiful at one point that he feels it has to be a metaphor for something. It almost seems ironic to call anything Ordinary when, if it is paid the slightest bit of attention, it begins to hint towards something more.

Robinson: Yes, and also, you can tell that I do read a lot of the new cosmologies in so far as they are available to my understanding, and it makes me so aware of the utter strangeness of the earth. People try to find things that are analogous – 'well that planetoid has a moon', or something like that – but basically there is nothing like the earth. We haven't seen anything that has indicated anything like it; this little atmosphere that makes all sorts of things possible, and Ordinary. If you look at the earth relative to the realty it swims through, everything about it is extraordinary. Everything. And the fact that we can know that to the extent to which we do now, and forget it as absolutely as we do, is just amazing to me.

Cunning: Lila reflects, 'What isn't strange, after all.' That anything should be strange at all is interesting, because what are we comparing it to? The things we find strange are what we are immersed in. Is strangeness the product of attention?

Robinson: Yes, I would say so. Then again, from what perspective strange? As you say, we are immersed in it and have no way of making an account of it except in its terms, yet at the same time it continually surprises us, continuously seems to present itself as alien. It is very interesting.

Cunning: It's an uncanny experience, because nothing should be strange because it is all we know, yet there are glimmers of ultimate strangeness.

Robinson: Exactly. People always talk as if we were not made of atoms.

Cunning: You used the word metaphysical a moment ago, and I wonder how it might situate itself in a discussion of the Ordinary, how transcendence fits into your vision of it.

Robinson: I know the Americans like Emerson and his school were called Transcendentalists, but they didn't like that word – it was picked up out of Germany and imposed on them as the nearest analogy. I think if we understood things properly we would not use the word 'transcendence'. The immanent should not be cut off from anything that implies a larger reality at any scale.

Cunning: Yes, and that comes through strongly in *The Givenness of Things*. There you devote a lot of time to a discussion of how Christ is rooted in the physical, folded into the fabric of what we know rather than something beyond or 'other'.

Robinson: Exactly, and it seems to me as if the Bible is very straightforward about that.

Cunning: I'd like to ask you about the 'resurrection of the Ordinary' passage in *Housekeeping*. It is a beautiful phrase and I wonder if this idea requires God, or, in other words, if the resurrection of the Ordinary is necessarily theological.

Robinson: When the Ordinary is resurrected, what that means is that the world is putting itself together in what she (Sylvia) finds a comprehensible experience, even though she doesn't comprehend it. That's a *given*, that happens. The world of most mental experience heals itself after amazing things;

it restores the Ordinary. The mark of the divine presence in the world, which is pervasive although I don't understand its pervasiveness, is that things that are in themselves absolutely arbitrary, like the fact that we can live in the world as if we understand it. Those things are part of the givenness, part of the 'let there be', and so to me certainly imply God, but I don't like to say prescriptive things about God because I know I would be wrong.

Cunning: If even the most Ordinary things exceed our abilities of expression, theological language can get into real difficulty as it tries to express something more. Ames says that he has wandered out to the limits of his understanding many times and there is the sense in *Gilead* that all language is partial. To what extent does theology need to make allowances for the partiality of language and how can it do this?

Robinson: I think in all serious theology there is a granting of the apophatic as a frontier which one does not pass, at the same time that in that very fact there is an enormous acknowledgement.

Cunning: I don't see in your work a hugely strong apophatic impulse in the sense that 'nothing meaningful can be said of God'. Ames is a minister, after all, and has to say something. There is a real distinction preserved in your work between a person's experience and their ability to speak of it, between a person's subjectivity and his or her articulacy.

Robinson: Yes, there is a profound difference there. In the best circumstances that makes people more interested in their subjective experiences. They are, in that wordless way, articulate to themselves. I think there has been a terrible tendency lately to take people at their word, or as they present themselves. People are persuaded that that is an appropriate understanding but, with a little attention, inner life is vastly richer than we can indicate.

Cunning: Yes, and there also seems to be the assumption in public discourse that people won't be interested beyond the most basic facts – which isn't how you treat your readers – but there seems to be such a collapse in faith in people's ability to understand things.

Robinson: I think that's so true. On the one hand there are these cheap tactics for manipulating public opinion but then at the same time, a lot of what is treated as intellectual discourse is actually reinforcing the same thing, and that is very discouraging. They ought to be tending away from each other, not towards each other.

Cunning: Going from the writing of Emerson to the speeches of current politicians, there seems to be such a collapse in language.

Robinson: Oh there is. We thought we knew what collapse was and then along came Donald Trump.

Cunning: Ames writes that it is religious experience that authenticates religious belief. Your work seems to do two key things in this regard. First, it is a demonstration of the authentication of religious belief by experience, and second, it demonstrates the necessity of art itself to hold something of the complexity of that experience.

Robinson: Globally, people's highest art tends to be religious. Art is the vocabulary beyond vocabulary. There is an overplus of experience in the consciousness of a religious person that tends to re-express itself as a sense of the beautiful. I read old theologies, not just Calvin, and the frequency with which beauty comes up – the idea that God is manifest in the 'glory of Creation' – often in relation to light or colour or something like that. I think it is interesting to see what has ebbed out of the language along with religious culture, and I think one of them is a profound notion of what beauty is.

Cunning: And beauty is an experience – it isn't something argued towards. This is true about your work. It isn't arguing for a position but rather portraying a vision, an aesthetic more than an argument. You've said this about Calvin, that it is his aesthetic vision that interests you. It is experience, then, not intellectual assent that is central to faith.

Robinson: It is also not being hit by a bolt of lightning. It is being attentive to the givenness.

Cunning: I'd like to ask you about that blessing scene at the end of *Gilead*. There seems to be a chasm fixed between Jack and Ames across which words do not seem to cross, but the blessing provides the site of encounter they had been seeking throughout the text. How do you think about blessing in relation to language?

Robinson: I'm very interested in blessing as a phenomenon because I don't understand it particularly. It seems to me that I can see the reality of it – people love a good benediction, you know? – but at the same time our cultures have not prepared us to be articulate about what actually passes, if it can even be spoken of. But it is human to human in a very profound way and it is a huge assumption of a kind of power that we normally don't acknowledge in ourselves, the idea that you can bless. When a situation is presented to us, we have the alternative of brushing it off or of using it as a moment in which you bless someone. A young Mormon fellow said to me that he was so happy to think that when he bathed his children he was blessing them. It wasn't that I told him that but that I helped him realize that it was going on anyway. I think that is a very powerful current in experience that is not very often acknowledged. When John Ames blesses Jack he is finally just saying, 'Whoever you are, you are my son', feeling all the love old Boughton has invested in him. It is a sort of acknowledgement that beyond all difficulties there is this power that we have – and to receive is another power, as the theologians are always saying.

Cunning: Right at the beginning of the novel you allude to Jacob and the Angel and it strikes me that not only do they share initials with Jack and Ames, but the story itself is an interesting mirroring of the novel. Both sets of characters wrestle, one in language, the other in reality and both stories end with a meaningful touch. *Gilead* doesn't seem to allow its reader to skip over the importance of touch, as language has been so problematic up to that point.

Robinson: Of course I'm dealing with middle-Western Protestants here, who may use touch more selectively than the average human being. But when it occurs I think it is quite highly defined and it really is crossing a space when Ames blesses Jack.

Cunning: Levinas has the idea that transcendence emerges out of the relation between self and other, and Jack, it seems, truly is 'other' to Ames, totally transcending his mastery. The claim of the human face, important to both Ames and Levinas, seems important here too. Is this the moment that Ames and Jack transcend their own ego or shame or pride, and are able to meet?

Robinson: I don't know how finally they've met. I think Jack is a mystery to himself. I don't think people understand each other; I think they appraise each other – I don't mean a cold word by that – the other's sincerity, the beauty of what you see of their inwardness. If Ames and Jack were in a room together for one hundred years they would not understand each other. The question is 'do I bless you?'

Cunning: The unknowability of the other is mirrored by the unknowability of the self. In *Housekeeping*, Ruth spends a great deal of time inwardly and, to my mind, doesn't reach too many conclusions about who or what she is.

Robinson: What you do is to appreciate the mystery, I think. You don't try to solve it.

Cunning: Is blessing 'doing something' in the face of mystery?

Robinson: Yes, and acknowledging it as a sacred mystery. Jacob and the Angel.

Cunning: I'd like to ask you about grace. In *The Givenness of Things*, you talk of grace as 'restoration' and 'return' but are also clear that grace itself will never submit to final definitions. With Shakespeare in mind you write, 'grace is grace, how might this be staged?', and I wonder is this the best way to investigate what grace might be – to stage it?

Robinson: Well it's hard to say in theory because we're talking about Shakespeare. There's that wonderful little speech in *The Tempest* in which Prospero says: 'my ending is despair, unless I be relieved by prayer which pierces so that it assaults mercy itself and frees all faults'. That final absolute forgetfulness of anything that would fall under the category of fault which is very beautiful. No one could say it more powerfully and he [Shakespeare] has clearly been reading his theology – he is clearly alert to what the issues were in his time. I think theology has an important place in culture. People under the most amazing duress – writing theology. It is an important art that we tend to have lost and like anything else it has its best and worst, even within a single text; but at its best it is invaluable. I would like to see a recovery of real theology, not this sort of self-protective pseudo-theology we see so much of.

Cunning: Yes, so much theology now seems so defensive. As Ames puts it, 'nothing true of God can be said from a posture of defence.' Apologetics went through the roof over the past couple of decades thanks to Dawkins, but it seems to me that it went down totally the wrong path.

Robinson: Exactly. It conceded so much to Dawkins, totally inappropriate concessions. And you read this theology that is shying away from the implications of Dawkinsian science and the cure would be to read some science. It just exasperates me to death and I think people are so intimidated by it that they don't look at it and are taken in by anything.

Cunning: What seems to have happened is that, under the assumption that the faith was under attack, the response was equally simplistic to the supposed attack. As you say, the cure for bad science is science, not bad theology.

Robinson: Exactly.

Cunning: Going back to Shakespeare and grace, I find it hard not to take your own question of how grace might be staged, and apply it to you. It does seem to me that grace is being staged consistently in your novels. To your mind is narrative/fiction/poetry perhaps the best environment for the staging of grace than philosophy or theology?

Robinson: Yes. Well the core text is the Bible, in terms of staging: 'You meant it for evil but God meant it for good.' Even the story of Jacob and the Angel which is so equivocal in the terms of 'yes you are blessed, yes you are lamed'. The Bible has this enormous persistence through time because it deals precisely in this staging. There is a little theology in Paul that he probably invented for our purposes, but even that is the drama of the address to the community, proposing all sorts of counter-intuitive things.

Cunning: There is something about narrative – it holds more than the details of the event it is reporting about. Kierkegaard has the notion that truth is something that emerges through experience, not something intellectual or argued towards and I feel this connects well to your thinking. When you think of a word like 'truth', would it be fair to say that it isn't a final premise or the aim of an argument but more to do with recognition?

Robinson: I think that's true. The absolute anchor for me, and this probably marks me as a Calvinist, is the image of God in human beings, without exception. This is a standard to which we have absolutely fallen short of recognizing but it is a given, it is an arbitrary condition. It is the starting place for all truth and in that sense the word 'truth' is very meaningful to me.

Cunning: In *The Givenness of Things* you say that predestination is so complex, so unknowable and mysterious that the only sensible thing to do would be to put the question aside. Yet *Home* takes the issue up. My own reading of that novel doesn't allow for any state of affairs in which grace doesn't win out finally and the text certainly complicates any binary notions of Christian and non-Christian, saved and unsaved.

Robinson: As my primary character, of course, I have this stalwartly religious – in the mainline sense of the word – figure. What I've been interested in doing in both *Home* and *Lila* is complicating the sense of what the religious is. I'm very glad to have Ames there and I'm not saying he's a kind of hypocrite or some unconscious pietist or something, but at the same time, using him as a sort of anchor, I can raise questions he wouldn't respect. In *Home* there are ways in which Jack is the righteous man and that's very important to the book.

Cunning: I do love the irony of Jack, the text's unbeliever, in some ways being the most Christian character of the book. Reading *Home* alongside *The Givenness of Things*, there are some profound correlations between what you say of Jesus and how you write Jack.

Robinson: I intended that.

Cunning: Would it be fair to say that grace is central and foundational to your theology?

Robinson: Yes, I think it is.

Cunning: It seems almost a lens by which things are seen, or a test things must pass before they get written.

Robinson: I know this is a crude simplification, but if you imagine a sort of double vision where there is the world as you see it, and the world as God sees it. Everything tells you that they are not the same thing at all no matter what you bring to bear on it. Trying to imagine the second perspective is interesting to me and the only way I can even begin to address that is the concept of grace, which is truly transformative. It makes the rules; and the fact that we never understand the rules does not alter that fact.

Cunning: I guess this links back to our earlier discussion, that it is attention that is crucial. For example, while Sylvia didn't expect her 'resurrection of the ordinary', there is the sense that it doesn't happen if she hasn't been present enough to experience it. Are there moments in which the two ways of looking at the world become one? Ames, for instance, seems to see and experience things that truly satisfy him theologically.

Robinson: Yes I think so, although I wouldn't know how to articulate that other than through fiction. The fact that our sense of the world can heal itself, like when I talk of an image of water coming back together. That is a given, a grace. I think that people are often surprised that they can be emotionally restored, spontaneously, over time, after something that they thought was almost not survivable. The fact that we are made that way, that among all the things that are amazing about us, our perception and so on, there is this self-healing quality in most people's experience.

Cunning: And even in the course of an Ordinary day there seems to be, in your fiction, the possibility for moments of immense transformative potential. It may not sound very Calvininst of me if I were to say that we 'allow grace to happen', but it does sometimes appear that perception and attentiveness are key here.

Robinson: Well, they mystify, these theologians, over the fact that people go from having no religious sensibility, apparently, to having a profound religious sensitivity. They come up with terms like 'prevenient grace', the notion that God is active in the creation of your predisposition before you are aware of it yourself. One thing that marks me as a Calvinist is that I do assume that in all sorts of ways God is continually active and one of them is an attentiveness to minds.

Cunning: Where does your conception of grace come from?

Robinson: It's biblical, it comes from the theology I read, it is a factor in experience. For one thing, I've lived long enough to have had some of those experiences where you think everything has fallen apart and then you discover it is reconfigured in a way that is much more interesting than the place where you began. I don't know how to explain it except that there is a kind of benevolence and an intention behind things where there seems to be nothing of the kind. I do think that grace can be tested, in this sense: that we are capable of it and it's very easy to feel the qualitative difference, whether you are the one who acts or the one who is blessed.

Cunning: So often what passes for grace between individuals is economic – 'I do this for you and you'll do this for me'. Divine grace in your work is profoundly uneconomic in that sense. There is no notion of deserving or underserving and it can never be repaid.

Robinson: Yes exactly. Except that it is very much repaid in the fact that it makes these wonderful qualitative changes in the life that you experience.

Cunning: There is the sense in your work that the inability to forgive someone is usually due to a lack of appreciation of the complexity of the other person. Jack, for instance. The more we see of him, the more inevitable forgiveness becomes. Writing three novels about the same place and same group of characters seems in this sense to be a kind of experiment in grace.

Robinson: Yes, I think so.

Cunning: I'd like to ask you about time. *Lila* and *Gilead* are punctuated by memory and each time a memory arises it is slightly altered. These novels seem to be celebrations of the subjective nature of memory and a demonstration of how memory functions – always in the service of meaning rather than 'truth', in the narrow, positivist sense.

Robinson: Yes. I think anyone conscious of their own consciousness knows the meaning of memory can be transformed in light of present experience. Memory is a sort of companion, in the sense that you can rarely have an experience that isn't one way or another through the lens of memory. It's how we know. If you have a mistaken memory, one that accuses someone, then in any present time you can respond to a reality that doesn't actually exist. It is something about the interweaving of memory and present experience, which I think is continuous.

Cunning: Yes, and that is very much a part of *Housekeeping* too. Ruth at one point comments that prophecy is 'brilliant memory', and there is the implication that it is very hard to imagine a future without projecting it through the lens of what has already happened. In *The Givenness of Things* you say some very interesting things about myth and it seems to me there are interesting correlations between myth and memory. Both are more revealing about the people doing the remembering than the events themselves.

Robinson: Yes, I think that's important.

Cunning: Ruth at one point says 'All this is fact. Fact explains nothing. On the contrary, it is fact that requires explanation', which connects well with memory, as I think a list of facts about an event would not necessarily communicate what happened.

Robinson: Exactly, and besides that, facts are these monumental things we live with. We are completely surrounded by these monolithic things, usually provided by the culture we are in. Facts are a cousin to the Ordinary, in that we don't understand them either.

Cunning: Myth seems necessary to preserve the meaning of what it was to experience an event. Whether it be the Exodus or Fall or when Ames shares communion with his father. Memory and myth seem to allow for shifting interpretation.

Robinson: Yes, you're right. One of the things that's amazing to me is the positivist notion of what the Creation narrative is about. When did that start? The eighteenth century I suppose. You can't find anything but myth in antiquity, that's how they expressed important ideas. It is absolutely naive to imply that standards that did not exist on earth at the time should be applied to these narratives. This is another area in which people who have become defensive about religion have gone completely off the rails, acting as if they are defending positive statements. It is ridiculous.

Cunning: They are fighting a war on the wrong turf.

Robinson: Exactly, and the posture of intellectual superiority that comes from making this huge mistake.

Cunning: Yes, and the word 'myth' has become a dismissive term when, in fact, it is a genre term.

Robinson: Exactly. Civilizations organized themselves around these myths. If they said 'sometimes there are floods around the Tigress and the Euphrates', they wouldn't have written it down, you know?

Cunning: Yes, I don't know why the Genesis question has become a scientific one when it is a literary question.

Robinson: Exactly.

Cunning: Your characters seem so conscious of time. Ruth hates waiting, Ames is aware of time running out and Lila lives most of her life immersed in the changing seasons. I wonder how you think of the self in relation to time, as it does seem absurd that the letter 'I' can be said to refer to the same thing through the persistence of time.

Robinson: Exactly. Lots of people have noticed that, I think Maimonides was one of them, contemporary physicists say similar things. There is no explanation for it physically – your brain really is a different collection of cells over time. Identity is one of those intractable mysteries and I expect it to remain so. It has led people to say things like 'There is no self', because there is no way of accounting for the fact that I have a self that is not highly mistakable for other selves, and I think the same is true for everyone else. Identity, it's sort of like the body's loyalty to itself, the fact that it will mend and compensate. I was very taken with the word *entelechy*. For my purposes identity means there is an arc of self-consistency and this is the self. The end is in the beginning, or something like that, in some very important sense. If that is true then what I am saying could be dismissed as teleology, but I think we have to look at a lot of things we have dismissed and realize the basic fabric of reality is a much more complex thing than people have acted on.

Cunning: I don't understand why people rush in with statements like 'There is no self.' On what evidence? It seems too early.

Robinson: Exactly, it is just bizarre. Well they make generalizations about what our motives are and they are always uninterestingly about self-interest. I just read an article that said white women make their political decisions in light of the fact that their life expectancy is particularly long and therefore have to think of this lingering twilight that confronts them. I've been a white woman for a lot of years now and I've never heard anyone speak in anything that remotely acknowledges such considerations.

Cunning: This kind of language can learn from theology, to play down certainty. The history of science is the history of being proved wrong, there is always something waiting to show you you've made a mistake.

Robinson: Exactly. It is absolutely essential. We shed error, and we have to be willing to. People are so locked into these scientific statements as if they were metaphysical statements. They talk about the Ptolemaic universe as if it were theology contaminating science when it is anti-theology contaminating science, and it is no more desirable.

Cunning: To finish, I'd like to ask you about your theology and writing and the relation between the two. I'm not a novelist so I am outside the process and experience of what it must be like. Writing a novel, exploring a character, writing from various perspectives – is this theological revealing as an activity?

Robinson: I think I start from a theological premise, or a complex of theological premises, and I'm glad I do. If you decide that people are very mysterious and you can watch them and respond to them and make aesthetic judgements on the basis of what they say and what they do, then you are very free in not over-determining them in any way. I do think that is the theological basis of my strategies of characterization.

Cunning: Does that relation between theology and writing work both ways? For instance, do you find out things you didn't know you knew while writing?

Robinson: Yes. I've been interested in theology for as long as I've known there was theology. It is an absolute habit of mine to make my characters into theologians, I realize that. Every one of them.

References

Arendt, Hannah. 1971. *The Life of the Mind*. New York: Harcourt Inc.
Aronociwz, Annette. 2017. 'Marilynne Robinson, Gilead, and the Battle for the Soul.' *Perichoresis* 15, no. 2: 41–58. https://doi.org/10.1515/perc-2017-0009.
Assmann, Jan. 2001. *The Search for God in Ancient Egypt*. New York. Cornell University Press.
Bailey, Lisa M. Siefker. 2010. 'Fraught with Fire: Race and Theology in Marilynne Robinson's Gilead.' *Christianity And Literature* no. 2: 265–80. https://doi.org/10.1177/014833311005900210.
Barthes, Roland. 1972. *Mythologies*. Translated by Annette Lavers. London: Vintage.
Barthes, Roland. 1993. *Camera Lucida*. Translated by Richard Howard. London: Vintage.
Batstone, David, Eduardo Mendieta, Lois Ann Lorentzen and Dwight N. Hopkins. 1997. *Liberation Theologies, Postmodernity, and the Americas*. London: Routledge.
Benjamin, Walter. 1936. 'The Storyteller: Reflections on the Work of Nikolai Leskov.' http://ada.evergreen.edu/~arunc/texts/frankfurt/storyteller.pdf.
Bennett, Bridget. 2016. 'Roundtable Discussion on Marilynne Robinson.' *Marilynne Robinson Symposium*. 10/06/2016. 98mins. https://robinsonsymposium.wordpress.com.
Bernasconi, Robert and David Wood, eds. 1988. *The Provocation of Levinas: Rethinking the Other*. London: Routledge.
Bloom, Harold, ed. 2006. *American Religious Poems: An Anthology*. New York: Library of America.
Boer, Roland. 2009. 'John Calvin and the Paradox of Grace.' *Colloquium* 41, no. 1: 22–40.
Bonhoeffer, Dietrich. 1948. *The Cost of Discipleship*. London: SCM Press.
Bosman, Hendrik L. 2014. 'The Exodus as Negotiation of Identity and Human Dignity between Memory and Myth.' *Theological Studies* 70, no. 1: 1–6. https://doi.org/10.4102/hts.v70i1.2709.
Brueggemann, Walter. 1978. *The Prophetic Imagination*. Minneapolis: Augsburg Fortress.
Bultmann, Rudolf. 1955. *History and Eschatology*. Edinburgh: Edinburgh University Press.

Calvin, John. 1965. *Commentary on Genesis*. London: The Banner of Truth Trust.
Calvin, John. 2008. *Institutes of the Christian Religion*. Massachusetts: Hendrickson Publishers, Inc.
Caputo, John. 2006. *The Weakness of God*. Bloomington: Indiana University Press.
Caputo, John. 2013. *Truth*. London: Penguin.
Caruth, Cathy. 1996. *Unclaimed Experience*. Baltimore: John Hopkins University Press.
Cavell, Stanley. 1972. *Senses of Walden*. Chicago: University of Chicago Press.
Caver, Christine. 1996. '"Nothing Left To Lose": Housekeeping's Strange Freedoms.' *American Literature* 68, no. 1: 111–37. https://doi.org/10.2307/2927543.
Chodat, Robert. 2016. 'That Horeb, That Kansas: Evolution and the Modernity of Marilynne Robinson.' *American Literary History* 28, no. 2: 328–36. Project MUSE.
Coiffi, Frank. 1998. *Freud and the Question of Pseudoscience*. Chicago: Carus Publishing Company.
Cone, James. 1970. *A Black Theology of Liberation*. New York: Orbis Books.
Cummings, Ryan P. 2009. 'Contrasts and Fragments: An Exploration of James Cone's Theological Methodology.' *Anglican Theological Review* 91, no. 395–416: 397.
Derrida, Jacques. 1992. *Counterfeit Money*. Translated by Peggy Kamuf. London: University of Chicago Press.
Dickinson, Emily. 1975. *The Complete Poems*. Edited by Thomas H. Johnson. London: Faber and Faber.
Doty, William G. 2004. *Myth: A Handbook*. Westport: Greenwood Press.
Douglas, Christopher. 2011. 'Christian Multiculturalism and Unlearned History in Marilynne Robinson's Gilead.' *Novel* 44, no. 3: 333–53. https://doi.org/10.1215/00295132-1381276.
Dueholm, Benjamin J. 2012. 'Calvin vs. Hobbes.' *Washington Monthly* 44, no. 3/4: 59–61. Business Source Premier.
Eagleton, Terry. 2009. *Trouble with Strangers*. Hoboken, NJ: Wiley-Blackwell.
Eagleton, Terry. 2014. *Culture and the Death of God*. New Haven: Yale University Press.
Eakin, Paul John. 2016. *Fictions in Autobiography: Studies in the Art of Self-Invention*. Princeton, NJ: Princeton University Press.
Emerson, Ralph Waldo. 2000. *Essential Writings*. New York: Random House.
Fay, Sarah. 2005. 'Marilynne Robinson, the Art of Fiction No. 198.' *The Paris Review*. https://www.theparisreview.org/interviews/5863/marilynne-robinson-the-art-of-fictionno-198-marilynne-robinson.
Feuerbach, Ludwig. 2008. *The Essence of Christianity*. New York: Dover.
Franke, William. 2017. 'The Negative Theology of Wallace Steven's "Notes Toward a Supreme Fiction."' *Religions* 8, no. 4: 1–9. https://doi.org/10.3390/rel8040054.

Frei, Hans W. 1993. *Theology and Narrative: Selected Essays*. Oxford: Oxford University Press.
Gardner, Thomas. 2006. *A Door Ajar: Contemporary Writers and Emily Dickinson*. Oxford: Oxford University Press.
Gardner, Thomas. 2010. 'Keeping Perception Nimble.' *Christianity Today* 4, no. 2: 32–5. General OneFile.
Gardner, Thomas. 2014. 'Dickinson, Calvin, and the Drama of Perception.' *Religion and Literature* 46, no. 1: 195–203.
Geyh, Paula E. 1993. 'Burning the House Down? Domestic Space and Feminine Subjectivity in Marilynne Robinson's "Housekeeping."' *Contemporary Literature* 34, no. 1: 103–20. General OneFile.
Guite, Malcom. 2012. *Faith, Hope and Poetry: Theology and the Poetic Imagination*. London: Routledge.
Gura, Philip J. 2007. *American Transcendentalism: A History*. New York: Hill and Wang.
Handley, George B. 2009. 'The Metaphysics of Ecology in Marilynne Robinson's Housekeeping.' *Modern Fiction Studies* 55, no. 3: 496–521. doi:10.1353/mfs.0.1629.
Hauerwas, Stanley and David Burrell. 1997. *Why Narrative?: Readings in Narrative Theology*. Oregon: Wipf and Stock Publishers.
Herren, Michael. 2017. *The Anatomy of Myth*. New York: Oxford University Press.
Hesselink, John I. 2011. 'Marilynne Robinson: Distinctive Calvinist.' 26, no. 1: 5–8. https://perspectivesjournal.org/posts/marilynne-robinson-distinctive-calvinist/.
Hoffman, Lawrence A. 2010 'Principle, Story, and Myth in the Liturgical Search for Identity.' *Interpretation: A Journal of Bible and Theology* 64, no. 3: 231–44. https://doi.org/doi:10.1177/002096431006400302.
Holberg, Jennifer L. 2010. '"The Courage to see it": Toward an Understanding of Glory.' 59, no. 2: 283–300. https://doi.org10.1177/014833311005900212.
Horton, Ray. 2017. '"Rituals of the Ordinary": Marilynne Robinson's Aesthetics of Belief and Finitude.' *PMLA* 132, no. 1: 119–34. https://doi-org.queens.ezp1.qub.ac.uk/10.1632/pmla.2017.132.1.119.
Howe, Marie. 2017. *Magdalene*. New York: W. W. Norton and Company.
Jenner, Paul. 2019. '"Acknowledging a numinous ordinary": Marilynne Robinson and Stanley Cavell.' In *Marilynne Robinson: Essays*. Manchester: Manchester University Press.
Kate, Stanley. 2016. 'Through Emerson's Eye: The Practice of Perception in Proust.' *American Literary History*, no. 3: 455–82. https://doi.org/10.1093/alh/ajw029.
Kearney, Richard. 2002. *On Stories*. London: Routledge.

Kearney, Richard. 2010. *Anatheism*. New York: Columbia University Press.
Kearney, Richard. 2015. *Reimagining the Sacred*. New York: Columbia University Press.
Kearney, Richard. 2016. *Reimagining the Sacred*. New York: Columbia University Press.
Kearney, Richard and Matthew Clemente, eds. 2017. *The Art of Anatheism*. London: Rowman and Littlefield.
Keller, Catherine and Chris Boesel, eds. 2010. *Apophatic Bodies*. New York: Fordham University Press.
Kirkby, Joan. 1986. 'Is There Life after Art: The Metaphysics of Marilynne Robinson's Housekeeping.' *Tulsa Studies in Women's Literature* 5, no. 1: 91–109. https://doi.org/10.2307/463664.
Krishna, S. Swathi and Srirupa Chatterjee. 2017. 'Apocalyptic Imagery in Marilynne Robinson's Housekeeping.' *Explicator* 75, no. 4: 234–8. https://doi.org/10.1080/00144940.2017.1379464.
Larsen, Timothy and Keith B. Johnson, eds. 2019. *Balm in Gilead: A Theological Dialogue with Marilynne Robinson*. Westmont, IL: InterVarsity Press.
Latz, Andrew B. 2011. 'Creation in the Fiction of Marilynne Robinson.' *Literature and Theology* 25, no. 3: 283–96.
Leise, Christopher. 2009. '"That Little Incandescence": Reading the Fragmentary and John Calvin in Marilynne Robinson's "Gilead."' *Studies in the Novel* 41, no. 3: 348–67. JSTOR Journals.
Levinas, Emmanuel. 1961. *Totality and Infinity: An Essay on Exteriority*. Translated by Alphonso Lingis. Pittsburgh: Duquesne University Press.
Lichtman, Maria. 1998. 'Negative Theology in Marguerite Porete and Jacques Derrida.' *Christianity and Literature* 47, no. 2: 213–27.
Lloyd, Genevieve. 1993. *Being in Time: Selves and Narrators in Philosophy and Literature*. London: Routledge.
Macquarrie, John. 1960. *The Scope of Demythologising*. London: SCM Press.
Manning, Lillian et al. 2013. 'St. Augustine's Reflections on Memory and Time and the Current Concept of Subjective Time in Mental Time Travel.' *Behavioral Sciences* 232, no. 43. 10.3390/bs3020232.
Mariotti, Shannon L. and Joseph H. Jr. Lane, eds. 2016. *A Political Companion to Marilynne Robinson*. Lexington, Kentucky: University Press of Kentucky.
Mauro, Aaron. 2014. 'Ordinary Happiness: Marilynne Robinson's Tragic Economies of Debt and Forgiveness.' *Symploke* 22, no. 1–2: 149–66. ProjectMUSE.
McFague, Sallie. 1982. *Metaphorical Theology: Models of God in Religious Language*. Philadelphia: Fortress Press.

McGowan, Philip. 2013. 'Berryman, Sexton and the Possibilities of Poetic Language.' *English* 62, no. 239: 380–404. https://doi.org/queens.ezp1.qub.ac.uk/10.1093/english/eft038.
Melville, Herman. 2004. *Moby-Dick*. London: Collector's Library.
Midgely, Mary. 2003. *The Myths We Live By*. New York: Routledge.
Naylor, Vivien. 1996. 'The Theology of Touch.' *The Society of Saint Francis*. http://www.franciscanarchive.org.uk/1996jan-naylor.html.
Nehamas, Alexander. 2002. *Nietzsche: Life as Literature*. Cambridge: Harvard University Press.
Nietzsche, Friedrich Wilhelm. 1974. *The Gay Science: With a Prelude in Rhymes and an Appendix of Songs*. 1st edn. New York: Knopf Doubleday Publishing Group.
Nietzsche, Friedrich Wilhelm. 1994. *The Portable Nietzsche*. New York: Penguin Group.
Nietzsche, Friedrich. 1996. *On the Genealogy of Morals*. New York: Oxford University Press.
Nietzsche, Friedrich Wilhelm. 2008. *On the Genealogy of Morals: A Polemic. By Way of Clarification and Supplement to My Last Book Beyond Good and Evil*. Edited by Douglas Smith. Oxford: Oxford University Press.
O'Connor, Flannery. 1972. *Mystery and Manners*. London: Faber and Faber.
O'Donahue, John. 1997. *Anam Cara*. London: Bantam Press.
Olson, Liesl. *Modernism and the Ordinary*. Oxford: Oxford University Press. 2009.
Painter, Rebecca. 2009. 'Further Thoughts on a Prodigal Son Who Cannot Come Home.' *Christianity and Literature* 58, no. 3: 484–92. https://doi.org10.1177/014833310905800312.
Painter, Rebecca. 2010. 'Loyalty Meets Prodigality: The Reality of Grace in Marilynne Robinson's Fiction.' *Christianity and Literature* 59, no. 2: 321–40. https://doi.org/10.1177/014833311005900216.
Petit, Susan. 2012. 'Field of Deferred Dreams: Baseball and Historical Amnesia in Marilynne Robinson's Gilead and Home.' *Melus* no. 4: 119–37. https://doi.org/10.1353/mel.2012.0066.
Phillips, Siobhan. 2010. *The Poetics of the Everyday*. New York: Columbia University Press.
Ploeg, Andrew J. 2016. '"Trying to Say What Was True": Language, Divinity, Difference in Marilynne Robinson's Gilead.' *Journal of Language, Literature & Culture* 63, no. 1: 2–15. Supplemental Index.
Porte, Joel and Saundra Morris, eds. 1999. *The Cambridge Companion to Ralph Waldo Emerson*. Cambridge: Cambridge University Press.

Potts, Matthew. 2017. '"The world will be made whole": Love, Loss, and the Sacramental Imagination in Marilynne Robinson's Housekeeping.' *Christianity and Literature* 66, no. 3: 482–99. https://doi.org/ 10.1177/0148333117708263.

Ravits, Martha. 1989. 'Extending the American Range.' *American Literature* 61, no. 4: 644–66. Project MUSE.

Ricouer, Paul. 1970. *Freud and Philosophy: An Essay on Interpretation*. New Haven: Yale University Press.

Rivera, Mayra. 2007. *The Touch of Transcendence: A Postcolonial Theology of God*. London: Westminster John Knox Press.

Robinson, Marilynne. 1980. *Housekeeping*. London: Faber and Faber.

Robinson, Marilynne. 1987. 'Language is Smarter Than We Are.' https://www.nytimes.com/1987/01/11/books/about-books-language-is-smarter-than-we-are.html.

Robinson, Marilynne. 1998. *The Death of Adam: Essays on Modern Thought*. New York: Picador.

Robinson, Marilynne. 2004. *Gilead*. London: Virago.

Robinson, Marilynne. 2008. *Home*. London: Virago.

Robinson, Marilynne. 2010. *Absence of Mind: The Dispelling of Inwardness from the Modern Myth of the Self*. New Haven: Yale University Press.

Robinson, Marilynne. 2012. *When I Was a Child I Read Books*. London: Virago.

Robinson, Marilynne. 2014. *Lila*. London: Virago.

Robinson, Marilynne. 2015. *The Givenness of Things*. London: Farrar, Straus and Giroux.

Robinson, Marilynne. 2018. *What Are We Doing Here?* London: Virago.

Rogerson, John W. 1974. *Myth in Old Testament Interpretation*. New York: De Gruyter.

Rorty, Richard and Gianni Vattimo. 2005. *The Future of Religion*. New York: Columbia University Press.

Royle, Nicholas. 2002. *The Uncanny: An Introduction*. Manchester: Manchester University Press.

Rule, Jane. 1975. *Lesbian Images*. London: Doubleday.

Sacks, Oliver. 1990. *The Man Who Mistook His Wife for a Hat and Other Clinical Tales: Oliver Sacks*. New York: Harper Perennial.

Scarborough, Milton. 1994. *Myth and Modernity*. Albany: State of New York University Press.

Schaub, Thomas. 1994. 'An interview with Marilynne Robinson.' *Contemporary Literature* 35, no. 2: 231–51. https://doi.org/10.2307/1208838.

Shakespeare, Steven and Hugh Rayment-Pickard. 2006. *The Inclusive God*. Norwich: Canterbury Press.

Shy, Todd. 2007. 'Religion and Marilynne Robinson.' *Salmagundi* 155: 251–64. JSTOR Journals.

Smith, Adriana. 2017. 'The Nature of the Horizon: Genealogy in Marilynne Robinson's Gilead.' *Irish Journal of American Studies*. Issue 6.

Stevens, Jason W. ed. 2015. *This Life, This World: New Essays on Marilynne Robinson's Housekeeping, Gilead, and Home*. Boston: Brill Rodopi.

Stevens, Wallace. 1982. *The Collected Poems*. New York: Vintage.

Stout, Andrew C. 2014. '"A Little Willingness to See": Sacramental Vision in Marilynne Robinson's Housekeeping and Gilead.' *Religion and the Arts* 18, no. 4: 571–90. https://doi.org/10.1163/15685292-01804005.

Sykes, Rachel. 2017. 'Reading for Quiet in Marilynne Robinson's Gilead Novels.' *Critique* 58, no. 2: 108–1120.

Tanner, Laura. 2007. '"Looking Back from the Grave": Sensory Perception and the Anticipation of Absence in Marilynne Robinson's Gilead.' *Contemporary Literature* 48, no. 2: 227–52. https://doi.org/10.1353/cli.2007.0034.

Tate, Andrew. 2008. *Contemporary Fiction and Christianity*. London: Continuum International Publishing Group.

Taylor, Marc C. 1982. *Deconstructing Theology*. New York: The Crossroad Publishing Company.

Thoreau, Henry David. 1983. *Walden and Civil Disobedience*. London: Penguin Group.

Weele, Michael Vander. 2010. '"Marilynne Robinson's Gilead and the Difficult Gift of Human Exchange.' *Christianity and Literature* 59, no. 2: 217–39. https://doi.org/10.1177/014833311005900205.

Weintraub, Aviva. 1986. 'Freudian Imagery in Marilynne Robinson's Housekeeping.' *Journal of Evolutionary Psychology* 7, no. 1–2: 69–74.

Westphal, Merold. 1998. *Suspicion and Faith: The Religious Uses of Modern Atheism*. New York: Fordham University Press.

Whitman, Walt. 1995. *The Complete Poems of Walt Whitman*. London: Wordsworth Editions.

Williams, Rowan. 1989. 'Language, Reality and Desire in Augustine's *De Doctrina*.' *Literature and Theology* 3, no. 2: 138–50. https://doi.org/10.1093/litthe/3.2.138.

Williams, Rowan. 2005. *Grace and Necessity: Reflections on Art and Love*. London: Continuum.

Williams, Rowan. 2014a. *The Edge of Words and the Habits of Language*. London: Bloomsbury.

Williams, Rowan. 2014b. 'Living the Good Life: Rowan Williams on Marilynne Robinson.' *New Statesman* https://www.newstatesman.com/culture/2014/10/living-good-life-rowan-williams-marilynnerobinson.

Williams, Stephen N. 2015. *The Election of Grace: A Riddle Without a Resolution?* Cambridge: Wm. B. Eerdmans.

Woelfel James. 2013. 'William James and Marilynne Robinson.' *American Journal of Theology and Philosophy* 34, no. 2: 175–87. https://doi.org/10.5406/amerjtheophil.34.2.0175.

Index

American Renaissance 4, 8, 21–2, 24–32, 35, 50
apologetics 149, 178
apophatic 6, 56, 57, 59–60, 62–3, 68, 75, 127, 162–3, 174
atheism 13, 62

baptism 35, 74–5, 77, 89, 137, 138
Barth, Karl 48, 63, 66, 105, 110
Barthes, Roland 136
blessing 72, 74, 75, 76, 80, 81, 142
    as embodied 5, 60, 83–5, 88–90, 155
    and language 66, 75, 176

Calvin, John 4, 48, 66, 68, 94, 155, 177
    and beauty 6, 21, 167, 175
    and Calvinism 2, 18, 19, 27, 44, 47
    and image of God 80
    and predestination 119–21, 122
    Robinson's relation to 19, 179
    and sight 22
    and sin 99
    and stranger 76, 79
Caputo, John 107, 125, 126
Christianity 39
    in the Gilead novels 112, 118, 131
    and incarnation 82
    and providence 106
    Robinson's conception of 3–4, 9, 113–15, 133
church 46, 70, 71, 87, 94, 122, 123 150
    and Emerson 20
    Robinson's experience of 12, 57, 59, 153
Cone, James 106–9, 143

death
    of God 4, 47–50, 145
    of mother 17, 30, 36
    and repression 37
    and resurrection 43, 118, 165
    and symbol 35, 43, 125

democracy
    and depravity 99, 119
    and imagination 119, 120
    and theology 120, 127
Dickinson, Emily 4, 19, 24–6, 35, 49, 52, 66

embodiment 60, 72, 84, 96, 116, 139
Emerson, R. W.
    and language 34–5, 41, 64, 175
    and *Nature* 3, 20, 157
    and the Ordinary 20–1, 22, 23, 25, 172
    and sight 3, 20
    and transcendence 13, 20, 25
    and transcendentalism 12, 20, 173
    and transparency 26, 29–33, 157

forgiveness 15, 93–4, 104, 111, 124–5, 126
Freud 48, 62, 80, 145

gospel 76, 109, 111, 115, 134, 138, 139, 143

heaven 14, 63, 67, 68, 69, 139
hell 87, 123
Howe, Marie 20, 41

image of God 79, 80, 107, 179
immanence 22, 25, 41
incarnation 47, 86, 109, 114, 127
    and blessing 60
    and Jack Boughton 73–8
    and transcendence 83, 85

justice 14, 64, 93, 94, 103, 105–20, 127

Levinas, Emmanuel
    and distance 81, 82, 85, 86
    and existence 73
    and faces 76, 78
    and the other 73, 74, 77, 79, 80, 81, 87
    and transcendence 77, 78, 83, 85, 177

McFague, Sallie
  on Protestant and Catholic metaphor 41, 42
  on theological language 35, 37, 38
memory 7, 9, 49, 95, 97, 100, 148
  and cultural remembering 132, 135, 137
  and home 101
  and morality 131
  and myth 137–44, 150
  and the past 130
  and selfhood 129, 144, 152–63
mystery
  and Christianity 3, 58–9, 61, 65, 171
myth 9, 29, 156
  and creation 36, 39, 40
  and experience 6, 8, 9, 75, 147, 156, 177
  as genre 131, 132–7, 153, 184
  and grace 101, 103, 120, 151
  and identity 144, 152, 154, 157, 161, 165, 183
  and injustice 107
  and memory 137–44, 150
  as narrative 5, 155
  and poetry 157

Nietzsche, Friedrich
  and the death of God 47
  and demythologizing 145
  and metaphysics 146
  and selfhood 156–9, 166, 168

O'Connor, Flannery 22–4
Ordinary, the
  and American writing 19–35, 172, 173
  and attention 92, 171, 172
  definition of 5–8
  and excess 7, 8, 10, 171
  and justice 105
  and loss 39
  'resurrection of' 40–1, 50, 164, 173
  and theology 2, 8, 9, 45
  and transcendence 12–15, 102, 104–5, 173
  and transcendentalism 21

parable 64, 95, 97, 104, 149
parascience 145, 146, 162
penal substitution 124–5
positivism 14, 133
predestination
  and Calvin 119, 121
  and change 164
  and Christ 116, 117, 118
  and ethics 115–16
  and fathers 113
  and grace 97, 101–3, 119
  and mystery 61

reductionism 60, 65, 127
religious experience 9, 104, 121, 146, 175
resurrection 37, 43, 47, 118, 153, 165
  of Christ 134, 138
  of the Ordinary 5, 40, 41, 50, 164, 173, 180–1
Rivera, Mayra 78, 81, 87
  critique of Levinas 82, 85, 86
  and transcendence 83

sacrament 21, 25, 35, 57, 66, 137, 138
  and embodiment 82, 88
salvation
  and Bonhoeffer 127
  and Calvin 119
  and fatalism 117
  and incarnation 76
  and privilege 117
  and universalism 122, 123
soul 93, 96, 101, 117, 122, 130, 144, 160
  and revelation 17, 66
subjectivity 12, 129, 141, 143, 144, 159, 162–3, 174
  and interpretation 130, 131, 140, 143–4, 161
  and Levinas 8, 87
  and reading 45, 160
surplus 8, 13, 68, 86, 136

theory 3, 35, 80, 178
  and Christianity 4, 61, 77, 153
  and literature 45–6, 159, 160
transcendence
  and divinity 11, 29
  as excess 13, 14, 25, 68

as horizontal   12, 13, 41, 173
   and Levinas, E.   78, 81–3
   and Rivera, M.   81–6
transfiguration
   and Emerson   29, 31
   and memory   9, 72
   of perception   7, 8, 40, 41
trauma   37, 53, 165
Trinity   110, 111, 113, 114
truth
   and meaning   38, 52, 56, 60
   and myth   132, 138
   and positivism   38, 133
   and speech   49, 55
   and subjectivity   18, 94, 143, 159

universalism   5, 116–21, 123

water   35, 51, 130, 138, 143
   and flood   34, 43
   and the lake   26, 35, 46
   as Ordinary   2, 7, 8, 171
Whitman, Walt   30, 35
   and democracy   120
   and sight   3, 21
   and 'Song of Myself'   3, 25
Williams, Rowan   130, 138
   and art   6–7
   and representation   9
   and truthfulness   161
   and understanding   58

www.ingramcontent.com/pod-product-compliance
Lightning Source LLC
Chambersburg PA
CBHW070637300426
44111CB00013B/2146